An Uncertain Certainty

An Uncertain Certainty

Snapshots in a Journey from "Either-Or"
to "Both-And" in Christian Ministry

Graham Buxton

Foreword by
John R. Franke

CASCADE *Books* • Eugene, Oregon

AN UNCERTAIN CERTAINTY
Snapshots in a Journey from "Either-Or" to "Both-And" in Christian Ministry

Copyright © 2014 Graham Buxton. All rights reserved. Except for brief quotations in critical publications or reviews, no part of this book may be reproduced in any manner without prior written permission from the publisher. Write: Permissions, Wipf and Stock Publishers, 199 W. 8th Ave., Suite 3, Eugene, OR 97401.

Cascade Books
An Imprint of Wipf and Stock Publishers
199 W. 8th Ave., Suite 3
Eugene, OR 97401

www.wipfandstock.com

ISBN 13: 978-1-61097-221-5

Cataloguing-in-Publication data:

Buxton, Graham.

An uncertain certainty : snapshots in a journey from "either-or" to "both-and" in Christian ministry / Graham Buxton, with a foreword by John R. Franke.

xviii + 236 pp. ; 23 cm. Includes bibliographical references and indices.

ISBN 13: 978-1-61097-221-5

1. Pastoral theology. 2. Mystery—Christianity. 4. Christianity and culture. I. Franke, John R. II. Title.

BV660.2 B88 2014

Manufactured in the U.S.A.

The Post-Communion prayer, Holy Communion Rite A from *Common Worship: Services and Prayers* is copyright © The Archbishops' Council, 2000 and are reproduced by permission. All rights reserved. copyright@churchofengland.org.

Christmas, from *Collected Poems*, by John Betjeman © 1955, 1958, 1962, 1964, 1968, 1970, 1979, 1981, 1982, 2001 Reproduced by permission of John Murray Press, an imprint of Hodder and Stoughton Ltd.

Honey from the *Rock: An Introduction to Jewish Mysticism—Special Anniversary Edition* © 2000 by Rabbi Lawrence Kushner. Permission granted by Jewish Lights Publishing, www.jewishlights.com.

I dedicate this book to my grandchildren
Joshua
Andrew
Skylar
Hannah
Matthew
Jackson
Jasper
Caleb
Joel
in hope-filled prayer that they may discover day by day the joy and freedom of living in the "uncertain certainty" of God's immeasurable grace

Contents

Foreword | ix
by John R. Franke

Acknowledgments | xiii

Introduction | xv
"We also know there are known unknowns"

Chapter 1 | 1
"Where is the Life we have lost in living?"

Chapter 2 | 18
"The unexamined life is not worth living"

Chapter 3 | 32
"Transcendent mystery and glorious immediacy"

Chapter 4 | 48
"We have to become People of the Story"

Chapter 5 | 61
"A hell of a problem"

Chapter 6 | 76
"The wayfaring people of God"

Chapter 7 | 93
"A communion corresponding to the Trinity"

Chapter 8 | 111
"Nothing astonishes men so much as common sense"

Chapter 9 | 124
"I am a bishop for you, I am a Christian with you"

Chapter 10 | 141
"What indeed has Athens to do with Jerusalem?"

Chapter 11 | 156
"A wager on transcendence"

Chapter 12 | 173
"Earth's crammed with heaven"

Chapter 13 | 192
"For anything to be real it must be local"

Chapter 14 | 208
"Now I know in part, then I shall know fully"

Bibliography | 219

Names Index | 231

Foreword

WHILE READING *AN UNCERTAIN CERTAINTY*, I WAS REMINDED OF an interesting conversation I had not so long ago with a PhD student who was writing a dissertation that was critical of some of the things I and others had written concerning the positive value of mystery, uncertainty, and doubt for Christian faith. As a good researcher, this individual wanted to make sure he was doing justice to the arguments he was criticizing and had therefore invited me to serve as the external reader for his dissertation. In one of our phone conversations the topic of certainty came up, and we discussed our differences on the matter. I spoke about walking by faith and not by sight and the inherent lack of certainty this implies as a basic posture for Christian life and leadership, while he stressed the importance of having total certainty in matters of belief and action in order to be a faithful witness to the good news and provide leadership and guidance for others. He concluded, "You can't give your life to something and invite others to do the same unless you are absolutely certain about it." I responded, "I have."

It seems to me that this exchange reflects a paradoxical element of biblical Christian faith. On the one hand, would-be disciples of Jesus Christ are called upon to count the cost of following him and be willing to lay down their lives, after his example, for the sake of the world. This cost counting and commitment would appear to require a large measure of confidence in order to sustain the potential hardships associated with such a decision. On the other hand, in taking up this journey of faith we are often confronted with surprising twists and turns that lead to strange and unexpected places. This ancient paradox is observed in the epistle to the Hebrews (11:8), "By faith Abraham, when called to go to a place he would later receive as his inheritance, obeyed and went, even though he did not know where he was going."

In this volume, Graham Buxton wrestles with the challenges of this paradox for faith and life in the context of Christian ministry. In a series of well-crafted interactions with thinkers not only ancient and modern, but as diverse as Donald Rumsfeld and Ralph Waldo Emerson, he offers a portrait of Christian ministry that moves away from the narrow "either-or" mentality that is so common in much of the church. In its place Buxton proposes and illustrates a "both-and" posture that is reflective of the tensions and enigmas that are characteristic of the biblical witness to the mission of God and the journey of faith. This suggests an approach to Christian ministry and witness that is open-ended and generous without lapsing into the thin relativism of so much cultural discourse.

This both-and posture is important, not only because it is consistent with what we read in Scripture, but also because it serves as a reminder of the limitations of our own understanding. We all do theology and ministry from a specific context and social location that shapes the way we interpret the particularities of our calling. One of the dangers of the absolutism of an either-or approach to ministry is that it can serve to stamp the Bible and Christian faith in the image of a particular set of cultural assumptions and assume the normativity of that outlook. When this occurs, the voices and perspectives of those who do not participate in the presuppositions of the majority are marginalized or eclipsed, often under the guise of claims that they are not being faithful to Scripture. A both-and outlook makes us alert to the fact that we are only *a part* of the story of God's ways in the world and that other people, different from ourselves, are participants in the mission of God and also have thoughts and ideas about God, Jesus, and the Bible. We can be liberated from the limitations of our own imaginations and perspectives when we learn to hear their voices.

Buxton believes that a faith lived and practiced with ambiguity, paradox, uncertainty, and mystery has the capacity to renew and revitalize ministers and ministries, liberating them from simplistic certainties that are inconsistent with the complexities and vicissitudes of the human experience as well as the witness of Scripture. I agree with him. In addition, this both-and faith is the best and most faithful witness to the God revealed in Jesus Christ, whose Spirit blows like the wind. As the great missionary theologian Lesslie Newbigin concludes, the confidence that is proper to a Christian "is not the confidence of one who claims possession of demonstrable and indubitable knowledge. It is the confidence of one who had heard and answered the call that comes from God through whom and for whom all things are made: 'Follow me.'"[1]

In *An Uncertain Certainty*, Graham Buxton admirably captures this conviction in a compelling and entertaining fashion that has the potential to change the way we in the church think about ministry. May God grant us the courage to let go of the safety and security of absolute certainty and prepare us for the adventure of uncertain certainty, that of following Jesus into the world.

John R. Franke, DPhil
Executive Director and Professor of Missional Theology,
Yellowstone Theological Institute;
Professor of Religious Studies and Missiology,
Evangelische Theologische Faculteit, Leuven;
General Coordinator, The Gospel and Our Culture Network,
North America

---

[1] Lesslie Newbigin, *Proper Confidence: Faith, Doubt, and Certainty in Christian Discipleship*. Grand Rapids: Eerdmans, 1995, 105.

Acknowledgments

As I have been working on this book I have become aware in a way that I have not experienced before the debt that I owe to so many who have mentored and encouraged me over the 40+ years of my Christian life and ministry. As I look back I realize that I have gone through not so much a "paradigm shift" as a "paradigm drift" in my transition from being an "either-or" to a "both-and" Christian. Without her being aware of it, my wife Gill has challenged me about my beliefs more often than I was willing to appreciate at the time, and for that I am truly thankful.

I have been profoundly influenced by three people for whom the eschatological "not-yet" has become a glorious "now"—Harry Cooke, pastor and dear friend and counselor at my first local church in Leeds, UK; Tom Smail, who taught me so much about myself whilst teaching me theology at St. John's College, Nottingham, UK; and Ray Anderson, a wise and deeply pastoral theologian with whom my wife and I enjoyed many stimulating conversations during my visits to Fuller Theological Seminary, USA. Each has contributed in no small measure to my own personal faith journey.

I would also like to acknowledge my many friends and colleagues at St. John's College in Nottingham, St. John's College at Durham University (where several chapters of this book were written in peace and solitude), and Tabor Adelaide, where I have engaged with students over the years in the re-shaping of my thinking about God and his world. I also wish to acknowledge the richness of life that I have experienced in a number of local churches to which I have been privileged to belong: St. Matthias in Leeds, UK, where my journey of faith began; St. John's in West Ealing, UK; St. Paul's in South Harrow, UK; and Coromandel Valley Uniting

Church in Adelaide, South Australia. I have learned from them what it means to be a fellow-traveller as I have wrestled with the profound complexities of life, and I am grateful for the opportunities that I have had to share my *theologia viatorum* with them.

Numerous people have therefore contributed unknowingly to this present work, and I would like to express my deepest gratitude to them all. In particular, I would also like to convey here my thanks to John Franke for his willingness to write the Foreword and for his generous and perceptive comments. Finally, it has always been a pleasure to collaborate with Robin Parry, who has been a constant source of encouragement to me in my writing, and the team at Wipf & Stock has been gracious and helpful throughout the process of bringing this book to print.

Adelaide, South Australia
July 2014

Introduction

"We also know there are known unknowns"
—Donald Rumsfeld

Known Unknowns

In a much-reported response to a question at a US Department of Defense News Briefing in 2002 concerning the lack of evidence linking Iraq with weapons of mass destruction, the Secretary of Defense, Donald Rumsfeld said in cryptic fashion: "Reports that say that something hasn't happened are always interesting to me because as we know, there are known knowns; there are things we know we know. We also know there are known unknowns; that is to say we know there are some things we do not know. But there are also unknown unknowns—the ones we don't know we don't know." Some greeted his words with derision, though others remarked on his impeccable logic and "brilliant distillation of quite a complex matter".[1] I cite this because Rumsfeld's category of "known unknowns" resonates very much with what I am trying to convey in this book.[2] To speak paradoxically of an uncertain certainty is to acknowledge that whilst there are some things of which we can be certain—or as certain as our own worldview permits—there are also many things connected to that certainty of which we cannot be certain.

---

1. Steyn, "Rummy speaks the truth," para. 10.
2. I owe this insight to my daughter Rachel, who first pointed out the connection to me.

The notion of mystery—explored more fully in the first chapter—is apposite here. I use the word in this book as that which is "sensed to be unknowable, and incomprehensible, and inexplicable, or even inaccessible *in its fullness* to the human mind."[3] It is, in the words of Jaroslav Pelikan, "the mysterious quality of the Known,"[4] which connects notionally with Rumsfeld's realm of "known unknowns." An example or two from science may help. As we expand our knowledge of the universe through space exploration, we become more aware of what we do not know: our sense of the wonder and glory of creation is heightened as we probe ever more deeply into what Einstein called the "mystery" of the universe. There is an elegant beauty embedded in the created order that defies analysis, evoking wonder and awe. At the other extreme, many scientists whose interests have taken them into the micro world of the basic building blocks of life—the biochemistry of molecular structures, the DNA helix, and self-replicating mechanisms—have expressed a similar sense of wonder. How did it all start? In Ps 139 we read that we were "made in the secret place, woven together in the depths of the earth." There is mystery even here in the biblical account.

Quest for Certainty

In *Cosmopolis*, his ambitious account of the evolution of modernity, the philosopher Stephen Toulmin confronts the rationalist agenda with its "quest for certainty" which had its starting point in the philosophical thinking of René Descartes. He concludes that "we need to balance the hope for certainty and clarity in theory with the impossibility of avoiding uncertainty and ambiguity in practice."[5] In his application of this philosophical insight to Christian theology, Toulmin laments the turn from the "free-wheeling *Summas*" of the medieval and pre-Reformation tradition to the "diet of centrally-authorized *Manuals*" imposed by seventeenth-century ecclesiastical authority. In acknowledging our inability to "prove invincibly our most fundamental belief,"[6] I argue throughout this book that we need to take a leaf out of the books of those who would encourage

---

3. Schilling, *New Consciousness*, 30.
4. Pelikan, *Christian Intellectual*, 70.
5. Toulmin, *Cosmopolis*, 175.
6. The declared goal of the Counter-Reformation, cited by Toulmin, *Cosmopolis*, 77.

us to be more relaxed and generous in our faith-understanding. This is akin to what psychologists call the "tolerance of ambiguity" (TA), which "refers to the way an individual (or group) perceives and processes information about ambiguous situations or stimuli when confronted by an array of unfamiliar, complex, or incongruent clues."[7] However, TA, it must be stressed, should not be interpreted in such a way as to acquiesce to the "subtle shift of emphasis away from the object of faith (i.e., what it is that is believed) toward our choice to believe."[8] Dogmatic theology cannot simply be thrown out of the window in favor of "the grammar of preference with respect to religion in general and Christian orthodoxy in particular."[9] When dogmatism in the theological arena is equated with narrow-minded bigotry, allowing orthopraxy to trump orthodoxy and leaving no room for revealed truth or indeed traditional wisdom, then we have truly lost our bearings.

However, it is precisely because we live in a world which is far removed from the modernist version of reality, with its rational, clinical, and superficial presentation of life, that we need the courage and wisdom to embrace the presence of uncertainties in the midst of certainty. As James Olthuis writes, "the world is too complex, too contradictory, too enigmatic, pock-marked with guilt, flawed with folly and pride, scarred by ignorance and arrogance."[10] In the context of Christian ministry in such a world, many pastors are tired of simplistic certainties: what they need is permission to live with uncertainty, with mystery, ambiguity, and paradox. In fact, I have made a habit in recent years of asking church leaders if they would be interested in a book addressing these themes, and—not to my surprise—I have received an overwhelmingly positive response. In the chapters that follow, I therefore offer snapshots of a number of central Christian topics—God, the gospel, the church, salvation, ministry—inviting us to treat them as features of a landscape to explore rather than a set of propositional statements to sign up to.[11] My hope is that each chapter—short enough to provoke interest and curiosity—will be a catalyst for deeper reflection and enquiry in the heart and mind of each reader. If we are willing to see ourselves as theological explorers,

---

7. Furnham and Ribchester, "Tolerance of Ambiguity," 179–99.
8. Gay, "Plurality, Ambiguity," 209–27.
9. Ibid., 209.
10. Olthuis, "Dancing Together," 140–52.
11. Adapted from a phrase in Williams, "To What End Are We Made?" 11.

learner-disciples who engage in *theologia viatorum* in our Christian ministry, we will be open to wrestle with our faith, eager to discover truths yet unknown to us. We will not be too quick to "grasp a revelation so blinding in its depth and simplicity that creatures such as we could not 'attain unto it.'"[12] We will discover a new freedom in ministry as we embrace a more generous "both-and" perspective in place of a more narrow "either-or" interpretation of the Christian faith. In the process, we may find ourselves rediscovering "the Life we have lost in living" as we imaginatively participate in the life, ministry—*and mystery*—of the triune God of grace in our midst.

---

12. Hall, *What Christianity Is Not*, 164.

1

"Where is the Life we have lost in living?"
—T. S. Eliot

We are Not the Messiah

In 1979 the Archbishop of Detroit, Cardinal John Dearden, delivered a homily in a service celebrating departed priests in the Catholic Church. In that homily he spoke a prayer apparently composed by Bishop Ken Untener of Saginaw, but often attributed to Oscar Romero, the Archbishop of San Salvador, who was assassinated in 1980. In that prayer we are reminded that "we cannot do everything, and there is a sense of liberation in realizing that." Here is that prayer in full:

> It helps, now and then, to step back and take a long view.
>
> The Kingdom is not only beyond our efforts, it is even beyond our vision.
>
> We accomplish in our lifetime only a tiny fraction of the magnificent enterprise that is God's work.
>
> Nothing we do is complete, which is a way of saying that the Kingdom always lies beyond us.
>
> No statement says all that could be said.
>
> No prayer fully expresses our faith.
>
> No confession brings perfection.
>
> No pastoral visit brings wholeness.

An Uncertain Certainty

> No program accomplishes the Church's mission.
> No set of goals and objectives includes everything.
> This is what we are about.
> We plant the seeds that one day will grow.
> We water seeds already planted, knowing that they hold future promise.
> We lay foundations that will need further development.
> We provide yeast that produces far beyond our capabilities.
> We cannot do everything, and there is a sense of liberation in realizing that.
> This enables us to do something, and to do it very well.
> It may be incomplete, but it is a beginning, a step along the way, an opportunity for the Lord's grace to enter and do the rest.
> We may never see the end results, but that is the difference between the master builder and the worker.
> We are workers, not master builders; ministers, not messiahs.
> We are prophets of a future not our own.[1]

At one level this book is an attempt to address that most familiar of human tendencies in Christian life and ministry, the propensity to try and achieve God's work in our own strength, eloquently articulated in the title of a book chapter by Jude Tiersma, an urban missionary in Los Angeles: "What does it mean to be incarnational when we are not the Messiah?" She rightly notes that the concept of incarnation is dangerous: "Although we are called to follow Jesus, we are not the Messiah, and Jesus did not call us to be messianic."[2] As the "Romero prayer" insists, "we are workers, not master builders; ministers, not messiahs," seeking to worship a God "whose expansive ways with the world exceed our contracted and fragile imaginings."[3]

One of my central convictions—spelled out over ten years ago in my book *Dancing in the Dark*—is that participation in the ministry of Christ is a liberating privilege, releasing us from the pressures and burdens of "doing things for God" in our own strength. I argue there that in our practice of pastoral ministry, we do well to take stock of our lives and to ask, with T. S. Eliot, "Where is the Life we have lost in living?"[4] Called to proclaim the richness and joy of life in Christ, many of us discover a

---

1. Untener, "Romero Prayer."
2. Tiersma, "What Does It Mean to be Incarnational?" 11.
3. McDowell, "Passion for Holiness," para. 13.
4. Eliot, "Choruses," 107.

vast gap between the words we speak and the lives we are living. A quiet desperation takes over as we struggle to fulfil our vocation as ministers of the gospel. Immediately preceding this searching question, Eliot remonstrates against the incessant, and ultimately fruitless, pursuit of idea and action that drives us further from God, rather than towards him.

"Where is the Life we have lost in living?" Perhaps I could paraphrase this question and ask: "where is the joy of ministry that we have lost in our action-packed agendas that too frequently characterize our pastoral practice?" Endless invention, endless experiment . . . knowledge of words, and ignorance of the Word. In *Dancing in the Dark* I propose a theology of participation as an antidote to the pragmatic weariness that seems to pervade so much of pastoral life: "To be sent out in the power of the Spirit to live and work to the praise and glory of God is to participate in the life of the world, dancing in the dark and shining the light of the gospel of grace wherever we go."[5]

And then I spell it out more explicitly: "Dancing in the dark: this is the core of Christian ministry. As we are drawn into the life of 'God-in-community,' we discover the privilege and joy of incarnating that life in the world, participating in the continuing mission of Christ in the power of the Spirit."[6] Twelve years on and that is still my conviction: by God's grace, you and I and all who are called into Christian ministry are privileged to enter the dance of the triune God, who is ever at work in the struggling and suffering creation that he brought into being, a creation that he loves deeply and will one day reconcile back to himself, as the apostle Paul reminds us in Eph 1:10.

Ministry Myopia

Over the last decade I have been encouraged by those who have told me of the way their eyes have been opened to a theology of participation, bringing genuine transformation in the way they engage in the practice of ministry. Many others, however, have not experienced such a liberating release, preferring still to rely upon their own efforts or techniques in their pastoral work. As I have reflected on this, I have come to see that this sort of pragmatic self-effort is actually the tip of a very large myopic iceberg! Not only is participation eschewed by many ministers in their

---

5. Buxton, *Dancing*, 153.
6. Ibid, 157.

attempt to achieve fulfilment in their calling as servants of the gospel—endless invention, endless experiment—but a good number of them have also succumbed to a restricted, and restrictive, understanding of church, gospel, pastoral leadership, salvation . . . and God.

I label this "ministry myopia," drawing my inspiration from an article by Theodore Levitt entitled "Marketing Myopia," first published in the *Harvard Business Review* in 1960. In this seminal paper, Levitt, a Harvard business professor, exposes the prevalence of a short-sighted vision amongst corporate leaders, which he calls "marketing myopia." He defines this as an inward-looking approach to marketing that puts the spotlight on the needs of the firm instead of interpreting the firm and its products in terms of customers' needs and wants. When I was a postgraduate student at a business school in the UK in 1969 one of the first things I was asked to do was to read Levitt's *HBR* article, and write a short paper on its central thesis, which revolves around the question, "what business are we in?" Writing that paper started me on a journey of discovery, a journey shaped by a continual questioning of why I think and behave the way I do. In fact, a willingness to critically examine our thinking and our behavior as Christian ministers lies at the heart of this book.

Returning to Levitt's article, the author argues that rather than asking this open-ended market-oriented question, many firms take a blinkered approach to their *raison d'être* and define their activity in terms of their own product base. His point is clear. For example, the company manufacturing drills is not in the drill-making business: it is in the hole-making business. That perspective opens it up to a whole new way of thinking about its product range, thus ensuring a better chance of survival. His prime example is the American railroads, who lost out to the automobile companies because of their failure to recognize that they were in the transportation business. This failure to adjust to rapid changes in markets means that many companies, despite their initial prominence, decline and ultimately disappear. They don't ask the crucial question, "what business are we in?" They don't see the big picture, but focus on their own narrow product orientation.

The same myopic vision applies, I suggest, amongst our church leaders, many of whom are paralyzed by a rigidity in their thinking which locks them into set patterns of ministry and practice: hence "ministry myopia." In ministry myopia vision for ministry is limited as the result of focusing on only one dimension of what is essentially a multifaceted pastoral reality. By failing to perceive the "big picture" of Christian ministry pastors forego opportunities for developing an understanding of a more generous and ultimately more satisfying participation in all that God is doing in his world.

This book argues that true vision for ministry starts with *how we think* about God and his involvement in the world. My earlier writing focused on the need to shift out of over-pragmatic models of ministry to a more participative approach in which the emphasis is placed not on "my ministry efforts" but on entering into what God is graciously doing by his Spirit amongst us. The central thesis in this present volume is that a Western way of thinking—often very rational and cognitive—tends to direct ministers of the gospel to a narrow "either-or" interpretation of Christian life and ministry, rather than a more inclusive "both-and" paradigm. As we expand this thesis, we will recognize the need to embrace new ways of thinking that acknowledge the paradox, ambiguity, and mystery implicit not just in Christian ministry, but in life itself. As in my earlier works, I will also draw from contemporary insights into the dynamic relationality of the Trinity, interpreting Christian ministry as participation in the relational life of the triune God of grace who is continuously working in his creation through his Spirit to reconcile all things under Christ.

In her book *The Ethical Imagination*, Margaret Somerville, the well-known Australian ethicist now working in Canada, quotes the philosopher Charles Taylor, who suggests that we have lost complexity, spirit, and mystery, and replaced them with mind, will, and technology. Somerville then makes a telling point: "it is not that the latter are bad or worthless; it's that they are necessary but not sufficient to live a fully human life."[7] In this book, this thesis will be explored with specific reference to the practice of Christian ministry and an appeal will be made to the element of mystery that necessarily infuses many elements of the pastoral task.[8] Throughout this book, I will argue that in pastoral ministry we must learn to embrace the complexity of "both-and" rather than be satisfied with the simplistic "either-or" that characterizes the naïve fundamentalism that too frequently shapes people's faith.

---

7. Somerville, *Ethical Imagination*, 207.
8. Parts of this chapter first appeared in Buxton, "In Praise of Mystery," 58–66.

The Mystery of Faith

A central premise in Karen Armstrong's magisterial volume, *The Case for God*, is that facile theology impedes our understanding of the divine. She argues that doctrinal conformity is, for some believers, a more acceptable measure of faith than an apophatic stance that "asserts less and is more open to silence and unknowing."[9] This insight means that we need to be willing to acknowledge the significance not just of what may be known but also of what *cannot* be known.

In a recent article, Peter Bussey helpfully reminds us of the distinction between mystery and ignorance,[10] first identified by William Hocking in his book *The Meaning of God in Human Experience*, published almost 100 years ago.[11] We often confuse the two terms. Ignorance reflects a condition in which we are unaware of something that is inherently knowable, and so ignorance is essentially negative in character—it is an *absence*. Mystery, however, is positive in expressing something which, though unknowable in an empirical—or revelatory—sense, is fundamentally ineffable, expressing a *presence* that lies beyond human experience.

Mystery has to do with the incomprehensible. Incomprehensibility is not something about which Christians should be embarrassed. There is an occasion recalled by the well-known English theologian Alister McGrath, who happened to be in a small countryside church in Ireland where the practice was to recite the Athanasian Creed. They reached the point in the liturgy that spoke of the Father incomprehensible, the Son incomprehensible, and the Holy Ghost incomprehensible, when a slightly deaf local farmer not far from McGrath was heard to mutter: "The whole damn thing's incomprehensible!" We should not be disconcerted if we share the old man's confusion. Mystery does not *inhibit* faith—it *inhabits* faith, though some would not have it that way. In one of his letters Sir Isaac Newton writes: "'Tis the temper of the hot and superstitious part of mankind in religion ever to be fond of mysteries & for that reason to like best what they understand least."[12] Newton subscribed to the rational worship of One God, and maintained that the doctrine of the Trinity had been imposed upon the church by Athanasius, amongst others: scientific rationalism had no place for such "monstrous legends." Away with such

---

9. Armstrong, *Case for God*, 313.
10. Bussey, "Mystery and Ignorance."
11. Hocking, *Meaning of God*, 235–36.
12. Newton, *Correspondence*, 108.

superstitions, declared Newton: our understanding of God must be made as easy and agreeable as possible in order to convince people of the Truth, and so combat the rise of atheism.[13] So mystery and other such foolishness must be banished.

It may well be that we are tempted to embrace a simplistic faith in our desire to resist the challenge of atheism, and those of a more fundamentalist hue have gone down that path. We might note too that the contemporary age has a Newtonian feel about it, in spite of the fascination with spirituality in all its forms. The French Jesuit philosopher, Pierre Teilhard de Chardin famously observed that we are not human beings having a spiritual experience; we are spiritual beings having a human experience. But too often human hubris has eclipsed our spiritual core.

D. H. Lawrence once asserted that "the supreme little ego in man hates an unconquered universe. We shall never rest until we have heaped tin cans on the North Pole and on the South Pole and put up barb-wire fences on the moon. Barb-wire fences are our sign of conquest. We have wreathed the world with them. The back of creation is broken. We have killed the mysteries and devoured the secrets. It all lies now within our skin, within the ego of humanity."[14] Such hubris is an offence to the mystery of faith. There is, as Aldous Huxley wrote in his essay *The Doors of Perception*, an "incompatibility between man's egotism and the divine purity."[15] Mystery lies at the heart of the Christian faith, not in the sense that Christianity is a "mystery religion," with all of the cultic implications associated with such a term. The mystery of the gospel is precisely *the mystery of Christ*, as Paul proclaims in a number of places in his letter to the Colossians (1:27; 2:2; 4:3), and we are now privy to this "open secret," as expressed in the doxology at the end of Paul's masterly exposition of God's saving grace for all people, in which the apostle alludes to the mystery of the gentiles now ingrafted into the nourishing sap of the Jewish root stock: "Oh, the depth of the riches of the wisdom and knowledge of God! How unsearchable his judgments, and his paths beyond tracing out. Who has known the mind of the Lord? Or who has been his counsellor?" (Rom 11:33–34). Human beings have been blessed with the faculties of reason and discernment, and especially the gift of the Spirit, in order to grasp—or be grasped by—the gospel of salvation for all people.

13. Armstrong, *Case for God*, 201.
14. Lawrence, *Reflections*, 281.
15. See Huxley, *Doors of Perception*, 1954.

But we recognize too that there are aspects of the Christian faith that elude human comprehension, and we do well to allow that insight to inform our ministry. How, for example, do we interpret the relationship between divine sovereignty and human freedom? How do transcendence and immanence cohere in the triune God of Christian faith? How do judgment and divine grace play out at the *eschaton*, when all things have been summed up in Christ? Confronted by what Harold Schilling calls "the mystery of nature's ambiguities"[16]—the coexistence of good and evil, of beauty and brutality, whether in the natural world or in human behavior—we understandably question the goodness of God. These are matters that rightly concern Christian pastors seeking to serve the people in their communities. They are the stuff of pastoral ministry. Dogmatic knee-jerk responses to pastoral dilemmas do the gospel no service at all.

The Trivialization of Christianity

An underlying premise in this book is that pastors are tired of simplistic certainties, often associated with formulae for church growth; what they need is permission to live with uncertainty, with mystery, ambiguity, and paradox. John Haught reminds us that we "run the risk of diminishing the mystery of reality and of ourselves if we plunge precipitously into shallow certitudes."[17] In truth, embracing uncertainty causes us to think more profoundly, whereas certainty may well lead us to discard thinking altogether. And that is a very dangerous thing indeed, reminiscent of Blaise Pascal's observation in his *Pensées* that human beings never do evil so completely and cheerfully as when they do it from religious conviction.[18] Vincent Donovan writes in his book *Christianity Rediscovered*: "The day we are completely satisfied with what we have been doing; the day we have found the perfect, unchangeable system of work, the perfect answer, never in need of being corrected again, on that day we will know we are wrong, that we have made the greatest mistake of all."[19]

In *Home*, her exquisite and moving novel about small-town family life in America, replete with the biblical themes of faith, hope, and love, Marilynne Robinson—in the words of one reviewer—"asserts the

---

16. Schilling, *New Consciousness*, 29.
17. Haught, *Mystery and Promise*, 57.
18. Pascal, *Pensées*, 265.
19. Donovan, *Christianity Rediscovered*, 146.

elusiveness of perfection. . . . The beauty of *Home* is that it does not offer the counterfeit currency of certainty but proffers the under-valued currency of hope."[20] Borrowing this language, I suggest that hope, rather than certainty, is the primary currency of the gospel. In similar vein, the Canadian theologian Douglas John Hall offers the perspective of *confidence* (*con + fide*) as an antidote to the hubris of certitude.[21] Whilst acknowledging the understandable public demands for unambiguous assertions regarding biblical texts in the face of Christian liberalism and modernism, Hall rightly laments "the trivialization of Christianity, its reduction to very simplistic ideas and slogans, its failure to speak to the most complex problems and anxieties of human beings"[22] Where, he asks, is the wrestling that the profound complexities of life require of the Christian faith?

However, whilst confident hope—and specifically the hope of the resurrection—lies at the heart of the gospel, certainty should not be discarded. Gospel certainty has nothing to do with the various forms of religious triumphalism or fundamentalism that afflict the Christian world today. Rather, it finds its place in the sure and certain hope of the resurrection to eternal life to which the biblical writers again and again give testimony (see, for example, 1 Thess 4:13-18; 1 Cor 15:12-28), not in the kind of certitude that too easily betrays a lack of contemplation before holy mystery. Commenting on the incident of the boy Jesus at the Temple in Jerusalem (Luke 2:41-50), when Mary and Joseph betrayed their own lack of understanding, Joseph Ratzinger (the former Pope Benedict XVI) writes: "Even for the believing man who is entirely open to God, the words of God are not comprehensible and evident right away. Those who demand that the Christian message be as immediately understandable as any banal statement hinder God. Where there is no humility to accept the mystery, no patience to receive interiorly what one has not yet understood, to carry it to term, and to let it open at its own pace, the seed of the word has fallen on rocky ground; it has found no soil."[23]

Ratzinger's advocacy of patience in gospel hermeneutics finds an echo in the words of the twentieth-century British philosopher of history Herbert Butterfield, who once famously—if rather perilously—said "hold

---

20. See the *Herald* review in Robinson, *Home*.
21. Hall, *What Christianity Is Not*, 11.
22. Ibid, xii.
23. Ratzinger and von Balthasar, *Mary*, 71.

fast to Christ and for the rest be totally uncommitted." Butterfield, of course, was highlighting the importance of placing our faith in a person rather than a system, so inviting us to recognize the contribution of different confessions in our search for the nature of Christian truth—to be discovered, not in a series of faith-statements, but in a living person, Jesus Christ. So there is a centre to hold fast to, a conviction to affirm, even as we acknowledge a boundary that is necessarily ill-defined. Just as Luther proclaimed his unswerving loyalty to the testimony of God's Word and would not—indeed, could not—recant at the Diet of Worms, so we are summoned to affirm the central reality of the living Word, Jesus Christ . . . a reality, however, that is at its core a mystery. As noted earlier, the apostle Paul writes about the revelation of the Word who is Christ in the language of mystery: "God has chosen to make known among the Gentiles the glorious riches of this mystery, which is Christ in you, the hope of glory" (Col 1:27). So we affirm certainty as we proclaim Christ, but we also affirm mystery as we confess with Paul that we all "see through a glass, darkly" (1 Cor 13:12).

Methodology, however, converts the mystery of life into the problems of life, problems that can be addressed and—it is claimed—ultimately solved by methodology. This is grist to the mill of all who are concerned to see the church grow and reverse its sad decline in the Western world, leading to the adoption of techniques that promise to put people in the pews and cash in the coffers. Well, that is the hope . . . and a forlorn hope it has proven to be, in many cases. The church, however, cannot grow as the result of methodology.

Church leaders are often under great pressure within their denominations to develop strategies for growth. In the second half of the twentieth century, the Church Growth movement, with which Donald McGavran and Peter Wagner are particularly associated,[24] unwittingly contributed to this pressure, though, paradoxically, it also offered hope to those who were struggling to get their local church out of ruts and into renewal. The literature, tapes, seminars, and conferences spawned by this movement seemed to promise new life: take the pulse, read the signs, develop five-year plans, distribute questionnaires, design new organizational patterns, set targets . . . the techniques and methodologies proposed were endless.

---

24. See, for example, McGavran, *Understanding Church Growth*, and Wagner, *Your Church*.

Many of those churches that were enamored of this formulaic approach discovered that for all their efforts nothing really changed. Pragmatism as a guiding principle for success in ministry offered so much, yet delivered so little. The bookshelves of pastors were full of "how to" texts, designed to get the local church out of maintenance mode into growth and mission; "spiritually-loaded" numbers, especially seven and twelve, appeared in the titles (*Seven Steps to . . .* or *Twelve Keys to . . .*) as if to guarantee divine authenticity or inspiration. Authors encouraged pastors to be success-oriented and growth-conscious, and an overly pragmatic "what-works" business-oriented mentality began its subtle invasion of the pastoral ministry of the church.

The Language of "both-and"

Of course—and here we adopt the language of "both-and" rather than "either-or"—methods designed to enhance the health and growth of the church are not wrong or inappropriate *per se* in the practice of Christian ministry: they have their place in mobilizing the community of faith in its witness in and to the world. As we shall discover in chapter 8, there is scope for pragmatic approaches that have been carefully thought through and do not assume a major role in the practice of pastoral ministry. However, the attractions of pragmatic methodologies may too easily obscure the mystery of faith. Ministry today takes place in a world that is rapidly changing and extraordinarily multifaceted. Contributing to these changes, the postmodern agenda highlights ambiguity, mystery, and paradox in its understanding of reality, so presenting us with emphases that need to be acknowledged if we are to participate compassionately in the turmoil of the world around us.

The Christian gospel is replete with paradox—indeed we might want to argue that paradox lies at the very heart of the gospel. The first will be last and the last will be first. All who will exalt themselves will be humbled and those who humble themselves will be exalted. More weightily, we wrestle with how love and suffering might cohere in God. Doctrinally, we have already mentioned the incomprehensible nature of the Trinity, with its impenetrable one-and-three structure. Earlier I identified a number of what we might call "the mysteries of faith": the relationship between divine sovereignty and human freedom; the coherence of transcendence and immanence within the Trinity; the logic of judgment and divine grace at the *eschaton*. Consider too the Christian doctrine of the incarnation, the wonder of which has been expressed eloquently in Charles Wesley's well-known words, "our God contracted to a span, incomprehensibly made Man," poignantly conveyed in the final three verses of John Betjeman's well-known poem, "Christmas":

> And is it true,
> This most tremendous tale of all,
> Seen in a stained-glass window's hue,
> A Baby in an ox's stall?
> The Maker of the stars and sea
> Become a Child on earth for me?
>
> And is it true? For if it is,
> No loving fingers tying strings
> Around those tissued fripperies,
> The sweet and silly Christmas things,
> Bath salts and inexpensive scent
> And hideous tie so kindly meant,
>
> No love that in a family dwells,
> No carolling in frosty air,
> Nor all the steeple-shaking bells
> Can with this single Truth compare—
> That God was man in Palestine
> And lives today in Bread and Wine.[25]

The Word made flesh. "Both-and" rather than "either-or." Søren Kierkegaard, the nineteenth-century Danish philosopher, regarded Christianity as essentially paradoxical, not because it embraces the impossible but precisely because it embraces the incomprehensible. Such paradoxes are, for him, offensive to reason and reflect the *virtue of the absurd*. Again, note the emphasis: not the impossible or the contradictory, but the illogical and absurd, the incomprehensible. This is the mystery of faith. In *A Grief Observed*, C. S. Lewis writes: "Heaven will solve our problems, but not, I think, by showing us subtle reconciliations between all our apparently contradictory notions. The notions will all be knocked from under our feet. We shall see that there never was a problem."[26]

25. In Harrison, *Christmas Poems*.
26. Lewis, *Grief Observed*, 83.

> "For my thoughts are not your thoughts,
> neither are your ways my ways,"
> declares the Lord.
> "As the heavens are higher than the earth,
> so are my ways higher than your ways
> and my thoughts than your thoughts." (Isa 55:8-9)

What I am proposing in this book is a way of seeing that offers a way forward as we seek to incorporate the element of mystery into all that we do in pastoral work. It is a mode of seeing that has to do with the imagination, and implies paying attention to "what is" in a way that takes us beyond observation and into *participation*. Using the imagination is a discipline, and does not come easily to some people, especially those who are locked into an "either-or" paradigm. But imagination—which is one of God's great gifts to humanity—enables us to experience realities which cannot be accessed through either reason or logic, exemplified in these well-known lines from *Aurora Leigh*, Elizabeth Barrett Browning's nineteenth-century verse-novel of contemporary early Victorian life in England:

> . . . Earth's crammed with heaven,
> And every common bush afire with God:
> But only he who sees, takes off his shoes,
> The rest sit round it, and pluck blackberries . . .[27]

What is needed, then, is a whole-hearted engagement in the manner suggested by the French philosopher Gabriel Marcel, who defines mystery as "something in which I find myself caught up, and whose essence is not before me in its entirety."[28] Marcel's distinction between problem and mystery is also very helpful here: "A problem is something which I meet, which I find complete before me, but which I can therefore lay siege to and reduce. But a mystery is something in which I am myself involved, and it can therefore only be thought of as *a sphere where the distinction between what is in me and what is before me loses its meaning and its initial validity.*"[29]

This idea of being drawn into something greater than ourselves has been described very powerfully by Daniel Hardy in his last book *Wording*

---

27. Browning, *Aurora Leigh*, 265.
28. Marcel, *Being and Having*, 101.
29. Ibid, 127.

a Radiance, written as a conversation with his family as he was dying of cancer. He cites the work of Samuel Taylor Coleridge, who introduces the term "abduction" to refer to "the capacity of our reasoning to be drawn by light, enabling us to 'see' more than perception allows." Ephesians 3:16-21 would be a good way of expressing this biblically. Hardy suggests that it is only when we are what he calls "rationally frustrated" by a sense that we are not what we ought to be and we are not doing what we ought to do that we are stimulated to "participate in patterns of order and unity that are not simply human constructs but windows to primordial patterns of attraction."[30]

Pastoral Practice

We can translate this insight profitably into the realm of pastoral practice. As Karen Armstrong points out, the experience of paradigm shifts, popularized by Thomas Kuhn in the context of scientific knowledge, is not a strictly rational process, as modernity would have it: rather it consists of "imaginative and unpredictable flights into the unknown,"[31] heuristic leaps that circumvent the scientific method. This experience is not dissimilar from what happens when we read poetry or gaze at a painting. If those in pastoral ministry allow themselves to be drawn into that which they observe, they may discover insights that re-shape their perception of reality.

Too often, however, our lives are shaped by exterior pressures rather than the interior demands of a loving and ever-present God. In 1987, the American pastor and theologian Eugene Peterson wrote a book in which he attempted to redefine ministry in terms of keeping communities of sinners attentive to God, rather than pulling in "customers" in order to build successful churches. He argues that there are three acts which are fundamental to Christian ministry: praying, reading, and giving spiritual direction. These acts are quiet, never public, and represent the three angles of a triangle, the lines of which are the more visible acts of preaching, teaching, and administration. "Working the angles is what gives shape to the daily work of pastors and priests. If we get the angles right it is a simple matter to draw in the lines."[32] Peterson's emphasis needs to be

---

30. Hardy, *Wording a Radiance*, 69.
31. Armstrong, *Case for God*, 273.
32. Peterson, *Working the Angles*, 4.

heard in the light of the pragmatism and activism that pervades much of church life today.

What pastors need is the encouragement to enter more deeply into the mystery of faith, seeking first to cultivate a relationship with God ever before they seek to do things for him. When Jesus was challenged by the Jewish authorities about his miracles performed on the Sabbath, he replied: "I tell you the truth, the Son can do nothing by himself; he can do only what he sees the Father doing, because whatever the Father does, the Son also does" (John 5:19). In the same way that Jesus participated only in what he saw his Father doing, pastors are summoned to participate only in what they see Christ doing in the power of his Spirit. This leads to creative and imaginative ministry for the kingdom of God!

Haught suggests that the prophets' visionary pictures of God's future require us to "use our own imaginations to portray, however inadequately, the freedom, extravagance, and surprisingness of God's eternal vision for the world and humanity."[33] Of course, we need to ensure that our visions are not simply "projections of childish wishing, rather than images more truly revelatory of mystery,"[34] which means that we need to be truthful and honest about our inner motivations. Many in pastoral work have found that their life and ministry have been transformed as they experience a paradigm shift—or, perhaps more realistically, a *paradigm drift*!—from imitation to participation.

Whilst they may at times be helpful "tools of the trade," pragmatic solutions and techniques which offer the hope of success in ministry should be viewed warily and employed sparingly. It is as foolish to promise church growth and healthy and vital congregational life through the strategic application of "tried and proven methods" as it is to suggest that certain evangelistic formulae will guarantee personal conversions to Christ. No aspect of the pastoral ministry of the church is exempt from the radical insight that pragmatic dependency must be eschewed in favor of imaginative participation in the life, ministry—*and mystery*—of the triune God of grace in our midst.

We might also note that in pastoral work, the presence of "limit-experiences" which occur at the edge of ordinary life—moments of deep sadness, ecstatic joy, or bewilderment over what life is all about—may open both pastor and parishioner to new, unexpected glimpses of the

---

33. Haught, *Mystery and Promise*, 99.
34. Ibid., 100.

mystery of life, offering new understandings of what it means to be free, as well as fresh courage to step into God's future with confidence and hope. In one of his sermons, Paul Tillich has this to say: "The Kingdom of God is peace and joy. This is the message of Christianity. But eternal joy is not to be reached by living on the surface. It is rather attained by breaking through the surface, by penetrating the deep things of ourselves, of our world, and of God."[35] It is in this sense that Christianity stands on the threshold of ultimate mystery. Karl Giberson argues that there is "no abstract, universal scheme into which 'timeless truths' . . . can be placed once and for all, snugly juxtaposed and eternally secure. Human beings know a tiny bit about the world and an even smaller bit about God. But the bit that we don't know—the *Cloud of Unknowing*—is so much larger. And in that larger cloud lies the possibility that what may seem to be contradictory truths are not what they seem."[36] For Giberson, this may be the beginning of wisdom.

Acknowledging the place of mystery, mediated through the imagination, we may discover a new way of doing ministry, grounded in a more generous and humble appreciation of what we *don't* know as much as what we do know. This apophatic approach to theology, characteristic of the Eastern Orthodox tradition, is precisely what Douglas John Hall addresses in his recent book, aptly titled *What Christianity Is Not*: "there must always be a prominent element of modesty, or even tentativeness or hesitancy, in what we profess concerning the knowledge of God," he writes. "The Creed (any Christian creed!) should be whispered, not shouted."[37] For Hall, the way of negation, the *via negativa*, is "nothing more or less than a manner of honoring the mystery of God and the things of God—all the things of God."[38] He then goes on to counsel theologians (and we are all theologians in our diverse attempts to describe, let alone understand, God) to take the greatest care about the words we use when we write or speak about matters of faith, for words have the capacity, especially if used hastily or unthinkingly, to mask, obstruct, perhaps even deny, the wonder and mystery that lie at the heart of the Christian faith. Whenever the theology we espouse or the ministry we practise betrays a lack of humility before ultimate mystery, we need to be

---

35. Tillich, *Shaking of Foundations*, chapter 7.
36. Giberson, "Where It All Comes Together."
37. Hall, *What Christianity Is Not*, 12.
38. Ibid., 15.

willing to acknowledge how little we really do know about God and his ways. This demands that—in true humility—we examine ourselves and think deeply and honestly about one of the most foundational disciplines in human life, the discipline of thinking itself. To this we now turn in the next chapter.

2

"The unexamined life is not worth living"

–Socrates

Adventure of Ideas

MOST THEOLOGICAL TEXTS BEGIN WITH AN INTRODUCTORY SECtion or *prolegomena*, in which the author sets out his or her theological *modus operandi*. This then becomes the template for the substance that follows. One theologian who has adopted a different approach to "doing theology" is the German Protestant theologian Jürgen Moltmann, whose method may be described as a "theology in dialogue" or, in his own words, like a road that has emerged as he has walked along it. And that walk has been necessarily shaped by his own personal history and by his own *Sitz im Leben* (or life context). An extended quote from Moltmann's preface to his *Experiences in Theology* is worth reproducing here:

> For me, theology was, and still is, an adventure of ideas. It is an open, inviting path. Right down to the present day, it has continued to fascinate my mental and spiritual curiosity. My theological methods therefore grew up as I came to have a perception of the objects of theological thought. *The road emerged only as I walked it*. And my attempts to walk it are of course determined by my personal biography, and by the political context and historical *kairos* in which I live. I have searched for the right word for the right time. I have not written any theological

textbooks. The articles I have contributed to various theological dictionaries and encyclopaedias have seldom been particularly successful. I was not concerned to collect up correct theological notions, because I was much too preoccupied with the perception of new perspectives and unfamiliar aspects. I have no wish to be a disciple of the great theological masters of past generations. Nor have I any desire to found a new theological school. My whole concern has been, and still is, to stimulate other people to discover theology for themselves—to have their own theological ideas, and to set out along their own paths.[1]

A theologian friend of mine once said, "I'd rather be a catalyst than a dogmatist!" Moltmann clearly wants his theological writings to serve as a catalyst for others to "do theology" for themselves. As made clear in the quote above, he sees his writings not so much as *textbooks* as reflections that stimulate further thought. Theology, for Moltmann, is an "adventure of ideas," "an open, inviting path." Here I am reminded of Douglas John Hall's insight that "theology was made for human beings, not human beings for theology."[2] And that is what it should be for all of us in our desire to deepen our understanding and experience of God in our lives. Rigidity in our theology is something that needs to be eschewed in favor of an aliveness to the Spirit who teaches us as we travel "on the way," which is always a *personal* way, and a way that necessarily embraces the insights of fellow-travellers.

My concern, then, is to encourage us to be more audacious and exploratory (though not in a cavalier manner) with regard to the way in which we make judgments and arrive at conclusions about life and living, which of course includes what we think about such weighty matters as God, the gospel, the church, culture, and pastoral ministry. It is with this in mind that we now consider the vital matter of thinking, and specifically *how* we think. Students of psychology and communication theory will recognize a number of thinking styles identified throughout this chapter, a number of which have been recently explored by Frank Tucker in the context of intercultural communication for Christian ministry: abstract-concrete, analytical-synthetical, linear logical-analogical, rational-intuitive, and auditory-visual.[3] Tucker notes that "some understanding of how people think will facilitate the communication of the ultimate truth

---

1. Moltmann, *Experiences in Theology*, xv.
2. Hall, *Thinking the Faith*, 63.
3. Tucker, *Intercultural Communication*, 202–31.

of the Word of God."[4] It will also, critically, help us to appreciate how very differently people with divergent ways of thinking *interpret* Christian doctrine and the message of the Christian gospel.

An example from church history will help us here. In the fourth-century debate about the deity of Christ Arius taught that Jesus was a lesser "god"—not True God—on the basis that, *humanly* speaking, you can't have three the same as one. Athanasius replied that you can't read into Scripture on the basis of a *human* way of thinking. So we need to think from a different perspective—we need to consider what Athanasius called the scope (*skopos*) of Scripture, in which (in his Christological example) we find a "double account" of Jesus threading through the text. In Athanasius' words, "that He was ever God, and is the Son, being the Father's Word and Radiance and Wisdom and that afterwards for us He took flesh of a Virgin, Mary Bearer of God, and was made man,"[5] a paradox that remains at the heart of Christ's being as the God-man.

Athanasius' point, of course, is that the two truths hold together. So it is *how we think* that generates our doctrine of the Trinity. This is a specific example of what we might call "both-and" thinking, to which reference has already been made in chapter 1. Before focusing on this particular perspective, however, we might note a number of other ways of "thinking about thinking."

In the Western tradition the discipline of thinking is cognitive, so that apprehension of truth is seen to take place at the level of the mind. We may trace this orientation to the classical philosophical ideas of Plato, whose dualistic thinking has been recapitulated in different forms at various stages of Western civilization, most recently in the rationalism of the Enlightenment and in contemporary scientific materialism. However, the inclination towards a postmodern view of reality opens us up to a perception of thinking that embraces the heart as well as the mind, reflecting a more holistic—and Hebraic—understanding of anthropology.

An example of this may be found in John Grisham's book *A Time to Kill*, based upon the author's experience of witnessing the traumatic testimony of a twelve-year-old victim of rape. In Grisham's book, Jake Brigance, a young white lawyer, is defending Carl Lee Hailey, a black man accused of killing two white thugs who had grossly violated his little daughter. The lawyer, making his closing address to a rigged all-white jury in a small Mississippi town beset by racial tensions, challenges the

---

4. Ibid., 231.
5. Athanasius, "Select Works and Letters," 1034.

members of the jury to think about the nature of truth not just with their minds, but also with their *hearts*. In Akiva Goldsman's transcript of the book's storyline, Jake speaks these words to the jury:

> Now, it is incumbent upon us lawyers not to just talk about the truth, but to actually seek it, to find it, to live it. . . . What is it in us that seeks the truth? Is it our minds or is it our hearts? I set out to prove a black man could receive a fair trial in the south, that we are all equal in the eyes of the law. That's not the truth, because the eyes of the law are human eyes, yours and mine, and until we can see each other as equals, justice is never going to be even-handed, it will remain nothing more than a reflection of our own prejudices, so until that day we have a duty under God to seek the truth, not with our eyes and not with our minds where fear and hate turn commonality into prejudice, but with our hearts where we don't know better.[6]

Different Standpoints

How do we think? The ancient Hebrew understanding of the heart saw it not only as the seat of all our emotions, but also as the seat of our *thinking*. We need to rediscover this more holistic perspective as we are confronted with the complexities of life today. As we journey through life, we need the humility to acknowledge that we often fail to think through issues as carefully and holistically as we should. If this is an important insight with regard to all of life, then it is irresponsible to ignore it in the context of our understanding of and approach to both theology and ministry. How we think is a measure of our willingness to change. Killen and de Beer argue that life experiences are an invitation to reflection: "The contours of our world do not allow us simply to accept answers to our questions handed down to us by communal or religious authorities. The challenges confronting us and the pluralistic world in which we live demand that we reflect on questions of meaning and value."[7] They insist that, as human beings, and not just as Christians, we are called to transformation if we are to live authentic lives.

Many people are caught in the trap of living what I call "routine lives" rather than "reflective lives." A routine life is one that draws from

---

6. Goldsman, "A Time to Kill," paras. 1–2.
7. Killen and De Beer, *Art of Theological Reflection*, 1–2.

previous patterns of behavior, repeating them unthinkingly because "that is the way I've always done it." On the other hand, a reflective life draws from past experience, but is excited by the prospect of identifying alternative approaches to living life, and engaging with others on the journey of life. Reflective living has to do with seeing life as an adventure. The Swiss psychiatrist Paul Tournier observes that the instinct for adventure "may be cloaked, smothered, and repressed, but it never disappears from the human personality. The timidest pen-pushing clerk will disclose under psychoanalysis, and particularly in the analysis of his dreams, a secret nostalgia for the adventure which he has sacrificed for security."[8] A suburban church in Adelaide, South Australia, famous for its eye-catching slogans promoting its Sunday services, once offered the following thoughtful aphorism: "Some people never sing; they die with all their music still inside them."

As Christians, those who are indwelt by the pentecostal Spirit of God, we should of all people be excited by the gospel promise of transformation, the promise of being transformed from one degree of glory to another (2 Cor 3:18). Transformation has to do with our *whole* beings, with our minds as well as with our hearts. Paul writes in Rom 12:2 that we are to be transformed by the renewal of our minds, and though his concern was to enlighten his readers about how to live morally and spiritually, we may reasonably suppose that his words apply equally to how we approach the task of Christian ministry.

In their text on theological reflection, Killen and de Beer present two very different standpoints that we may adopt as we seek to direct our lives, standpoints that inform the way in which we might engage in the practice of ministry. The first is called the standpoint of certitude, from which we are inclined to see what may be unfamiliar to us only in terms of what we already believe.[9] The result is that we fail to test new experiences against the view of life that we already hold—our mind is made up, tradition is on our side, and if "some aspect of the new landscape is too difficult to fit into the picture we wish to see, we bulldoze it until we are satisfied that the world is as we know it ought to be."[10] Killen and de Beer offer a biblical illustration of this in the apostle Paul's religious certitude prior to his Damascus Road experience, as recorded in Acts 9:1-10. The

---

8. Tournier, *Adventure of Living*, 5.
9. Killen and De Beer, *Art of Theological Reflection*, 4–9.
10. Ibid., 4.

consequence of adopting the standpoint of certitude is that all we hear is an echo of ourselves, rather than the voice of the Spirit leading us in the direction we should go, whether in our practice of ministry or, more fundamentally, in our theology.[11] The danger is that we end up as ideologues rather than theologians, engaged in *repetitive* or *routine* ministry rather than *reflective* ministry.

We must not assume that the use of the word "routine" above eliminates the need to serve others in the ordinariness of daily living. A pastor once dreamt that he was in a fairground, enjoying the many different rides on offer; he was especially captivated by the thrills of the huge roller-coaster and was making his way towards it when he found himself being re-directed to the merry-go-round. The dream persisted, and he woke up with the scenario fresh and alive in his mind. The pastor was considering his future, and was keen to explore exciting new vistas in ministry; through this dream the Lord called him to rededicate his life afresh to the ongoing task of ministry in the local community (the merry-go-round). Like many in ministry, the attractions of running towards the big thrills of "roller-coaster ministry" are tempting, especially if the merry-go-round becomes predictable and boring. But it is in the very routine of everyday life that we are called to make a difference, and that is where the Spirit of God is pleased to minister his grace and hope.[12]

In the present context, however, the word "routine" is adopted to refer to *unreflective* ministry—unthinking actions, which do not bear the stamp of maturity, where "we have no ears to hear what God might be saying to us in our experience."[13] But experience, of course, may also be a danger for us, especially when we rely *solely* upon what we are currently feeling and thinking. This is what Killen and de Beer define as the standpoint of self-assurance, a biblical example of which may be found in Mark 10:17–22, where the rich young man, confident in his own understanding and wishing to stay in control of his life, fails to respond to the freedom of the gospel offered to him by Jesus. This standpoint, in which personal experience and perspectives override that which stands objectively over and against us, "dulls our awareness of how much we are shaped by our contexts and communities . . . and denies the tradition's integrity and

---

11. For an example of an evangelical approach to theological revisionism, see Grenz, *Revisioning*.

12. First cited in Buxton, *Dancing*, 292–93.

13. Killen and De Beer, *Art of Theological Reflection*, 9.

blocks our openness to the tradition's revelatory power."[14] It is evident that the two standpoints of certitude and self-assurance correlate with the two classical approaches to the relationship between experience and theology (within the quadrilateral of reason, tradition, Scripture, and experience): the first is that experience provides a foundational resource for Christian theology; the second is that Christian theology provides an interpretive framework within which human experience may be interpreted.

Permission to Wrestle

The cost of being imprisoned in these two standpoints is immense, and contributes in some measure to the failure of the Christian community to effectively incarnate the life and ministry of Christ in the world. "As adult Christians we are called to more than mindless obedience to authority or totally self-determined thought and action."[15] Arguing that doubt is feared by many Christians as truth's mortal enemy, Daniel Taylor invites us to consider the narrative of God's command to Abraham to sacrifice his son Isaac (Gen 22). "The pious Christian version of Abraham often turns him into an automaton. . . . Abraham, eyes glazed, mind dormant, body stiff, says in a slow, robotic monotone, 'Yes, Master. Whatever you say, Master.' This, for many inside and outside the church, is the Christian view of faith." But, Taylor continues, "Didn't he, rather, gape at the enormity of it? Didn't he argue, plead, question, object? Are we to believe nothing took place between the command in verse 2 of Genesis 22 and the departure for the sacrificial mountain in verse 3? Is Abraham a greater or lesser man, a greater or lesser example of faith, if we suppose he received the command calmly?"[16] Abraham was clearly a man of faith, to which the biblical witness attests again and again: Paul writes in Rom 4:20 that "he did not waver through unbelief." But through his life experiences with God, such as his doubt about Sarah providing him with a son in her old age, Abraham's doubts were woven into the tapestry of his growing faith. So for us today: if we eliminate doubt in our pursuit of certitude, regarding it as the enemy of faith rather than its necessary companion, we will likely end up with a faith that is shallow. All Christians need to give themselves permission to wrestle at times not only with the false

---

14. Ibid., 13.
15. Ibid., 15.
16. Taylor, *Myth of Certainty*, 80.

gods and idols that threaten true faith but also the real doubts that are too quickly suppressed in the name of certainty.

Of course, we may not think that we are embedded in one or other of the two standpoints proposed by Killen and de Beer—however, many Christians are surprisingly oblivious to their theological or ministry orientation, and need to hear the age-old injunction of Socrates, who once soberly declared that the unexamined life is not worth living. So Killen and de Beer direct us towards a mediating position, which they call the standpoint of exploration, involving a conversation between tradition and experience, allowing each to inform and illuminate the other. This is the way of transformation.[17] The American pastor Jerry Cook once wrote a book entitled *A Few Things I've Learnt Since I Knew It All*; we are called to be learners (the Greek word disciple—*mathetes*—literally means a learner), and a learner is one who is thrilled by the prospect of discovering new truths, new insights, and new ways of living.

The position we are advocating here is that of "open inquiry." In his book *Let Ministry Teach* Robert Kinast describes theology as "God-Word," understood in at least three ways.[18] "Word-from-God" expresses God's self-communication, usually understood in terms of revelation. Here we are invited through theological reflection to consider how God makes himself known to us, and the limits of that self-revelation. Have we placed limits on God's self-revelation? Does a particular ministry situation or event challenge us about our perceptions of how God reveals himself, and about what aspects of his being and work he may be opening up to our understanding?

"Word-to-God" is Kinast's language for Christian living, the human response, in terms of understanding and action, to "Word-from-God." This perspective may find us asking: what does a particular incident teach me about my approach to ministry? Perhaps our church practices and beliefs need to be re-evaluated, and we may find ourselves facing questions at a deeply personal level regarding our own response to and relationship with God. Thirdly, in order to make sense of God's self-revelation, we attempt to organize that which we receive by faith through a process of confessional acknowledgement, open inquiry, and systematic presentation, what Kinast calls "Word-about-God" (involving confession, interrogation, and investigation). At this level—our organization of

---

17. Killen and De Beer, *Art of Theological Reflection*, 16–19.
18. Kinast, *Let Ministry Teach*, 5–6.

faith-material—we are often anxious to preserve our systematic presentation of "God-knowledge," based upon our confessional acknowledgement of that which we receive as truth from God (revelation) for the purpose of Christian living (response). However, the step of "open inquiry" is often short-circuited, to the detriment of truth-discovery, personal growth, and ministry practice.

Our discussion so far has identified a number of different ways in which we might think about thinking: "both-and"/"either-or", cognitive/intuitive (head/heart), and routine/reflective. To these we might add the distinction between "bottom-up" and "top-down" thinking: is our instinct to start with a particular phenomenon or experience and seek to build our understanding of reality from that (the "bottom-up" approach)? Or do we prefer to start with broad, general principles, and then work downward from there (the "top-down")? The two approaches need not imply conflict, because they are both, in different ways, tackling the same sort of questions. Both are attempting to get to grips with the nature of reality. The "bottom-up" approach relates closely to the scientific way of looking at things. "Bottom-up" thinkers "feel it is safest to start in the basement of particularity and then generalize a little."[19] The "top-down" approach presupposes some form of metaphysical framework—such as a Christian theistic framework—within which to interpret the nature of reality. The theoretical physicist-cum-Anglican priest John Polkinghorne acknowledges that he is naturally a "bottom-up" thinker rather than a "top-down" thinker. In other words, although his Christian framework requires a "top-down" approach, he instinctively builds up from observable phenomena in the "one world of human experience and human understanding that we are trying to come to grips with."[20]

Still others have distinguished between convergent and divergent thinking. Divergent thinking opens the imagination to all possibilities, while convergent thinking analyzes and chooses from among those possibilities.[21] Divergent thinking is more imaginative and outward-focused, a form of brainstorming characterized by creative "big-picture" thinking, whereas convergent thinking looks inward, seeking to resolve problems through a process of inductive logic, often drawing from a range of givens. Whilst both have their place in generating ideas and arriving at deci-

---

19. Polkinghorne, *Science and Christian Belief*, 11.
20. Polkinghorne, *Serious Talk*, 1.
21. See *SmartStorming*, "Power of Divergent and Convergent Thinking."

sions, divergent thinking clearly resonates with a more exploratory and open thinking paradigm. In his foreword to Scot McKnight's book, *The King Jesus Gospel*, Tom Wright writes:

> The Christian faith is kaleidoscopic, and most of us are colour-blind. It is multidimensional, and most of us manage to hold at most two dimensions in our heads at any one time. It is symphonic, and we can just about whistle one of the tunes. So we shouldn't be surprised if someone comes along and draws our attention to other colours and patterns that we hadn't noticed. We shouldn't be alarmed if someone sketches a third, a fourth, or even a fifth dimension that we had overlooked. We ought to welcome it if a musician plays new parts of the harmony to the tune we thought we knew.[22]

Parallel Thinking

The more holistic, divergent model of thinking has been addressed by the well-known "guru of thinking," Edward de Bono, in a number of interesting books, one of which is called *Parallel Thinking*.[23] De Bono's starting point is to make a distinction between "searching" for truth in order to fit data into our pre-determined boxes and moving forward in an exploratory way, with an emphasis on creativity and design. Accordingly he proposes two alternative models of thinking. The "search" model is based on analysis of data in order to discover those things that will fit into our boxes, rather like prospecting for gold. The key word here is *judgment*: we judge whether or not something is "true" according to its fit, and accept it if it is suitable within our existing frames of reference.

Traditional thinking, according to de Bono, has a lot to do with our perception of what is true. He is not epistemologically rigorous in his discussion, as he is interested in truth only as it affects the way we think: so truth is "the admittance label that allows things into your mind or into consideration. Truth is a party badge, a badge of membership. At the door everyone is checked. Only those with the truth label are allowed in; the rest are turned away. Then the thinker proceeds to organize those who have been allowed into the room."[24] It might be apparent to observ-

---

22. Wright, Foreword in McKnight, *King Jesus Gospel*.
23. De Bono, *Parallel Thinking*.
24. Ibid., 62.

ers of contemporary Christendom that de Bono's words apply to the way some people direct the affairs of the local church!

The second model—de Bono's concept of *parallel thinking*—is predicated on "design" rather than search: "We seek to design a way forward. You need to design and construct a house. You do not discover a house."[25] In parallel thinking attempts are made to reconcile what initially appear to be contradictions, instead of assuming that they are irreconcilable: the key word is *exploration*. In parallel thinking judgment is not discarded. It is a matter of sequence: do we tend to judge first, or are we willing to explore options and then make appropriate judgments after we have explored? De Bono offers a simple example of a motorist who ignores a turning to the left of a narrow road because it leads backwards. But a view from above shows that the side road leads to a much wider, and probably better, road going in the same direction as the narrow road. So we may need to travel south to go north. The question posed by de Bono is: how open are we to other possibilities?

Peter Hampson, an English psychology professor, quotes the philosopher Ludwig Wittgenstein, who once wrote that "an honest religious thinker is like a tightrope walker. He almost looks as though he were walking on nothing but air. His support is the slenderest imaginable. And yet it is really possible to walk on it."[26] Suggesting that "the tightrope charts a route with naïve, fundamentalist belief on one side and naïve rationalism or scientism on the other" (both positions reflecting an unhealthy reductionism), Hampson argues that one reason why Christians wobble from time to time may be that "creation is ambiguous and Christianity paradoxical; while these are both strengths, they easily appear as weaknesses, and we're tempted by the apparent certainty on one side or the other."[27] In other words, we opt for "either-or" rather than "both-and."

In their best-selling book on management entitled *Built to Last*, Collins and Porras define *the tyranny of the OR* as "the rational view that cannot easily accept paradox, that cannot live with two seemingly contradictory forces or ideas at the same time." Their antidote is *the genius of the AND*, defined as "the ability to embrace both extremes of a number of dimensions at the same time. Instead of choosing between **A OR B**, they

---

25. Ibid., 216.
26. Wittgenstein, *Culture and Value*, 84.
27. Hampson, "How to Walk," para. 2.

figure out a way to have both **A** *AND* **B**."²⁸ This is the genius that I am proposing in this book. The reality is that many people in Christian ministry are happier with certainty than with uncertainty. And whilst certainty is not to be dismissed, it may also be the midwife of ministry myopia.

Over the years, I have talked with Christians from all walks of life—many of them occupying positions of leadership and responsibility. I have become aware of the need many of them have—as I suggested in the Introduction—to give themselves permission to live with the tensions of ambiguity, paradox, and mystery that lie at the very heart of the Christian faith and its outworking in the world today. We do well to remember that sincerity and humility are indispensable handmaidens in our response to the difficult questions that confront us in our life of faith. One of the most prolific theological writers today is the English theologian and public intellectual Alister McGrath. In one of his most recent books, *The Passionate Intellect*, he invites us to embark on a quest of wrestling in a vigorous and exciting way with God and his world:

> Theology is . . . about *discernment*, seeing reality in a certain way and attempting to resolve its ambiguities through this interpretative framework. But how are we to visualize this changed way of seeing the world? How are we to grasp it with the power of the imagination, rather than simply comprehend it with our minds? In what ways does the Christian gospel so enhance our capacity to behold things that we may discern the footprints of God in the sand, the tracks of his passing in the walkways of life and his presence and power in our everyday experiences? While we should never neglect the importance of reason and understanding, we must also value the power of the human imagination as the gatekeeper of the human soul. . . . Theology is an activity of the imagination as much as of reason, in which we seek to transcend the boundaries of the given, pressing upward, outward and forward. Theology frames the landscape of reality in such a way that our everyday existence is set in a wider perspective. The world, formerly an absolute end in itself, now becomes a gateway to something greater.²⁹

---

28. Collins and Porras, *Built to Last*, 43–44.
29. McGrath, *Passionate Intellect*, 46, author's italics.

A Landscape to Explore

When we start defining the Christian faith in the generous language of a landscape to explore rather than a set of propositional statements to sign up to, when we speak of "doing theology" rather than inheriting a given theology, when we adopt the language of exploration, imagination, and mystery as an antidote to the safe haven of "this is what I've always believed," there may be a real concern amongst some that we are in danger of straying into heretical territory. That, of course, is understandable, and not one of us is exempt from the dangers of re-orienting ourselves on shaky theological ground. Indeed, a few of the topics discussed in this book may alarm some readers. But the cost of not being willing to acknowledge our human finitude is to collapse into the sort of fundamentalist dogmatism that would have deeply troubled the more adventurous and exploratory theological minds of earlier centuries.

Earlier I cited the innovative ideas of Theodore Levitt, the American business guru, whose concept of "marketing myopia" was an important catalyst for this present volume. Another of his ilk is the modern-day entrepreneur and bestselling author Seth Godin, whose ideas have been challenging corporate leaders all over the world. In his book *Tribes* he likens a heretic to a unicorn in a balloon factory, and the parable is a striking illustration of the challenge to the *status quo* brought by those who are willing to prick a few hallowed balloons.[30] This, of course, begs the vital question: which balloons need to be punctured within Christendom's balloon factory? G. K. Chesterton once observed that all heresy is a narrowing down unduly of what is essentially a complex reality. While this view has its limitations, it is certainly an appropriate insight in the context of the way in which the church has too frequently been content with a single interpretation of what is essentially a multidimensional and complex reality. In recent years, for example, there have been some radical reappraisals of the doctrine of the atonement, and of the belief in "hell" as "eternal conscious torment." And church history teaches us that from time to time balloons have been not so much punctured as slowly deflating. For example, "the age-old dogma that God is impassible, that is immutable and therefore incapable of suffering, is for many no longer tenable. The ancient heresy that God suffers has, in fact, become the new orthodoxy."[31] Subsequent chapters of this book will explore some of these issues.

30. Godin, *Tribes*.
31. Green, *Beating the Bounds*, 8.

In our Christian lives, we need to acknowledge that we inhabit what C. S. Lewis once described as the "shadowlands" before God makes all things new. But as we journey in our Christian faith, we do well to acknowledge that some of our treasured balloons need to be pricked in order to rupture the rigid "either-or" dichotomies that we so love to erect in our Christian edifices. And as we travel this more inclusive and ultimately more charitable path, we will find ourselves more readily embracing—or, more likely, being embraced by—the mystery of faith that characterizes this side of ultimate glory.

3

"Transcendent mystery and glorious immediacy"
–David Bentley Hart

Dualistic Thinking

I recall in my early days as a young Christian visiting people in their homes in order to talk to them about the God in whom I had just come to believe. Whenever the conversation turned towards spiritual matters, a common response was, "Well, I don't believe in God." I would ask, "Tell me, what sort of God don't you believe in?" On many occasions, the classic "unreal gods" to which J. B. Phillips refers in his oft-quoted little book *Your God is Too Small*[1] would be mentioned, if not explicitly, then certainly implicitly. In particular, allusions to variations of Phillips' "resident policeman," "grand old man," "God-in-a-box," and "parental hangover" were commonly made, and after an appropriate time, I would declare, "Well, I don't believe in that sort of God either!"

The irony of this is that my own perception of God in those early days might well have been characterized as "too small," a myopia shaped by an early charismatic experience that reinforced in me a powerful dualistic paradigm. I was still involved in teaching management at the time, and the intensity of my spiritual initiation led me to believe that there was a yawning gap between Christianity and the way the world goes about its business of life and living. This view caused me to dismiss everything that

---

1. Phillips, *Your God is Too Small*.

the world had to offer in terms of wisdom and experience, to the point that an unreal dualism began to take root in my mind: businessmen live according to secular principles, and God's people live according to spiritual, or sacred, principles. And so the divide between sacred and secular was reinforced in my mind, contributing to an unhealthy and, at times, narrow super-spirituality. There is an amusing anecdote about a bishop who made a visit to a church known for its ultra-pietism. Sitting cross-legged on a table, he casually addressed the children: "Tell me," he asked them, leaning forward, "what is grey, has a bushy tail, and eats nuts?" There was an uncomfortable silence, until one little boy put up his hand, and answered uncertainly, "Please, sir, I know the answer should be Jesus, but it sounds like a squirrel to me!"

I have written about this distorted way of thinking about the relationship between God and his world more fully elsewhere,[2] arguing that dualism fails to appreciate the inherent goodness in all that God has created, leading to (as well as arising from) mistaken and false ideas not only about the nature of God, but also about the nature of creation and salvation. When we consider approaches to creation and culture that depend upon a dualistic separation between God and the world, we are denying the trinitarian nature of the God who has made space for the world within himself,[3] and who loves this world with a passion that ultimately led to the incarnation and the cross. That is why we cannot endorse dualism if we truly believe in God as Trinity. God is not a deistic being, separate from his creation, nor is he in dualistic opposition to it. He is intimately involved in all that he has made—he is immanent as well as transcendent.

Of course, dualistic thinking is not the only myopia that afflicts ministry practitioners. Reflecting recently on the three books that I have written on pastoral theology, I realized that in one form or another they all deal with different forms of ministry myopia—the myopia of pragmatic activity, the myopia of scientific apathy and ignorance, and the myopia of dualistic thinking. In this particular chapter, I would like to focus on the myopia of one particular narrow, and ultimately unbiblical, understanding of God himself, a perception that inevitably influences how we go about witnessing to and communicating about this God.

---

2. Buxton, *Celebrating Life*.

3. Tom Wright prefers to think of God creating *new* space through his creative love: see Wright, *Surprised by Hope*, 113.

Both "Other" and Intimate

This misrepresentation has to do with the relationship between God's transcendence and his immanence, described by the American theologian Langdon Gilkey as "the central problem for the doctrine of God." The problem is spelled out more explicitly by Gilkey: "how to unite intelligibly the *absoluteness* of God as the unconditioned source of our total being with the dynamic *relatedness* and the *reciprocal activity* of God as the ground, guide, dialogical partner, and redeemer of our freedom."[4] As Christians, we acknowledge that God is the "transcendent Other," distinct from and greater than his creation, whilst being at the same time the ever-present intimate God, involved in and with his creation, though never identified with it in any pantheistic way. And in their creedal statements, Christians routinely confess that in Christ transcendence and immanence are held in exquisite tension: in the incarnation, we are reminded that God is "not only the Infinitely Near but also the Wholly Other."[5]

The English poet Alfred Tennyson, in a poem paradoxically entitled "The Higher Pantheism" (for Tennyson was no pantheist), wrote these well-known words: "Speak to Him, thou, for He hears, and Spirit with Spirit can meet—Closer is He than breathing, and nearer than hands and feet." Here we see God presented as someone who invites us, his creatures, into a reciprocal relationship of communicating love. God is not one who hears us, as the popular song goes, "from a distance." For some, the idea of distance is embedded in the language of the classical divine attributes, such as immutability, impassibility, and timelessness. For others, however, like many of the mystics, these attributes were no threat to their sense of God's closeness.

How can we possibly come to grips with the mystery and paradox of God as one who is *both* "Other" *and* intimate, without succumbing to either of the two heresies that lie at the extreme ends of the spectrum: a deistic, distant God, existing apart from his creation in splendid isolation, and a chummy, matey "daddy"-God, made in human image, which dissolves the distinction between God and his creatures in a sloppy pseudo-pantheism? Of course, these two extreme positions are just that—extreme, and not representative of the views of the majority of Christendom. So the question we ask in this chapter is this: in what

---

4. Gilkey, "God," 108.
5. Bloesch, *Jesus Christ*, 78.

sense is it actually possible to envisage the "both-and" coherence of transcendence and immanence in the triune God of Christian faith without finding ourselves veering to one or other end of the spectrum? One of the critical issues in the debate is open theism (to which we will turn at the end of this chapter): there are many Christians who have no problem affirming that the living, active, holy God enters into a covenant relationship with his creation, but struggle with the idea that he wants us to share with him in the outworking of his purposes, to the point that he is influenced by and responds to our actions, as proposed by open theism.

Of course, once we introduce the language of mystery, we find ourselves drawn into the incomprehensibility of a God whose innertrinitarian life speaks to us of mystery—the paradox of the one and the three, whereby the being of each person of the Trinity lies in the existence of each for the other. However, for some of the early church fathers, there was behind the Trinity the idea of something else that defines the mystery and reality—or essence—of God. For example, Pseudo-Dionysius proposed that God, in his transcendence, is somehow hidden, clothed in unfathomable darkness. Although the notion of God's inaccessibility should not be interpreted as a rejection of trinitarian conceptions of God, it does add weight to the belief that the ultimate truth about God is somehow *beyond the Trinity*, that behind relationship are concepts like impassibility and immutability. So absolute statements about God may be seen as greater than the relational reality that exists and defines the life of the triune God, an interpretive paradigm that owes much to the dualistic framework proposed by Plato.

However, God is not to be summed up in the static language that eschews his inner relationality and loving interaction with his creation. Clark Pinnock puts it well when he writes that "God's fair beauty according to Scripture is his own relationality as triune community. It is God's gracious interactivity, not his hyper-transcendence and/or immobility, which makes him so glorious."[6] Here, of course, we are into different interpretations of the doctrine of the Trinity. What is of particular note in our present discussion is the emphasis—particularly in the latter half of the twentieth century—on what has come to be known as "social trinitarianism." Stripped to its basics, the debate may be reduced to three main areas of contention with regard to Western theology:

---

6. Pinnock, *Most Moved Mover*, 5–6.

1. Too much weight has been given to the oneness of God at the expense of his threeness.

2. Relations between the three persons have been articulated more in static and philosophically abstract language than in the language of personal, dynamic relationality.

3. For love to be truly and most fully expressed, trinitarian thinking necessarily needs to orient itself towards threeness as the most complete expression of God's glorious perfection.

Perichoresis is a concept that has re-entered the theological mainstream in an attempt to correct the one-sided Western emphasis on static personhood. A number of analogies have been suggested to convey the mutuality and interdependence implicit in the notion of *perichoresis*, such as the light of lamps which permeate one another in undifferentiated light, or the three dimensionality of physical objects. However, as Catherine LaCugna (a key social trinitarian theologian) points out, these analogies "do not convey the dynamic and creative energy, the eternal and perpetual movement, the mutual and reciprocal permeation of each person with and in and through and by the other persons."[7] This model of inner-trinitarian life has been taken further by those who wish to posit a continuity between the divine and the human, locating it within the economy of salvation: in other words, drawn into the inner life of the Trinity, we begin to experience what the three persons of the Trinity have eternally experienced, summed up in Jesus' prayer to his Father in John 17:20–23: "My prayer is not for them alone. I pray also for those who will believe in me through their message, that all of them may be one, Father, just as you are in me and I am in you. May they also be in us so that the world may believe that you have sent me. I have given them the glory that you gave me, that they may be one as we are one—I in them and you in me—so that they may be brought to complete unity."

The problem, of course, is how far we are able to sustain perichoretic correspondence between divine and human. Arguing that *perichoresis* refers to the reciprocal *interiority* of the divine persons, Miroslav Volf rightly observes that, in a strict sense, "there can be no correspondence to the interiority of the divine persons at a human level. Another human self cannot be internal to my own self as subject of action. Human persons

---

7. LaCugna, *God for Us*, 271.

"Transcendent mystery and glorious immediacy"

are always external to one another as *subjects*."[8] So the indwelling of other persons is an exclusive prerogative of God. Theologically, it may be argued that the new relationality experienced by Christians is predicated on the fact that we have now been brought into a new relationship with God in the power of the Spirit—so "we all, who with unveiled faces contemplate the Lord's glory, are being transformed into his image with ever-increasing glory, which comes from the Lord, who is the Spirit" (2 Cor 3:18)—rather than through the acquisition of some form of perichoretic correspondence. What is clear from Jesus' high-priestly prayer in John 17, irrespective of the precise nature of the theological correspondence between divine and human *perichoresis*, is that many contemporary trinitarian theologians regard the mutuality and reciprocity implicit in the inner life of the Trinity as the ontological and normative ground for all human interactions.

Most Moved Mover

Whatever position one takes in the debate,[9] it is evident that in recent years the movement towards a more dynamically relational understanding of the Trinity challenges classical conceptions of a remote, inaccessible deity, unresponsive to the unfolding history of his creation, and specifically unmoved by the actions of human beings. The language of *perichoresis* in trinitarian discourse has given the transcendent-immanent conversation a new impetus in the attempt to articulate the nature of the correspondence between the inner life of the Trinity, and the revelation of the life of God as Trinity in the economy of salvation. And the thesis to be developed in this chapter is that God acts in human history not as the "unmoved mover" of Aristotelian philosophy but as what Clark Pinnock has called the "most moved mover."

Of course, any talk of the presence of the transcendent God in his creation—which is what we mean by immanence—has to deal also with the relationship between the Trinity and non-human creation, or the natural world. Earlier, I referred to God making space for the world within himself. It is theologically problematic positing an act of creation that takes place outside God because that implies the presence of some

---

8. Volf, *After Our Likeness*, 208–13.

9. For a fuller and more scholarly discussion, see Buxton, *Trinity*, especially chapters 3 and 4.

form of space outside God, thus threatening God's omnipresence. And so we might reasonably infer some form of action by God by which he makes room within himself for his creation *ex nihilo*. This withdrawal, or "shrinkage," conveys the idea of a humble, self-restricting love that finds Christological expression in the *kenosis*, or self-emptying, of the incarnation. This way of thinking has been explored by Jürgen Moltmann in *God in Creation*, and it is an intriguing development of perichoretic thought: not only does God dwell in creation, but creation dwells in God. For Alan Torrance, this kind of exposition highlights in a very appealing way the continuity between creation and incarnation: "The 'self-emptying' of God in the incarnation is not now simply to be seen as an event which takes place 'out of the blue.' Rather, the divine 'contraction' in love at Bethlehem and on the cross is the culmination and fulfillment of precisely that dynamic which is constitutive of the very event of creation."[10] God's immanence is thus given fullest expression in his gracious, saving, loving, sustaining, majestic presence in *all* of creation, human and non-human, to which the Scriptures manifestly testify; as the psalmist declares in Ps 65:9, "You care for the land and water it; you enrich it abundantly."[11]

The transcendent-immanent tension has, of course, been the subject of considerable debate amongst many twentieth- and twenty-first-century theologians in their reflections on the relationship between God and the world. Barth's conception of God's freedom is expressed supremely as transcendence: "The loftiness, the sovereign majesty, the holiness, the glory—even what is termed the transcendence of God—what is it but this self-determination, this freedom, of the divine living and loving, the divine person?"[12] God's freedom both preserves and is determined by his otherness, his absolute independence from all that he has created. For Barth, God's transcendence is the sum of his freedom, which incorporates his freedom to be immanent: it must not, indeed cannot, be weakened.

Karl Rahner's theology was conceived, in part, as a major attempt to overcome the classical dualism between transcendence and immanence. Whilst Barth's starting point was the transcendence of God, Rahner argued that human beings are transcendental creatures who, by virtue of their transcendence, are inevitably oriented towards the ineffable mystery of God, a theme that finds an echo in the writing of Daniel

---

10. Torrance, "*Creatio ex Nihilo*," 89–90.
11. Care for creation will be given specific treatment in chapter 12.
12. Barth, *CD* 2/1, 302.

Hardy and his notion of "abduction," to which we referred in chapter 1. With regard to humanity's transcendental orientation towards mystery, he insists that "He who is essentially open to being cannot by his own capacities set limits to the possible object of a revelation."[13] Elsewhere, he writes that, "In the fact that he experiences his finiteness radically, he reaches beyond this finiteness and experiences himself as a transcendent being, as spirit."[14] But, of course, the movement is not just towards God, it is also initiated by God towards human beings. For Rahner, the doctrine of the Trinity represents "the simple statement which is at once so very incomprehensible and so very self-evident, namely, that God himself as the abiding and holy mystery, as the incomprehensible ground of man's transcendent existence is not only the God of infinite distance, but also wants to be the God of absolute closeness in a true self-communication."[15]

For other theologians after Barth and Rahner, God's freedom is expressed more impressively by his immanence. Perhaps the most prominent exponent of God's immanence is Jürgen Moltmann. In his desire to proclaim the narrative of the dynamic, shifting, and essentially open relationships of fellowship and movement within the Trinity, into which all humanity has been invited to participate, Moltmann has been criticized for emphasizing the immanence of God at the expense of his transcendence. However, for Moltmann, as for Barth, God's transcendence is precisely the sum of his freedom, which necessarily incorporates his freedom to be immanent in the history of the world. This immanence is, as he and others have demonstrated most forcefully, supremely summed up in the cross, which "stands at the heart of the trinitarian being of God."[16] For Wolfhart Pannenberg, in order to find a basis for the doctrine of the Trinity "we must begin with the way in which Father, Son, and Spirit come on the scene and relate to one another *in the event of revelation*."[17]

Promise of the Future

In his book *Eternal Life*, the Catholic theologian Hans Küng offers an attractive alternative, grounded in the future: "God is not to be understood

---

13. Rahner, *Hearers of the Word*, 112.
14. Rahner, *Foundations of Christian Faith*, 32.
15. Ibid., 137.
16. Moltmann, *Crucified God*, 207.
17. Pannenberg, *Systematic Theology. Vol. 1*, 299, my italics.

simply as the timeless eternal behind the homogeneous flow of coming to be and perishing, of past, present and future, as he is known particularly from Greek philosophy; but it is precisely as the eternal that he is the future reality, the coming reality, the one who creates hope, as he can be known from the promises of the future of Israel and of Jesus himself: 'thy kingdom come.'"[18] This eschatological interpretation of mystery is central to Moltmann, who asks: what do we really and truly hope for? To which he answers, the *kingdom of God*, which "embraces the *salvation* and eternal life of human beings, the *deliverance* of all created things, and the *peace* of the new creation."[19] For Moltmann, God's transcendence is not something that lies remotely "above us," but rather that which comes to us from the future. So the transcendent God comes to us in the present, challenging us to embrace the future as an adventure. This idea of adventure is explored more fully in *The Experiment Hope*, recapitulating Jesus' words to his disciples in Luke 9:24: "For whoever wants to save his life will lose it, but whoever loses his life for me will save it." For Moltmann, "life in hope entails risk and leads one into danger and confirmation, disappointment and surprise. We must therefore speak of the experiment of hope."[20]

Whenever we speak of the presence of the future in theological terms we are beginning to grasp the reality that the transcendent mystery of God is accessible precisely because this "wholly Other" God of Christian faith freely chooses to open up himself to those who desire to participate in his infinite goodness. In his stimulating book entitled *The Spirit of Life*, Moltmann argues that the essential obstacle to our experiencing the full life that is ours in Christ is to be found in our passive sins, not our active ones: "for the hindrance is not our despairing attempt to be ourselves, but our despairing attempt not to be ourselves, so that out of fear of life and fear of death we fall short of what our own lives could be."[21] I often think here of the psalmist's words: "I am the Lord your God, who brought you up out of Egypt. Open wide your mouth and I will fill it" (Ps 81:10). Too often, however, we come to God with our mouths open only partially, whereas God encourages us to open *wide* our mouths! If Rahner is right that we are inevitably oriented towards the

18. Küng, *Eternal Life?* 214.
19. Moltmann, *Coming of God*, xvi (author's italics).
20. Moltmann, *Experiment Hope*, 187.
21. Moltmann, *Spirit of Life*, 188.

"Transcendent mystery and glorious immediacy" 41

ineffable mystery of God, perhaps we need to listen to our hearts more attentively. We often fear treading out into the unknown, preferring the safety of familiar things—that is not something to despise, of course, for it reflects the inbuilt tendency many of us have for security and safety. But the gospel encourages us to move beyond the security of our own comfort zones into a life of adventurous trust in God, a life in which we discover our full humanity.

Following Rahner, John Haught argues that it is a fundamental structure of our being to be open not only to the world, but also to transcendent mystery.[22] "The image of a promising God who meets us out of the mysterious future subverts the archaic religious instinct to seek fulfillment in nature or in the present moment alone, or in an escape from history into timelessness. The promising mystery holds out a new vision of creation's possibilities and thereby sabotages our instincts for securing our existence only in the predictability of natural recurrences."[23]

Indeed, throughout the biblical record, God's people are encouraged again and again to put their trust in the transcendent God who offers them a vision of what their future might be. Translating this into the context of pastoral ministry today, Ray Anderson adopts Moltmann's important distinction between *futurum* (which emphasizes that which arises out of the present) and *adventus* (which has to do with that which comes into the present out of the future), interpreting the present as that which apprehends the future in terms of what is yet to be or come, and asks what yet can be done to bring that future into reality.[24] So the controlling factor is God's revelation of his will. All ministry is therefore concerned with discerning that will and entering into the stream of God's gracious working—in partnership with him—such that God's future comes into being in its time.[25] Picking up themes from Daniel Hardy discussed in chapter 1, the thesis presented here is that the joy of ministry—as much as in our personal lives—is to be caught up into the infinite potential of God's mystery, in which we see every pastoral event as an opportunity to discover the glorious possibilities of the goodness of God at work in our lives *now*, anticipating the fullness of God's transcendent glory. So transcendence

---

22. Haught, *Mystery and Promise*, 44–45.
23. Ibid., 86.
24. On *futurum* and *adventus*, see Moltmann, *Future of Creation*, 29–31.
25. See Anderson, *Minding God's Business*, 48.

and immanence cohere as the promise of the future, mediated as God's presence, or, to put it another way, as God's openness.

An example of such an experience in my own life immediately comes to mind. Over the years my wife and I have found ourselves living in many different surroundings. Back in the 1980s we lived in a run-down part of London. I was an Anglican curate in inner-city London, and our home was in the most desperate part of the parish. We struggled with that, having just sold our own home in beautiful countryside! We had a pocket-handkerchief of a backyard, and our children were young. There was a constant flow of traffic outside our front door. Next door to us was an older man. He had a foul mouth, and whenever our children went out into the backyard, there he was, swearing obscenities in a loud voice—we couldn't get away from him. One day it got so bad that Gill and I prayed out to God, "O God, move this man or shut him up!" It was a heartfelt prayer, and we were earnest in our pleading. The next week he had a stroke that paralyzed half his side. He couldn't talk! The amazing thing is that as he slowly recovered, he changed. We began to talk with him, and he began to relate to us and our children. In many ways he was a new man. Desperation had driven us to pray that way, and however you interpret the result we knew that God was at work in this man in a way that was truly miraculous. We didn't pray on that occasion with a passion for that man's soul. We prayed with urgent desperation for our own sakes! The point I want to make here is that in the midst of our longing for God's deliverance, he met us in a totally new and unexpected way, revealing himself in our midst as the hospitable triune God who welcomes *all* people into his life. It was a powerful lesson of the mystery of God's transcendent love revealed in the concrete reality of our life and ministry in inner-city suburbia, pointing us, indeed drawing us, deeper into the possibilities of God's redemption, *the seeds of which already lie deep within us!*

Active Participants

Both transcendent and immanent, not "either-or." God, in his transcendent freedom, chooses to dwell amongst us precisely because he wants to reveal who he truly is, thus evoking the response of faith, irradiating us (to use Hardy's language) with his light, never too much to overwhelm us, but enough to draw us deeper into his life. Thus we are encouraged to enter into God's purposes for his creation, not as passive observers but as active participants. I once attended an evening service at an Anglican church that was beginning to experience an openness to the Spirit, and that openness to God was accompanied by an openness with one another, so that it wasn't odd for people to speak out what was on their hearts from time to time. That evening we could sense the "weight" of the Spirit—not a heavy weight, but what could be described, in the language of C. S. Lewis, as "the weight of glory." As we were standing in the Lord's presence, a particular need arose and was voiced with fervor and longing by a woman in the congregation. I cannot remember at all the actual situation involved. But what I do remember after a short silence was the impassioned plea of a young man, who challenged God to have mercy on the basis that he is a merciful God. And so his intercession went on, reminding God of his compassion and faithfulness, even to the point of praying something along the lines of "Lord, because of who you are, you dare not fail this person in this situation . . ." I recall thinking, "Well, how dare he pray like that! How presumptuous!" And doubtless there were one or two others who thought like that too. Looking back, though, I wish I could have prayed like that. I wish I had had the *chutzpah* to pray with such nerve and audacity! I don't think God minds one little bit about that sort of praying.

The story of Esther in the Old Testament is seen by Christians and Jews alike as a narrative of intercessory *chutzpah*, even though God is never named. Jews still observe today the Feast of Purim "as the month when their sorrow was turned to joy and their mourning into a day of celebration" (Esth 9:22). For both Christians and Jews, Esther's bold plea before King Xerxes speaks of the transcendent God who acts in human history . . . and human beings are invited into his story. In the book of Ruth (another Old Testament narrative in which God is the hidden "actor," working out his purposes "behind the scenes") both Naomi and Ruth are portrayed as active participants in the story. They avoid the temptation to sink into a morass of self-pity. Naomi had one card left—a small piece of land in Israel and a distant relative, and it is quite possible to characterize her as a desperate woman playing her last card! As God's purposes unfold, in the hidden way so typical of his dealings with us, we recognize the twin themes of human and divine activity. God calls us into a co-operative venture with him, so that we contribute to the ultimate outcome.

In the incident of the golden calf in Exod 32, Moses' response to God's intention to destroy the Israelites for their idolatrous stupidity is remarkable indeed, resulting in God changing his mind. Some insist here that God knew ahead of time that he was going to change his mind and so fulfil the plan that he had from the very beginning . . . so preserving God's immutability. But the Bible doesn't say that. It simply lays out the story as a narrative and invites us to draw some conclusions, one of which is that we are welcomed into God's plans and purposes, and he invites us to be part of the solution. Our prayers make a difference to God, a view that has been strongly championed by those who espouse what has been called "open theism," "openness theology," or "free will theism," a theological paradigm that asserts that God has freely chosen to limit his power because he delights in welcoming the actions and free-will decisions of human beings into the unfolding trajectory of history. In a nutshell, God is open to the future, and the future is open to God.

Open theism, as one of its most prominent advocates, Clark Pinnock, writes, "treads the middle path between classical theism, which exaggerates God's transcendence of the world, and process theism, which presses for radical immanence."[26] In his book *Most Moved Mover*—a title that captures exquisitely the "both-and" nature of God's relationship with his creation—Pinnock argues that the traditional, classical view of God "is one sided in its preference for God's magnificent otherness over his loving condescension and it makes it difficult to speak adequately about a personal God. God is not like a stone pillar, in no way affected by the world and alien to real relatedness and reciprocity."[27] Open theists challenge process thinking because of its limited view of transcendence—in fact, God's transcendence is dealt a fatal blow because process thought fails to make a clear distinction between God and his world, which is an ontological necessity for open theists. Open theists also reject the deistic worldview which lies at the other end of the spectrum of the God-world relationship; deism radically abandons God's immanence by locating God as a transcendent being beyond and apart from all that he has created. Whilst acknowledging their critical emphasis on God's transcendence, openness theologians critique classical theists because of their failure to make sufficient allowance for God's preferred relationship of dynamic reciprocity and interaction with human beings.

26. Pinnock, "From Augustine to Arminius," 26.
27. Pinnock, *Most Moved Mover*, 7–8.

In the example cited earlier in this chapter, open theists would claim that the young man's impassioned plea in church on behalf of a woman's deep need might well have turned around the situation faced by that woman, in the same way that Moses' intercessory *chutzpah* brought about a transformation in the Israelites' plight: "Then the Lord relented and did not bring on his people the disaster he had threatened" (Exod 32:14). For open theists, the God of Abraham, Isaac, and Jacob is the God of loving condescension, who has revealed himself throughout Scripture as the holy God who "freely enters into genuine give-and-take-relations with us."[28]

Open theism also holds, on the basis of human freedom, that God knows everything that can be known, but he does not know the future. Because God has chosen to make himself open to human freedom, then the future is not fully knowable, even to God. Understandably, this is a controversial assertion, challenging traditional interpretations of divine omniscience, and is likely to remain divisive. However, for open theists, "the watershed issue in the debate is not whether God has exhaustive definite foreknowledge but whether God is ever affected by and responds to what we do."[29] With regard to God changing his mind, besides the obvious question about the meaning of words like "relent" and "change," Scripture would seem to be ambiguous on the matter. Incidents like the golden calf in Exod 32 and God's judgment on Nineveh in Jonah 3 need to be set alongside specific verses that declare that God does not change his mind (e.g., Mal 3:6 and Jas 1:17)—so we need to be careful that we do not box God into our own preferred hermeneutical framework!

Condescending Love

In drawing to a close, we might note the insights of the Eastern Orthodox theologian and philosopher David Bentley Hart (no advocate of open theism), who, in his remarkable and erudite book *The Beauty of the Infinite*, argues for the presence of mystery in the Godhead not by virtue of any form of divine omnipotence or inaccessible remoteness, but precisely because of the depth of his accessible and intimate love. God comes to us and dwells with us—this, for Hart, is the true Christian aesthetic, an aesthetic of beauty, in which human beings and indeed all creation are

---

28. Sanders, *God Who Risks*, 282.
29. Sanders, "Summary of Openness Theology," para. 7.

summoned to discover their place within the life of the triune God. So the mystery of God is not an *escape* from the history of the world, but precisely the opposite. Mystery, for Hart, is one of the defining characteristics of God's *temporal* presence in the world, where transcendence and immanence meet in condescending love: "the entire motion of condescension—creation, covenant, incarnation—is already contained in the perichoretic motion of the Trinity."[30] This is the gospel that informs all pastoral ministry, and it is a mystery—the mystery of a God who, in trinitarian love and grace, invites us into his life and into his future. The invitation is open to us all to participate in that mystery which, as demonstrated in Hart's self-confessed elliptical fashion throughout his book, is that "infinity of beauty that declares itself both as transcendent mystery and as glorious immediacy."[31]

There are, of course, very real pastoral implications in holding divine transcendence and immanence together in this way—for example, those who experience suffering will be comforted in the knowledge that their God interacts compassionately and sensitively with them in their afflictions. So we might want to affirm God as an open Trinity who feels the pain of his creation, and whose seeking Spirit is ever at work to bring healing and hope to the suffering and the oppressed. But God is also the ontological "Other," beyond our comprehension. So the persistence of suffering remains a mystery located within the inner life of God. We dare not presume upon God with regard to the mystery of suffering. Jürgen Moltmann has rightly called the question of theodicy "*the open wound of life* in this world."[32]

How, then, might we grasp something of this mystery in pastoral life today? Perhaps the sacrament of the Eucharist offers a key, for there the three pastoral dimensions of worship, mission, and compassion converge in a powerfully creative and imaginative way as the Christian community participates in what the English Baptist theologian Paul Fiddes describes as "interweaving currents" in the history of the triune God—not only with thanksgiving, but also as we experience pain over the suffering in this world. It is precisely because the Eucharist is inclusive as a catholic sacrament that we interpret it proleptically as a sign of the kingdom: "discerning the body of Christ in the breaking of the bread enables us to

---

30. Hart, *Beauty of the Infinite*, 256–57.
31. Ibid., 229.
32. Moltmann, *Trinity and Kingdom of God*, 49.

discern him through the broken bodies of the prisoners, the thirsty and the hungry."[33] The God of eternity and history, unchangeable in his faithfulness, opens up his life to us in eucharistic worship. He is immanent in his transcendence. Here is fertile soil for what we might call "eucharistic imagination," in which we envision creation as an interconnected whole, and find ourselves crying out for the freedom of the whole of God's "creation-community."

When we remember again whose people we are, and dance with the joy of the redeemed, then we will begin to understand in the depths of our being that the eucharistic feast is not just for ourselves, and there will awaken in us a hunger for freedom and a cry for the other person. Perhaps, then, theodicy can only really be addressed—though never "resolved"—within the framework of a theology of redemption and new creation, anticipated in the eucharistic feast, the supreme act of worship in which transcendence and immanence converge.

---

33. Fiddes, *Participating in God*, 283.

4

"We have to become People of the Story"
–Scot McKnight

Personal Salvation

In his encounter with the rich ruler who wanted to know what was required of him to inherit eternal life, Jesus pointed to the commandments and then told him: "Sell everything you have and give to the poor, and you will have treasure in heaven" (Luke 18:22). The rich man's sadness at this response prompted one of Jesus' humorous "camel sayings": "How hard it is for the rich to enter the kingdom of God! It is easier for a camel to go through the eye of a needle than for someone who is rich to enter the kingdom of God." "Who then can be saved?" was the incredulous reaction of those standing around.

A number of interpretations have been given to this narrative, but it is probably best to take Jesus' reply at face value and understand that what is impossible for us is possible for God—in other words, entry into the kingdom of God is something only God can bring about. Whatever one's interpretation, however, this story is significant because it contains a number of important themes that have to do with the nature and scope of the gospel. The response of the hearers, "Who then can be saved?" signifies that the concern of the hearers was with personal salvation, as indeed was likely the case with the rich ruler—Tom Wright suggests that he had "hoped to impress Jesus with his piety and devotion."[1] Jesus, however, takes them—and us—beyond a concern for personal salvation, referring three times in this encounter to the kingdom of God.

In this chapter, I would like to briefly examine the emphasis that has been placed by Christians on personal salvation at the expense of the gospel of the kingdom, arising from (and reinforcing) an incomplete understanding of the biblical revelation of God in Christ. In his recent book, *The King Jesus Gospel*, the New Testament theologian Scot McKnight makes this his central theme. Citing Luke's record of the story of the Jerusalemites' response to Peter's first gospel sermon in Acts 2:37—"When the people heard this, they were cut to the heart and said to Peter and the other apostles, 'Brothers, what shall we do?'"—McKnight makes a critical point: "Peter focuses on Jesus, and the Jesus Story awakens a consciousness of sin and a need for Jesus to be their Messiah, Lord, and Savior."[2] Peter's sermon was essentially the good news (gospel) of the story of Israel coming to completion in the story of Jesus—it was not the gospel *of* personal salvation (which many evangelicals assume is the point of the pericope of the rich man in Luke 18) but the gospel of Jesus as Messiah that *leads to* personal salvation. The point that McKnight makes throughout his book is that "gospel" and "salvation," though inextricably entwined, are not the same thing—the gospel is not reducible to personal salvation, or (citing Dallas Willard) to "sin management." It is far wider than that—the gospel is "the salvation-unleashing Story of Jesus, Messiah-Lord-Son, that brings to completion the Story of Israel as found in the Scriptures of the Old Testament."[3] So "*we have to become People of the Story.*"[4] However, personal salvation is not relegated to an also-ran in McKnight's thesis—the full gospel is *both* justification *and* the kingdom, but justification finds its significance within this "big-picture" perspective of the story of Jesus that is Scripture's grand narrative. So the gospel is not either justification or the kingdom—it is *both*. And it is also much bigger than the idea of personal discipleship often associated with the phrase, "living in the kingdom," which too often has been reduced to some sort of spiritualized existence, set apart from the physicality of God's good creation. And, of course, as indicated already, not only does

---

1. Wright, *Luke for Everyone*, 216.
2. McKnight, *King Jesus Gospel*, 145.
3. Ibid., 61.
4. Ibid., 153, author's italics.

the gospel address our relationship with the whole of creation, but it also says some important things to us about where the nation of Israel fits into the big picture of God's promised new age.

Gospel Culture

All this begs the real question lying behind the debate that McKnight explores in his book, which is "what does it actually mean to be saved?" He argues that many evangelical Christians have succumbed to what he calls a "salvation culture" rather than being captivated by a "gospel culture"—they are, in his words, more "soterian"[5] than evangelical, with the result that they focus on how we respond to the personal gospel of salvation rather than on what it means to be caught up in God's grand narrative of the completion of his promise to Israel in Jesus. "Our salvation culture," claims McKnight, "tends toward asking one double-barreled question: 'Who is in and who is out?' Or more personally, 'Are you in or out?'" The emphasis in many evangelical churches (if that is the right way of describing them in the light of McKnight's thesis!) is on personal *decision*—in or out—rather than personal *discipleship*.

One way of illustrating the point that McKnight and others are making, and then expanding it, is to bring a trinitarian focus into the gospel paradigm outlined above, and represent diagrammatically in the following table:

---

5. *Soteria* is the Greek word for salvation.

From a "salvation culture" to a "gospel culture"		
SOTERIAN	*TRINITARIAN*	*EVANGELICAL*
Focus on ACTION: "GOD SO LOVED…"	Focus on PERSON: "GOD IS LOVE"	Focus on the NEW CREATION: "GOD IS KING"
Key word: JUSTIFICATION	Key word: ADOPTION	Key word: FULFILMENT
Key text: Rom 3:21–26	Key text: Eph 1:3–8	Key texts: Eph 1:9–10; Rev 21:1–6
LEGAL context	HOME context	NEW EARTH context
Focus on the DEATH of Jesus	Focus on the LIFE of the Trinity	Focus on the DWELLING of God
Emphasis on what we've been saved FROM	Emphasis on what we've been saved INTO	Emphasis on what we've been saved FOR
"Them and us"	All included	Restoration of "all things"

In the left hand column of the diagram, the classical Protestant soterian interpretation of the gospel is outlined, emphasizing the reality of Christ's death on the cross for the sins of the world. Underlying this interpretation, which is common in contemporary evangelicalism, is the well-known Johannine verse, "For God so loved the world that he gave his one and only Son, that whoever believes in him shall not perish but have eternal life" (John 3:16). This verse is so commonly cited amongst evangelicals that one might be forgiven for thinking that it sums up the gospel in a nutshell. However, as we shall see, it represents not so much a *summation* of the gospel as the personal *consequence* of individual belief in the one who is himself the gospel, the good news of salvation. A key word in this interpretation is justification, that is justification by faith, as spelled out in Paul's words in Rom 3:21–26. The language used by Paul here is forensic. In these verses we find a word used five times that is based on the idea of God as someone who is just—so *just, justifies, justified, justice*. The language, of course, comes from the courtroom—it is legal language. Justification is a declaration that God's perfect justice has been satisfied: the penalty for sin—which is death—has been paid. The Greek word translated "just" means that God's acts are perfectly in line with his nature. *God does what he does because he is who he is.* God is not a God of love because he acts towards us in love—he acts towards us in love precisely because he *is* love. As indicated in the diagram, the focal point in this way of understanding the gospel is the death of Christ, so the cross-emphasis is crucial . . . but, of course it doesn't end there. As Tom Wright reminds us, "One of the specific things on which the New Testament insists, again and again, is that in the life, death and *supremely the resurrection* of Jesus the promised new age has dawned."[6]

But even if resurrection language is introduced into this gospel paradigm, it still doesn't tell us anything about God's grand saving purpose for his whole creation, Jew and Gentile alike. Typically, in the soterian paradigm, resurrection is also interpreted in a personal and individualistic way, so that the full cosmic significance of the resurrection is lost in the myopic focus on "me and my God." The real problem with the soterian paradigm is that it stops short at what God has done for you and me as individuals, declaring—quite rightly, and still gloriously so—that through faith in Christ's death on the cross we have now been saved from our sins: he took the punishment we deserve, and we now have eternal life . . . whatever that might mean within this particular view of the gospel. If the truth be told, though, the gospel is much more dangerous, and ultimately much more exciting, than that conveyed by the "Plan of Salvation!" Images of being "set free" abound in this paradigm, and whilst I do not want to diminish the sheer grace of God in delivering us from the hold of sin in our lives, we surely need to ask the question: what exactly have we been freed *into*? And, as we shall see in the right hand column, what have we been saved *for*? Because the gospel is not essentially about *me*—it is about Jesus. What has actually been accomplished through the death and resurrection of Jesus, into which we have now been gloriously caught up?

Before moving to that part of the story, we note the tendency of the "soterian gospel" to separate those who have been saved from those who have not, those who will go to heaven from those who will end up in hell.

---

6. Wright, *Way of the Lord*, 126, my italics.

In the next chapter we will consider what Robin Parry (aka Gregory MacDonald) describes as "a hell of a problem," namely whether God really does consign people to hell (however that may be interpreted). Suffice it to say, at this stage, the traditional evangelical position is that the gospel certainly does divide the "sheep" from the "goats," and that faith in Christ is seen as the marker between those who are "in" and those who are "out" with regard to eternal life. The emphasis in the reduced gospel of the soterians is on making a decision for Christ, so that I can "go to heaven when I die"—I'm "in" . . . praise the Lord! Those who have not made this decision will be consigned to hell—they are "out." Of course, this view, by placing "decision" rather than "discipleship" in the spotlight, also debases the currency of the gospel because it says nothing about how we are living our lives *today*—more about that later.

Evangelism is therefore perceived as a matter of witnessing to those who are "out" in the hope that they make a decision for Christ in order to be safely "in." In my early days as a Christian, this was precisely what motivated my encounter with people in the Anglican parish in which I lived: I—along with many other eager Christian believers—was sincerely motivated by the soterian gospel paradigm, and the grace and wonder of it all is that there are still many people today whose lives have been truly changed as a result of that understanding of the gospel (I confess too that my own enthusiastic efforts sometimes had a totally opposite effect!). However, if that transformation has only been from "me and my world" to "me and my God," then it represents a dilution of the full gospel. Certainly, to be drawn out of our own selfish little worlds into the very life of God is a staggering reality, full of wonderful and eternal significance for individual Christians. But the gospel is more, far more, than that.

Trinitarian Gospel

In turning to the "trinitarian gospel" in the middle column of the diagram, we introduce a dimension that is noticeably absent from McKnight's treatment of the gospel. In *Celebrating Life* I argue that "the gospel is not so much about God giving us a new life, but of us being caught up into the very life of God himself, so that humanity and Trinity—and creation—are bound together forever."[7] In that book my concern was to demonstrate that Christians have no legitimate grounds for celebrat-

---

7. Buxton, *Celebrating Life*, 35.

ing the good news of Jesus Christ in a world that is itself searching for answers if they proclaim a triumphalistic and truncated gospel. Such a gospel is tantamount to a *theologia gloriae*, because it not only distances Christians from the goodness of God's creation, but it also massages their faith by diluting the problems and difficulties that we all face in a broken and confused world. Introducing the Trinity into our understanding of the gospel corrects that dualistic myopia by putting the focus back on the nature of God himself, rather than on what God has done for our salvation, and serves as a necessary segue into a full "gospel culture."

In the "trinitarian gospel," the weight shifts away from God's loving *act* to God's loving *being*, and they are not, as Karl Barth reminds us, to be separated: "this subject, God, the Revealer, is identical with His act in revelation and also identical with its effect."[8] Indeed their identity is, for him, grounded in the doctrine of the Trinity: "When we ask: Who is the self-revealing God? the Bible answers in such a way that we have to reflect on the triunity of God."[9] However, it may be argued that Barth's trinitarian discussion is grounded in an abstract "revelation model" that is too narrowly conceived, failing to do justice to human participation in the intra-divine life. It is to this that we now turn in developing a trinitarian shape to the gospel story.

Trinitarian being is grounded in John's declaration that "God is love" (1 John 4:8). And this God who is love "does not remain locked up in the 'splendid isolation' of self-love but spills over into what is other than God, giving birth to creation and history."[10] God has not created us to praise and honor him as if he, in his triune being, lacked something. Rather, he has created us that we might live in the fullness of his "spilled-over" life in the creation that is bound up within his tri-personal life of dynamic perichoretic relationality. This is the gospel of salvation. In Paul's letter to the Ephesians, the apostle spells out the manifold blessings of the gospel, declaring in verse 5 that, in love God "predestined us for adoption to sonship through Jesus Christ, in accordance with his pleasure and will." Of note here is Jim Packer's memorable comment that adoption is *"the highest privilege that the gospel offers*: higher even than justification."[11] In the context of the present discussion, Packer's use of italics might equally

---

8. Barth, *Prolegomena to CD Vol. 1, Part 1*, 296.
9. Ibid., 303.
10. LaCugna, *God for Us*, 353.
11. Packer, *Knowing God*, 232.

well apply to the second part of his statement. Can there really be anything higher than justification, being put right with God?

The answer, of course, is that, yes, there can indeed be a higher blessing, because justification is the (necessary) doorway into our privileged adoption as God's children, welcomed into the Trinity's hospitable family life. The notion of hospitality is a characteristic feature of God, who creates space for human beings to experience in the fullest sense possible what it means to "feel at home." This is what we have been saved *into* . . . and it eschews all individualism, the curse of the present age. If the soterian gospel, in the way that it has often been presented, has a tendency to put the accent on "me and my God," the trinitarian gospel puts the emphasis on "us and our God." Is this not what Jesus promised when he prayed to his Father that all who believed in him may be one "just as you are in me and I am in you" (John 17:21)? To echo the community-life of the Trinity in our life as the body of Christ on earth, "fellow-citizens with God's people and members of God's household" (Eph 2:19), takes us into a greater depth of spiritual experience as we learn what it means to actually participate with one another in the outworking of the triune God's purposes in his promised new age.

When the Spirit was poured out upon the waiting disciples, they proclaimed the wonders of God in the tongues of every nation under heaven. Many people heard them: "Amazed and perplexed, they asked one another 'What does this mean?'" (Acts 2:12). It means that God has included all people in his act of grace in Jesus Christ—no one has been left out. Through Jesus' promise of the Spirit in Acts 1:8 and the reality of his coming on the day of Pentecost, God was teaching his church about the inclusiveness of his accepting love. All have been included as the result of the death and resurrection of Jesus Christ. The incarnation firstly has to do with God's deepest desire in relation to humanity, which is to renew his image in us. In his treatise *De Incarnatione Verbi Dei*, the early church father Athanasius argued that no one could do this save God alone: "Therefore He assumed a human body, in order that in it death might once for all be destroyed, and that men might be renewed according to the Image."[12] So when Christ died, he took *all humanity* into his death, and in his resurrection *all humanity* is lifted up with him. This is what Athanasius describes as "the good pleasure of God." This insight actually changes the way we witness to the gospel, because instead of see-

---

12. Athanasius, *On the Incarnation*, 41.

ing people as those who are "out" needing to opt "in," we now see that all people are actually already "in" as the result of the death and resurrection of Jesus Christ. The privilege we now have is to so live the gospel that others around us ask, "What shall we do?," echoing the response of those who heard Peter's first gospel sermon in Acts 2. But in order for this to be authentic "gospeling," we need to fully understand the truly evangelical nature of the good news of the gospel as laid out in the right hand column of the diagram above.

Why did God send Jesus into the world? Brian McLaren's response is that "Jesus . . . did not come merely to 'save souls from hell.' No, he came to launch a new Genesis, to lead a new Exodus, and to announce, embody, and inaugurate a new Kingdom as the Prince of Peace (Isa 9:6)."[13] When Jesus was asked by the Pharisees when the kingdom would come, he replied, "The coming of the kingdom of God is not something that can be observed, nor will people say, 'Here it is,' or 'There it is,' because the kingdom of God is in your midst" (Luke 17:20–21). Here Jesus is declaring that he is the *autobasileia*, the kingdom in person. In proclaiming that "the kingdom of God has come near. Repent and believe the good news" (Mark 1:15), "he was not calling attention to general, timeless spiritual truths, nor was he urging people to make a decision for God; he was telling his hearers that Yahweh was actively gathering the people of Israel and, indirectly, all people into a new salvific order, and he was insisting that his hearers conform themselves to this new state of affairs."[14]

To maintain that the "evangelical gospel" has a "new creation" focus, as stated in the diagram above, is to insist that the resurrection of Jesus is not just an event of the present age, but, as argued vigorously by Tom Wright in *Surprised by Hope*, crucially the defining event of the new creation: "The power of the gospel lies, not in the offer of a new spirituality or religious experience, not in the threat of hellfire (certainly not in the threat of being "left behind") which can be removed if only the hearer ticks this box, says this prayer, raises a hand, or whatever . . . but in the powerful announcement that God is God, that Jesus is Lord, that the powers of evil have been defeated, that God's new world has begun."[15] This is the good news—that the *eschaton* ("end times") is not just something to anticipate as future event, but has already been inaugurated in the person

---

13. McLaren, *New Kind of Christianity*, 180.
14. Barron, *Priority of Christ*, 72.
15. Wright, *Surprised by Hope*, 238–39."

of Jesus, the *autobasilaeia*, through whom (as Paul writes in Eph 1:9-10) the mystery of God's will has now been put into effect, namely, to bring unity to all things in heaven and on earth under Christ.

Participatory Eschatology

The implication of all this is that Christians now have the privilege of participating in the full outworking and ultimate fulfilment of the kingdom of God. Our calling as Christians, therefore, is to live redemptively in the world because we are looking forward to experiencing it in all its beauty and fullness in the new creation of God's promise. This is what we've been saved *for!*[16] This is what McLaren calls "participatory eschatology": "When we ask, 'What does the future hold?' the answer begins, 'That depends.' It depends on you and me. God holds out to us at every moment a brighter future; the issue is whether we are willing to receive it and work with God to help create it. We are participating in the creation of what the future will be."[17]

So we have a part to play, energized by the Spirit, who is at work in the whole of creation in deep, hidden, generous, surprising, and liberating ways. The feminist theologian Elizabeth Johnson argues that the full range of the reality and activity of the Spirit at the very heart of the world has been lost in the Western theological tradition. She claims that the language we use to refer to the Spirit reflects this neglect: "faceless, shadowy, anonymous, half-known, homeless, watered-down, the poor relation, Cinderella."[18] In contrast, the energizing presence of the Spirit who sustains all created things pervades the cosmos and is to be celebrated with thanksgiving and open response:

> The Spirit's renewing presence is always and everywhere partial to her beloved creatures suffering from socially constructed harm, working to liberate oppressed and oppressors from the distorted systems that destroy the humanity of them both. Like a baker-woman she keeps on kneading the leaven of kindness and truth, justice and peace into the thick dough of the world until the whole loaf rises (Matt 13:33).[19]

16. This is a theme I develop more fully in the final chapter of *Celebrating Life*, esp. pp. 191-96.
17. McLaren, *New Kind of Christianity*, 106.
18. Johnson, *She Who Is*, 131.
19. Ibid., 137.

Johnson's explicit eschatological orientation embraces a liberation that encompasses not only human life but all creation; as such, it shatters any dualistic notions we might have in which human beings are somehow "caught up" by the Spirit, and transported out of this world and into some mystical, spiritual reality that has no bearing on the created order. For salvation has to do with living in the new creation—God is not in the business of abolishing creation, but *redeeming* it. And his longing is that no one should be left out. Hence the energizing life of the Spirit in creation, whose "power makes all withered sticks and souls green again with the juice of life."[20]

And what Jesus has done in his death, resurrection, and ascension is also, crucially, the completion of the story of Israel. What God has done for all creation in the story of Jesus he has done *through* Israel—Jesus is Israel's Messiah first, "sent to the lost sheep of Israel" (Matt 15:24). Israel's salvation has been accomplished, not in any political or nationalist sense involving a strip of land in the Middle East, but in the context of a comprehensive and cosmic liberation that *starts* with Israel, but doesn't end there. What God has begun in Christ he will complete in Christ, as foretold in Rev 21, and it is a promise that embraces all humanity, all creation. The full, "big-picture" gospel which is the story of Jesus throughout the Bible (in both Old and New Testaments) finds its climax in the new creation of God's promise, a new heaven and new earth, where "God's dwelling-place is now among the people, and he will dwell with them"—"a great multitude that no one could count, from every nation, tribe, people, and language, standing before the throne and before the Lamb" (Rev 7:9). This is the gospel of the kingdom.

In *Dancing in the Dark* I represented the gospel paradigm transition outlined above in the form of another, much simpler, diagram:

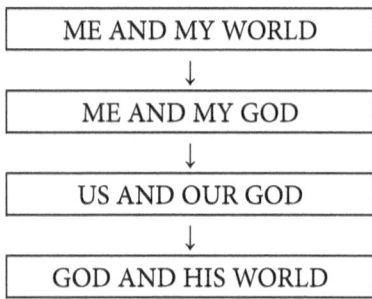

---

20. Ibid., 128.

The Goal of Creation

The first two entries above signify Scot McKnight's "Plan of Salvation," whilst the final entry symbolizes the "big-picture" promise summed up in the story of Jesus. It is not a matter of "either-or" but "both-and", as individual eschatology finds its rightful place within God's cosmic eschatological framework. In between we are reminded of our calling to live as a hospitable community of love, echoing the perichoretic life of the Trinity. No one of us can "go it alone" as a Christian, as Paul's teaching makes clear. If baptism signifies our incorporation into the triune life of God, it is entirely inappropriate to conduct the sacrament as a private "hole-in-the-corner" affair typical of much folk religion. Baptism is not only *personal*: theologically, it is a *public* declaration of our participation in the life of the Trinity, who welcomes us in the outworking of the promised new age. In my days as an Anglican minister in a variety of parishes I struggled with the idea of baptizing the babies of parents who had no real personal interest in being part of God's family, but increasingly I have become aware of the theological truth that baptism is first and foremost about God before it is about us, signifying what God has done for all humanity in Jesus Christ. Baptism, then, is less a guarantee of commitment on our side as it is a guarantee that God remembers us all the way through our lives from the very moment of our birth, even before then. The gospel, then, is about God first before it is about you and me. It speaks to us of a God who is 100 percent committed to every single person who has ever lived, who lives now and who will live in the future. God is for us, and, as Karl Barth once put it in his doctrine of reconciliation, "what unites God and us men is that He does not will to be God without us, that He creates us rather to share with us His own incomparable being and life and act."[21]

And it is a gospel which takes seriously God's creation, because he is also committed 100 percent to all that he has brought into being *ex nihilo*: ultimately, to live fully as those who have been created *imago Dei* means to enjoy the experience of life in God, life with other human beings, and life in relationship to God's creation. Evangelical Christianity has given prominence (rightly) to the first, acknowledged the second, but in large part given only lip service to humanity's relationship with the natural world. Just as the full gospel of God invites us to move from an egocentric salvation paradigm ("me and my God") to one that embraces all humanity, it also arouses in us the possibility of a paradigm shift from

21. Barth, *CD Vol. 4 Pt. 1*, 7.

an anthropocentric understanding of creation towards a theocentric perspective, which has the potential of transforming our relationship with nature from one of domination to one of communion, a theme explored more fully in chapter 12. As expressed succinctly in an Anglican report on global sustainability, "We are not consumers of what God has made; we are in communion with it."[22]

The ultimate goal and redemption of creation, to which the gospel continually points us, may be summed up in the language of "Sabbath," the completion and crown of God's saving activity. It is *God's* Sabbath, the goal for which human beings are created. The gospel, then, has to do with the exquisite tension of the "now" and "not yet" of the kingdom of God: present reality and future hope. And it has to do with living life in this good world that God has created, enjoying the richness of all that he has created, in anticipation of—and witness to—the new creation of God's promise, the banquet to which all are invited. As Matthew Sleeth reminds us in *24/6*, his inspiring challenge to a 24/7 lifestyle, we are created for God's *Shabbat shalom*, invited into a way of living in the present as human *beings* rather than human *doings* as we look forward to the new creation of God's love.[23]

---

22. Foster and Williams, *Sharing God's Planet*, vii.
23. See Sleeth, *24/6*.

5

"A hell of a problem"
−Robin Parry

Ultimate Fate

If the gospel speaks to us of the ultimate consummation of all things, as we have seen in chapter 4, what can we then say about those for whom the Christian faith holds no meaning? What is the ultimate fate of those who have no desire to join in the "wedding banquet" (Matt 22:1-14)? Does God remember them? The tension inherent in the biblical claims regarding the ultimate scope of salvation is an issue with which many evangelicals are currently wrestling, and there is a sense in which the ground is shifting on the topic, as more and more evangelicals confess to a "hope for universal salvation." Specifically, the problem is often presented as follows: how can one reconcile the clear scriptural texts on damnation with those that seem to offer hope concerning God's resolve in Christ to "unite all things in him, things in heaven and things on earth" (Eph 1:10 and Col 1:20)? There is also the added difficulty of the struggle many Christians have about a perfect and just God consigning people to an eternity of hell (whatever that might mean) for a finite and (relatively) insignificant period of time of sinning on earth. There is both ambiguity and paradox here that demand inquiry.

For some, a preference for universal salvation is grounded in the conviction that, in the final divine self-glorification, when God will be "all in all," nothing will be lost. This, of course, challenges mainline evangelical interpretations of Scripture with regard to the role of faith in personal salvation and the biblical support for a "double outcome." For Jürgen Moltmann, the doctrine of the transcendent sovereignty of God is critical to his universalist position: divine grace and human decision cannot be brought to the same level, for this means "humanizing God and deifying the human being."[1] God has the last word.

This God, sovereign in choosing to affirm his love for *all* that he has made, has acted in Christ, whose resurrection is the "open plenitude" of God for the redemption of "all things" (*ta panta* in the Greek)—human and non-human—within the new creation of his glory: as Moltmann succinctly states "what God wants to do he can do, and will do."[2] John A. T. Robinson, well-known for his book *Honest to God*, argues that the doctrine of universalism is grounded, not in the demands of human longing (which does it no credit at all), but in the work of God in Christ, in whom is expressed the fullness of divine love: "In a universe of love there can be no heaven which tolerates a chamber of horrors, no hell for any which does not at the same time make it a hell for God. He cannot endure that, for *that* would be the final mockery of his nature. And he will not."[3]

The issue here, of course, is that of "both-and" rather than "either-or." Just as we would want to maintain that God is both transcendent and immanent, might we not also want to argue that it is possible to be both an evangelical Christian and a universalist? To put it in a nutshell, is the notion of an "evangelical universalist" an oxymoron? The issue of Christian universalism—not the same as pluralism, which teaches that all roads lead to the same god, however he/she/it may be described—is perhaps one of the greatest challenges facing evangelicals today.

The Christian—or evangelical—universalist subscribes to mainstream orthodox beliefs such as the efficacy of God's work in Christ on the cross, the centrality of the resurrection, the importance of faith in Christ and living a holy life, the notion of God's wrath and the reality of hell . . . as well as the missionary calling of the church. What is at stake, however, is the traditional doctrine of eternal damnation, often interpreted in terms of unending conscious torment, represented so vividly in many medieval religious tapestries and paintings (one I recently saw was Giotto's lurid vision of hell in his fresco of *The Last Judgment* in the

---

1. Moltmann, *Coming of God*, 245.
2. Ibid., 244.
3. Robinson, *In The End, God . . .* , 133.

outstandingly beautiful Scrovegni Chapel in Padua). Such images call to mind our discussion in the last chapter about what sort of God we do or don't believe in. Is it really possible to believe in a God who will permit such horrendous suffering and perpetual misery for the majority of humanity . . . *for eternity*?

Inescapable Love

On his website, Thomas Talbott, the Christian philosopher of religion, states that much of his writing seeks to present "a stunning and utterly consistent vision of God's all-inclusive, all-pervasive, and inexorable love."[4] In his book, *The Inescapable Love of God*, he offers what he calls "an inconsistent set of three propositions," combinations of which lead to three different schools of thought—Calvinism, Arminianism, and universalism (discussed further below).

1. It is God's redemptive purpose for the world (and therefore his will) to reconcile all sinners to himself;
2. It is within God's power to achieve his redemptive purpose for the world;
3. Some sinners will never be reconciled to God, and God will therefore either consign them to a place of eternal punishment, from which there will be no hope of escape, or put them out of existence altogether.[5]

Talbott cites well-known biblical texts in support of the first proposition, such as 2 Pet 3:9, 1 Tim 2:4, Rom 11:32, Ezek 33:11 and, most especially, Lam 3:31-33. Proposition 2 is supported by texts such as Eph 1:11, Job 4:22, Ps 115:3, and Isa 46:10-11. There are also, according to Talbott, some texts that "seem to imply that God has *both* the power *and* the will to bring all things into subjection to Christ (1 Cor 15:27-28), to reconcile all things in Christ (Col 1:20), and to bring acquittal and life to all persons through Christ (Rom 5:18)."[6] Talbott then cites a number of well-known "damnation texts" in support of proposition three—Matt 25:46, 2 Thess 1:9, and Eph 5:5. In the face of what are, for Talbott, competing and

---

4. "Tom Talbott's Site."
5. Talbott, *Inescapable Love of God*, 43.
6. Ibid., 45.

contradictory statements—not all three propositions can be true—and setting aside the "correct interpretation" of the texts cited, what is needed is "an interpretive structure that avoids a fundamental logical inconsistency" in God's revealed truth.[7]

The classical evangelical response is to hold fast to the third proposition, leading to a rejection of either proposition one or two—hence, for example, the Calvinist-Arminian division. Talbott rejects the manoeuvres of those who seek a way through the ambiguities of the biblical text with regard to personal eschatology, for example by arguing that at least God *offers* salvation to all, or by dismissing the dilemma with a comment along the lines that the fate of the wicked is a mystery in the hands of God. On this appeal to mystery, Robin Parry, writing under the pseudonym of Gregory MacDonald, suggests that this position is one of last resort: "The secret things may well belong to the Lord, but that which has been revealed can be known to be true."[8]

Talbott then goes on to invite us to consider the universalist position, which accepts the first two propositions, but rejects the third. It is clear, for him, that we are not dealing with an unfathomable mystery, but with ambiguities in the biblical text that are ultimately reconcilable: indeed, the case for universalism is so clear for him that the "real mystery is why so many have failed to *appreciate* the universalism of the New Testament and why so many have tried to *explain it away*."[9] This raises a number of important questions: how then are the damnation or hell texts to be interpreted? And if such an interpretation were possible, does the universalist position necessarily lead to both evangelistic indifference (what is the urgency of telling others about Jesus if everyone is going to be saved anyway?) and moral compromise (if everyone is going to heaven anyway, that includes me, so what motive do I have to live a faithful Christlike life?)? All we can do in this chapter is to very briefly sketch out some of the contours of the debate, and summarize a number of key points in support of a reconciliation between what appear at face value to be contradictory biblical statements on the matter.

---

7. Ibid., 46.
8. MacDonald, *Evangelical Universalist*, 33.
9. Talbott, *Inescapable Love of God*, 55, author's italics.

Two Generic Problems

One particular difficulty that Talbott has with the doctrine of hell relates to the idea of the punishment fitting the crime, reflected in the Old Testament principle of "an eye for an eye and a tooth for a tooth" (*lex talionis*). This principle of retaliatory justice was instituted to limit excessive vengeance, discourage cruelty, and restrict compensation to the value of the loss incurred, and was interpreted by the courts in a variety of ways in Old Testament times. This now raises the question: could one conceive of a crime in God's *finite* world that justifies *eternal* conscious torment? It would seem intuitive that, according to the *lex talionis*, *infinite* punishment does not fit the harm, however monstrous, we might do *in this world*. We might note here that for theologians like Augustine and Anselm the answer was unambiguous: the only appropriate punishment for rebellion against an infinite being is one that is itself infinite. However, as Talbott has shown, this argument actually denies the central premise in the equivalence theory of retribution ("an eye for an eye") because it treats all sin of *whatever* magnitude as deserving of the *same* infinite penalty.[10]

The problem of "the justice of infinite retribution" is the first of two generic problems that Robin Parry identifies with regard to the doctrine of eternal conscious torment. The second problem, which Parry calls "the problem of the joy of the redeemed," has to do with the difficulty of seeing "how God could give the redeemed perfect happiness if some of their loved ones are in hell forever."[11] One resolution that has been proposed to this problem is what Talbott calls the "memory-wipe" option, in which God obliterates any memory of loved ones who do not share the same blissful fate. However, such a devastating "lobotomy on the redeemed" would necessarily rob many of us of our own identity. When I think of loved ones in my own family who did not, to my knowledge, profess the Christian faith in their lifetime, I would not regard my eternal life as either blissful or complete if I was kept in ignorance of their fate or if my memory of those loved ones (often very precious and significant to my self-understanding and identity) was excised from my eternal consciousness.

There are some people whose accounts of being "in heaven" for a short time—as an "after-death" experience—may suggest an eternal bliss consistent with the sort of "memory-wipe" to which Talbott objects. For

10. Ibid., 151–56.
11. MacDonald, *Evangelical Universalist*, 18.

example, a recent claim by Don Piper, a Baptist pastor in America, that he had spent ninety minutes in heaven after a horrific road accident, during which *he wasn't conscious of anything he'd left behind, including family*, may point to the viability of the "memory-wipe" option. However, wonderful though Piper's experience may have been, his account of "heaven" lacks the gospel focus on Jesus Christ. His claim to have experienced heaven—which takes up a very brief part of his top-selling book *90 Minutes in Heaven*—is weakened by his description of "heaven" as a place populated by a large crowd of wonderful people that he had known in his lifetime. Significantly, he didn't see Jesus (though he does write that as he stepped forward into an increasingly brilliant luminosity he sensed that he was being ushered into the presence of God), and he describes the "perfect love" that he felt in "heaven" as that which "emanated from every person who surrounded me."[12] Ultimately, Piper's description of heaven is pastorally comforting rather than theologically convincing.

Of course, it is arguable that the difficulties identified with the two generic problems discussed above—"the justice of infinite retribution" and the "memory-wipe" option—hinge upon a logic that fits comfortably with our finite way of seeing things, but may not carry much weight in the infinite and unfathomable mystery of God's will. However, if, as Talbott and others maintain, universalism is clearly portrayed in the pages of the New Testament, then we need at the very least to examine the case a little further, both biblically and theologically.

Firstly, it needs to be emphasized that the idea of universal salvation is not at all new in the history of the church: it can be traced back at least as far as Origen, who followed Clement of Alexandria in teaching the doctrine of *apokatastasis*, or the final restoration of all souls.[13] The doctrine was taught by a number of early theologians, including Gregory of Nyssa, Diodore of Tarsus, and Theodore of Mopsuestia. However, it was officially condemned as an anathema in 543 at the Council of Constantinople,[14] although it has reappeared at different times in the history of the church. For Barth and Brunner in the twentieth century, universalism was an open question, though for different reasons, and midway through the century John A. T. Robinson created a furore by famously arguing for universal salvation on the basis of God's omnipotent

---

12. Piper and Murphey, *90 Minutes in Heaven*, 31.

13 See especially Sachs, "Apocatastasis."

14 For an absorbing review of the deliberations of the early church with regard to *apokatastasis*, see MacDonald, "Introduction: Between Heresy and Dogma," 4–10.

love.[15] In recent years, there has been a distinctive shift in the evangelical wing of the church, and the hope of universal salvation is now very much on the agenda—as well as on the bookshelves—of an increasing number of church leaders.

Amongst the New Testament texts that are compatible with a universalist interpretation, Col 1:15-20 is of particular note. The passage, which is in the form of a hymn to Christ, refers to the creation of "all things" in Christ (verse 16) and ends with the promise in verse 20 that "all things" will be reconciled in him. Exegetically, there is no reason to believe that the "all things" in verse 20 are different from those in verse 16. The significance of the passage has been spelled out powerfully by the New Testament scholar Andrew Lincoln, who sees it as "a depiction of the church as the forerunner of a reconciliation that will be cosmic and universal in scope. . . . The worldwide community of believers is meant to be a microcosm in which the divine purpose in reclaiming the entire creation is anticipated and through which, as a reconciled and reconciling community, that purpose is furthered."[16] Christ, then, has already achieved on the cross the reconciliation of "all things," and the task facing the church today is, as Lincoln declares, to participate with God in the outworking of the vision of a restored creation.

Does Hell Exist?

A number of other New Testament texts were cited earlier in support of God's intent to be merciful to all and his desire that all should find life in him, but it is to some of the New Testament material on hell that we now need to turn in our brief assessment of the possibility of evangelical universalism. And you can't talk about hell unless you also talk about judgment. In fact, any talk of universalism needs to take into account the reality of judgment. Tom Wright argues persuasively that "one cannot forever whistle 'there's a wideness in God's mercy' in the darkness of Hiroshima, of Auschwitz, of the murder of children and the careless greed that enslaves millions with debts not their own."[17] There needs to be some sort of accountability in the face of the reality of evil. In their book, *Why We're Not Emergent*, Kevin deYoung and Ted Kluck argue that it's thoroughly biblical

---

15. Robinson, *Honest to God*.
16. Lincoln, "Colossians," 611 (cited in MacDonald, *Evangelical Universalist*, 51).
17. Wright, *Surprised by Hope*, 193.

to "move past agnosticism about hell and implore people on Christ's behalf: Be reconciled to God (2 Cor. 5:20)."[18] We need the doctrine of hell, they claim, "to set our face like a flint toward Jerusalem." They go on to present a number of reasons why we need the doctrine of eternal punishment, or God's wrath, all to do with keeping us "up to the mark" in our Christian discipleship, as well as helping us to grasp the wonder of God's mercy and ultimate glory. Certainly, some may be motivated by the threat of hell to sort out their lives, but, in response to Young and de Kluck, isn't loving encouragement a better teacher than the threat of punishment? And do we really need this doctrine to apprehend God's glory?

So does hell exist? And if so, what purpose does it serve? Clearly, we cannot go into great depth here, but, confining ourselves to two well-known Gospel parables frequently cited against universalism (and omitting Revelation, which for all sorts of reasons is fraught with hermeneutical problems[19]), a careful reading of the material shows us that "Jesus is not an apocalyptic preacher, satisfying the ever-present pious curiosity in regard to a hereafter, projecting the unfulfilled hopes and fears of this side onto the other side."[20] Wright argues, for example, that when Jesus spoke of the fires of Gehenna, he was warning those to whom he spoke about the destruction of Jerusalem in AD 70 in the *present age*, not where they would spend their eternal future. However, it is clear from the Gospels that Jesus spoke often about hell in vivid imagery—"outer darkness," eternal fire, a place of divine wrath, "weeping and gnashing of teeth," "eternal punishment," and rejection. But, asks Parry, do Jesus' references to Gehenna and the "fires of hell" speak of an everlasting fate? Was hell, in Jesus' understanding, *eternal*?

In his commentary on Jesus' parable of the rich man and Lazarus in Luke 16:19-31, interpreted by many as the clearest evidence in the New Testament for a final, eschatological "double outcome" of saved and unsaved, Bauckham argues that the parable belongs properly to the religious folklore of the common people, with which Jesus was familiar, highlighting "the intolerable injustice of the situation where one enjoys luxury and another suffers want."[21] In the first half of the parable "the rich man's luxurious lifestyle in this life is replaced by suffering in the

---

18. DeYoung and Kluck, *Why We're Not Emergent*, 196.

19. For a balanced, non-dogmatic and hopeful universalist interpretation of Revelation, see MacDonald, *Evangelical Universalist*, 106–32.

20. Küng, *Eternal Life?*, 169.

21. Bauckham, "Rich Man and Lazarus," 233.

next, while Lazarus' destitution and suffering in this life are replaced by exaltation in the next,"²² but the reference to *Hades*, or *Sheol*—which represents in Judeo-Christian tradition the temporary dwelling place of the dead—rather than *Gehenna* suggests that the context for the parable may be some sort of transitional stage between death and final judgment. Perhaps the rich man was a Pharisee, as some have suggested, rendering the parable a biting parody of Pharisaical piety. The central point for us here is that we cannot decisively conclude that the parable has to do Jesus' teaching about final states in the afterlife: rather, in drawing attention to the gross inequality between the two men, Jesus is probably using the parable to challenge misleading Pharisaical interpretations of the afterlife based upon such things as riches or piety. This has implications for how we live our life today, and that was the central focus in Jesus' teaching: he simply did not have a great deal to say about the sort of "double outcome" eschatology that characterizes the rhetoric of some evangelicals today. However, having said that, the judgment motif in the parable is difficult to ignore, and we should not be too quick to dispense with it; which brings us to another well-known teaching in the Gospels, the parable of the sheep and the goats.

We need to remember, of course, that, as in the rich man and Lazarus pericope, we are dealing in Matt 25:31-46 with a parable, not a literal narrative. In looking for a universalist apologetic for this passage, interest focuses on the exegesis of the Greek word *aionios*, translated "eternal" in verse 46. The most likely interpretation of the word is that it relates to "an age to come" and universalists suggest that we should not assume that the life that comes from God is of the same duration as the punishment that comes from God. Also, the word used for punishment (*kolasis*) has been interpreted as having a corrective or educative connotation, suggesting that there is an age to come before the final judgment, a form of "purgatory," but this is by no means clear-cut. The passage is probably one of the most ambiguous in the New Testament with regard to judgment and hell, indicating either the possibility of a temporary "hell" in which those, confronted by the majesty of God, find their wills bending towards the worship of the one whom they had rejected in their earthly life—thus supporting an ultimate universalism when God will be "all in all," and nothing will be lost—or, alternatively, a real eternal hell in which there will truly be everlasting torment.²³ The parabolic nature of the narrative,

22. Ibid., 231.
23. See MacDonald (*Evangelical Universalist*, 150–54) for a brief discussion of

of course, suggests that we must not take every detail strictly literally, and, in any case, as many others have pointed out, Jesus' primary concern was not to help us to understand the afterlife, but to show us how we might live kingdom lives in the present.

New Order of Reality

The discussion so far in this chapter suggests that there is a case for universalism to be made, and the most acceptable version is perhaps one that acknowledges the reality of an intermediate age characterized by some form of divine punishment that is essentially educative in purpose, a period of indeterminate length in which "unbelievers are 'given up for lost' temporally and for the End-time, but not to all eternity."[24] However, contra this view, we need to recognize the very deep unease of those, like Tom Wright, who—rather than going down the "annihilationist" path[25]—suggest that it is possible for human beings "to refuse all whisperings of good news, all glimmers of the true light, all promptings to turn and go the other way, all signposts to the love of God, that after death they become at last, by their own effective choice, *beings that once were human but now are not*, creatures that have ceased to bear the divine image at all."[26] That might well be the fate some of us would expect—even demand—for those whose crimes have been indescribably evil. Following this line, Catherine Keller, responding to Moltmann, asks, "does Moltmann's universal salvation not come into conflict with those very longings for justice that gave rise to eschatology in the first place?"[27] But for Moltmann, the eschatological vision that so drives his theology has to do with the final transformation of all things, a transformation that offers no room for retaliatory justice:

> This means that the eschatological Last Judgment is not a prototype for the courts of kingdoms and empires. This Judgment has to do with God and his creative justice, and is quite different

Pauline texts on hell, in which the author acknowledges 2 Thess 1:9 as a problem text for universalists, though not, in his view, irredeemably so.

24. Moltmann, *Coming of God*, 242.

25. "Annihilationism" is the belief that unbelievers will not experience eternal torment, but will be extinguished completely (total elimination is, of course, one form of everlasting punishment).

26. Wright, *Surprised by Hope*, 195, author's italics.

27. See Keller, "The Last Laugh," 381.

from the forms our earthly justice takes. What we call the Last Judgment is nothing other than the universal revelation of Jesus Christ, and the consummation of his redemptive work. . . . Judgment at the end is not an end at all; it is the beginning. Its goal is the restoration of all things for the building up of God's eternal kingdom.[28]

In this new beginning a new order of reality comes into play, a "fullness of God" where "we are at liberty to leave moral and ontological concepts behind, and to avail ourselves of aesthetic dimensions."[29] This is a far cry from the "massive denial of reality by the cheap and cheerful universalism of western liberalism"[30] which Wright rightly condemns. In this new order, we experience a transfiguration that transcends finite understanding: it is the triumph of grace, in which God's *charis* is more powerful than human sin. For Moltmann this is "no more than a small beginning of the transfiguration of the whole cosmos,"[31] precisely because individual salvation is inconceivable without a new heaven and a new earth. When evangelical convictions place personal salvation first in the eschatological horizon, the debate about universal salvation predominates. However, when the *shalom* of God's new heaven and new earth becomes the principal horizon, the perspective that we outlined in the last chapter, a new way of seeing emerges, grounded in the restoration of all things.

Robin Parry invites us to hold in our minds two alternative scenarios: the traditional Christian vision of the exclusion of the majority of humanity from salvation forever, and the universalist vision of the redemption of the whole of creation. And then he asks:

> Which vision has the strongest view of divine love? Which story has the most powerful narrative of God's victory over evil? Which picture lifts the atoning efficacy of the cross of Christ to the greatest heights? Which perspective best emphasizes the triumph of grace over sin? Which view most inspires worship and love of God bringing him honor and glory? Which has the most satisfactory understanding of divine wrath? Which narrative inspires hope in the human spirit?[32]

28. Moltmann, *Coming of God*, 250–51.
29. Ibid., 336.
30. Wright, *Surprised by Hope*, 193.
31. Moltmann, *Coming of God*, 338.
32. MacDonald, *Evangelical Universalist*, 176.

I am aware that there is much that I have not been able to address in this all-too-brief account of some of the issues in the universalism debate. Where, for example, does Israel fit into the broad sweep of God's salvation purposes for humanity? If, as I argued in chapter 4, the gospel has to do with the story of Israel coming to completion in the story of Jesus, then the answer is that nobody is excluded, for on the cross Jesus represented the *whole* of humanity, and that includes Israel. Nor have I given much attention to Old Testament allusions to the afterlife, but that is principally because the Old Testament itself has very little to say about individual eschatology, offering, rather, many nuanced references to *Sheol* as the "underworld," or abode of the dead. As Philip Johnston points out, Israel's "theological bedrock is that faith in Yahweh is experienced in this life, not after death: death and the dead lie largely outside the spheres of their religious beliefs."[33]

Holy Silence

What I have attempted to demonstrate in this chapter is that the hope of the salvation of all people is not as heretical a doctrine as many people might suppose. I mentioned earlier Karl Barth's openness to universalism which is, as Hunsinger rightly points out, "best understood as standing in the tradition of holy silence."[34] Hunsinger continues his assessment of Barth's "reverent agnosticism" by alluding to the "strong tilt towards universal hope" in his theology: "Like Origen, he finds it hard to see how God will not fully triumph at the end. But like Augustine, he has a chastened sense that human sin is profoundly inscrutable. Like Origen more than Augustine, he does not find a fully clear picture emerging from Scripture. But like Augustine more than Origen, his final concern as a theologian is not so much to respect the compromised 'freedom' of fallen humanity, but rather to respect above all the sovereign freedom of divine grace."[35] Whilst Moltmann writes with a greater explicit confidence in the final triumph of grace that embraces all people, Barth's position is more nuanced, even ambiguous: he acknowledges the possibility of hell, but holds this alongside his deep conviction that God has graciously and lovingly elected all humanity for himself in Christ, in whom "He elected

33. Johnston, *Shades of Sheol*, 24–25.
34. Hunsinger, *Disruptive Grace*, 243.
35. Ibid., 243.

our rejection. He made it His own. He bore it and suffered it with all its most bitter consequences. For the sake of this choice and for the sake of man He hazarded himself wholly and utterly."[36] Barth attempts no final reconciliation between the possibility of hell and his divine affirmation of all humanity, but rather leaves the final word to God who has in grace and love "decided for the creature and not against it."[37]

This topic is one that many serious and devout Christians have wrestled with throughout the ages, and it is a legitimate issue for Christians today to ponder and debate. It is an issue that is shrouded in uncertainty and mystery, and it is at least arguable that some of those who demand an absolute assurance on the matter are motivated more by a focus on the guarantee of life in the hereafter than by the biblical imperative to live the Jesus-life in the here-and-now. And so the biblical text is mined one-sidedly for verses in support of the "double-outcome" position. My own reflections on the topic lead me to the conclusion that it is possible to sustain what might at face value appear to be an oxymoron, the idea of an evangelical universalist: in other words, a "both-and" response to this possibility need not be rejected as anathema as it was in Origen's day.

Firstly, Christ's death on the cross and his resurrection for all people is not diminished in any way: universalism takes sin seriously, acknowledging that what was achieved at Calvary represented God's turning point in history for all creation—victory over sin and the inauguration of the promised new age. Secondly, the reality of judgment and divine punishment is not eliminated in universalism: rather, the consequences of turning away from God in this life are expressed in the language of a temporary hell. In wrestling with this issue, I am often reminded of evil tyrants today whose despotic rule is characterized by unspeakable horrors—surely they, of all people, deserve to be punished? Universalism, however, does not "go soft" here, as we "leave room for God's wrath, for it is written: 'It is mine to avenge; I will repay,' says the Lord" (Rom 12:19). Evildoers will not get off scot-free: due punishment will be exacted. Thirdly, and this follows on from the last point, the urgency for gospel proclamation, and of the response of repentance and faith, remains, though some might argue that the warning of eternal conscious torment is more motivational—for both believer and unbeliever—than the prospect of a temporary hell. However, as Parry rightly points out, we do not

---

36. Barth, *CD Vol.* 2:2, 164.
37. Ibid., 27.

have to take the worst possible scenario—eternal conscious torment—in order to take the consequences of sin seriously.

In his study of the Orthodox Church, Bishop Kallistos Ware acknowledges that "hell exists as a final possibility, but several of the Fathers have none the less believed that in the end all will be reconciled to God. It is heretical to say that all *must* be saved, for this is to deny free will; but it is legitimate to hope that all *may* be saved."[38] This echoes the position taken by the eminent Roman Catholic theologian Hans Urs von Balthasar, who makes a clear distinction between the *hope* of universal salvation and the *doctrine* of universal salvation.[39] More recently, Rob Bell, the well-known American pastor and Christian communicator, offers the same distinction in his book *Love Wins*,[40] arguing that it is misguided and toxic to insist upon the doctrine of eternal, conscious torment as an essential Christian truth. All three—Ware, von Balthasar, and Bell—coming from different traditions, and addressing different audiences, recognize the outworking of divine love *and* divine justice, acknowledging that hell is not the absence of divine love, but, in MacDonald's words, "the *severity* of a divine love that allows the obstinate to experience the consequences of unwise lifestyles with the aim of ultimately redeeming them."[41]

And that, surely, is what God wants to do, expressed in Paul's great Christ-hymn in Phil 2, in which the apostle celebrates the exaltation of Jesus, at whose name "every knee shall bow, in heaven and on earth and under the earth, and every tongue confess that Jesus Christ is Lord, to the glory of God the Father" (Phil 2:10-11). *Every* tongue, writes Paul, including those under the earth, the place of *Sheol*, the underworld, the place of the dead: every person who has ever lived will one day magnify the name of the Lord. Perhaps hell, then, may be understood as that terrible place of judgment where the Spirit of God is ever at work, opening the eyes of the unsaved to the majesty of God, enabling them freely and voluntarily to declare "Jesus is Lord"—for no one can truly proclaim that "except by the Holy Spirit" (1 Cor 12:3).

---

38. Kallistos, *Orthodox Church*, 232.
39. Von Balthasar, *Dare We Hope?*
40. Bell, *Love Wins*, 2011.
41. MacDonald, *Evangelical Universalist*, 163–64.

Pastoral Implications

The pastoral implications of the universalist position are evident. During my time as a pastor in a number of evangelical churches I have been confronted on many occasions by the longings of those who had just lost loved ones, sometimes under very tragic circumstances. To be able to speak with confidence about the future fate of the deceased in the midst of deep pain and sorrow is reassuring not only for bereaved persons but also for pastors who need to speak with biblical integrity. In my early days as a church minister, even though I valued the opportunity to come alongside the bereaved in pastoral care, I was often uncomfortable speaking words of hope to the families of those who, to the best of my knowledge, had demonstrated no interest in God. I had not thought through the biblical material on personal eschatology as carefully as I have since those days. Typically, in these circumstances, my approach was to speak words of hope and reassurance based on standard "funeral texts" without any personal reassurance of their applicability to the deceased or to the grieving family, vaguely comforting myself that God is the "judge of all the earth" (Gen 18:25) and I could leave the outcome in his capable hands. The comfort received by the bereaved was doubtless real enough, for which I give credit to God's grace overriding my own lack of conviction.

Caleb Wilde is a sixth-generation funeral director who reflects on his Christian faith through the lens of his vocation: "when it comes down to it: when the rubber hits the road; when preachers show their cards; when they stand up before a grieving, hopeless family who has just lost their loved one to an overdose, suicide or alcohol, all the preachers I have ever heard, either imply or state the same thing as Rob Bell—they, too, hope that love wins."[42] Of course, emotions must never trump exegesis, nor must pastoral concerns determine how we do our theology. But, as we have examined in this chapter, the biblical teaching on our ultimate destiny as human beings enables pastors to be genuine in their offer of the *hope* of salvation, whatever circumstances they face in their pastoral work. The hope of the gospel becomes a glorious reality to proclaim for all people, as pastors no longer have to wrestle disingenuously (and perhaps hypocritically at times) with pastoral compassion on the one hand, and biblical integrity on the other. In this dimension of pastoral ministry, as in others to be explored in subsequent chapters, the genius of "both-and" graciously and triumphantly overrules the tyranny of "either-or."

---

42. Wilde, "Why 99% of Pastors are Universalists."

6

"The wayfaring people of God"
–Jürgen Moltmann

Life-in-Community

The "both-and" paradigm that has been running through the previous chapters on God and the gospel of salvation echoes resoundingly in any biblically faithful understanding of the nature of the church. I became a Christian at the age of twenty-seven, and I grew in faith in a local Anglican church that was beginning to experience the joys—and inevitable pains!—of charismatic renewal. Drawn into the richness of a new life in the Spirit, I entered into a deeply attractive, yet at the same time intensely challenging, experience of life-in-community. As we have observed in earlier chapters, the Christian life is essentially trinitarian, reflecting God's inner life of hospitality, welcome, inclusiveness, and generosity. It is personal, yes, but it is not a private affair, practised in isolation from our fellow believers or cut off from the realities of everyday life in the world in which we are privileged to live.

And so I found myself challenged to become a different person—to live my life not for myself, but for God, and for others. The transformation that the Spirit seeks to bring into our lives is not coercive, but gentle and inviting in its regeneration. In Daniel Hardy's words, it is "a pulse of healing that does not overwhelm people but finds them where they are, engages them, opens breathing space for them, and then draws them forward."[1] Hardy uses the language of 'temporal abduction' to describe this expansive and ultimately liberating experience of divine action in our lives, for that is what it is: God's work, not ours, though we are certainly invited to cooperate with God in his gracious work of conversion in our lives, "working out what God works in" (my paraphrase of Phil 2:12-13). To grow into the likeness of Christ is not something we can engineer by ourselves, for, as the apostle Paul declares (2 Cor 3:18), "we are being transformed into his image with ever-increasing glory, *which comes from the Lord, who is the Spirit.*"

We cannot, as Christians, experience this growth into Christlikeness unless we are bound to others—not legalistically, but freely, and voluntarily. In other words, we are called to live out our Christian lives in open, non-coercive relationship with one another and for one another, for we have been created as "being-with" creatures, rather than simply "being."[2] To be human is to participate in the richness of reciprocal relationships, opening ourselves vulnerably to one another. Experientially, we actually discover who we are in the context of an extensive network of intricate relationships: I am, for example, a husband to my wife, a father to my children, a colleague in my place of work, a neighbor to those who live around me . . . a brother in the community of God's family, and a son of my Father in heaven. It is a liberating truth to know to whom I belong, for then I begin to discover who I am. Our understanding of God as a trinitarian being drives us to this conclusion: to be made in the image of a relational God-in-community is to be invested with the same capacity for relatedness, representing the very essence of our being. Ultimately, then, who we are as particular individuals derives from the very interactions in which we are historically and necessarily involved as human beings whose lives are embedded in community.

Ecclesial Authority

So the local church becomes the context within which we discover our identity as those who are becoming, in Luther's famous phrase, "little Christs." Despite the many disagreements which have plagued the life of the church, the historic formularies that have been handed down through the centuries, enshrined in the creeds of the early church and

---

1. Hardy, *Wording a Radiance*, 78–79.
2. On this, see Hall, *Imaging God*, 118–19.

reinterpreted more or less faithfully in a wide array of denominational statements, represent "the good deposit" of the gospel that Paul writes about in 2 Tim 1:14. It is in this sense that we might affirm with the Orthodox theologian John Zizioulas that Jesus Christ, by virtue of his authority, establishes the church[3]—"I will build my church" declares Christ to Peter at Caesarea Philippi (Matt 16:18). The community of believers—whatever form it takes—therefore constitutes one expression of the body of Christ, in whom they are united ontologically, and in whose ministry they participate by virtue of their adherence to his authority as head. That much we can all surely agree on. But can we? Church history reminds us that such agreement is not always guaranteed. The problem, of course, revolves around the fundamental question of ecclesial authority.

Authority was at the heart of the Great Reformation in the sixteenth century, when Luther's new-found understanding of the gospel of grace, grounded in the authority of *sola scriptura*, set him on an irrevocable collision course with the established ecclesiastical authorities, resulting in the break with Rome and a lasting transformation of the religious and spiritual landscape. These events represent one instance of what the American Episcopalian Phyllis Tickle describes as the church's periodic "giant rummage sale." In *The Great Emergence*, she identifies four great "hinges" in the history of the church, drawing from the claim by the Anglican bishop Mark Dyer that "about every five hundred years the empowered structures of institutionalized Christianity, whatever they may be at the time, become an intolerable carapace that must be shattered in order that renewal and new growth may occur."[4] Tickle's four great semi-millennial upheavals are not altogether convincing because she leaves out huge chunks of global Christendom in her sweeping historical survey, but they are certainly useful benchmarks for her purposes. They are represented by Gregory the Great and the monastic movement in the 500s, the Great Schism around 1000, the Great Reformation of the 1500s, and the Great Emergence of today.[5] Acknowledging the convenient and rather whimsical reference to "great" every 500 years, Tickle's essential point is that each historic movement results in, firstly, a new and more vital form of Christianity; secondly, the reconstitution of the organized

---

3. See Zizioulas, *Being as Communion*, 140.

4. Tickle, *Great Emergence*, 16.

5. "The Great Emergence" is Tickle's term for the contemporary cultural upheaval, and the religious consequences of the changes we now face, epitomized in the "emerging church movement."

expression of Christianity into a purer and less ossified expression of its former self; and thirdly, the spread of the Christian faith into new geographic and demographic areas.[6]

For Tickle, the issue has much to do with how authority has been exercised in the church over the centuries; she observes: "Each time of reformation has the same central question: Where now is the authority?"[7] She describes this question as "the fundamental or foundational question of all human existence and/or endeavor,"[8] and as such it goes to the core of local church life. Authority typically relates to issues of power and control and as such informs the nature and function of leadership and the attendant tensions between hierarchical and collaborative approaches to pastoral leadership (the subject of chapter 9). Authority impacts the way church members function in relation to each other as "the priesthood of all believers," and how, as individual Christians as well as faith-communities, we discern the voice of the Spirit. Authority, and how it is mediated, is therefore the central issue in any discussion concerning the nature and function of the church as it is expressed in its many geographical and socio-cultural contexts.

The question of authority, of course, has plagued Christians for two millennia, giving rise at times to schism, hatred, war, and murder. Yet it is a question that has also been considered over the centuries with deep theological inquiry and a genuine concern to hear the voice of the Spirit. At times, the still, small voice of the Spirit brings illumination. In *Dancing in the Dark*, I relate my experience of walking along a country lane in England many years ago. I stopped underneath a large tree. It was in the middle of winter, and all the leaves had fallen, so I was able to see clearly the many different branches which spread out from the central trunk. As I looked up from the base of the tree, I sensed that God was speaking to me about his church. That day I had been discussing with some friends my concern over a claim made by one particular denominational group that they were the "new breed" of Christians, through whom God would fulfil his eschatological purposes in the world. This was not a new claim, of course, but it was an urgent issue at the time. This Christian group was well-known for its vibrant style of worship, and often challenged the comparatively lifeless worship of the traditional denominations. They

---

6. Ibid., 17.
7. Ibid., 72.
8. Ibid., 72.

called Christians to leave the "sterile" worship of their local churches in order to enter into the flow of their "pure stream" of worship. Underlying this assertion of purity was their authoritative claim to being the one, pure church.

I was troubled by this claim, though as a young Christian I confess that I was attracted by the rousing and energetic, and at times deeply reverent, expressions of congregational worship that characterized their meetings. As I looked up at the tree, the Spirit of God helped me to see that just as there are many branches which emanate from the trunk, each bearing life because of its association with the trunk, so there are many branches in God's church. I noticed that each branch was different, yet the same sap—the living Christ, the one true vine—was flowing through each one, eventually to turn bud into leaf. God does not compress his life into one branch: eschewing monotonous uniformity, he delights to express himself in glorious diversity in the life of his church. Brian McLaren likewise celebrates this variety; observing that the Christian faith has recaptured its earlier pre-Constantine plurality of forms, partitioning into different denominational expressions and, more recently, collaborative networks, he notes: "Some see this as a *division* to be remedied, but there's another way to see it: as *diversification* to be celebrated. What if the Christian faith is *supposed* to exist in a variety of forms rather than just one important one? What if it is both more stable and more agile—more responsive to the Holy Spirit—when it exists in these many forms?"[9]

I continued to walk along the lane, reflecting deeply on what I had experienced. I realized that what was important in local church life was not the outward expression but the inner source which gives rise to our life in God. I came to understand that, important though experience is, "more important than our experience of Christ is the Christ of our experience,"[10] and that wherever two or three are gathered in Christ's name, there gathers an authentic expression of the body of Christ, the church universal. Furthermore, I was encouraged at the time to explore the truth of what I was experiencing within the Anglican tradition into which God had led me; whilst not rejecting the attractions of more charismatic or Pentecostal styles of worship, I was motivated to learn how the richness of charismatic worship could be developed within the established liturgical structures of the Anglican Church. This is aptly captured

---

9. McLaren, *New Kind of Christianity*, 164, author's italics.
10. Torrance, *Worship, Community and the Triune God*, 16.

in the title of a book written by John Leach, an English pastor and worship leader, during the latter stages of the charismatic renewal movement in the UK—*Liturgy and Liberty*:[11] "both-and" not "either-or."

Ecclesial Diversity

This personal revelation of ecclesial diversity grounded in the authority of Christ suggests that we need to be very careful whenever we find ourselves trying to determine what makes church "church." We need to be gracious enough to acknowledge that local churches are essentially called to be "communities that form Christlike people who embody and communicate, in word and deed, the good news of the Kingdom of God."[12] In order to address this question, it is helpful to focus on what has come to be known as the "emerging church movement," an expression, drawing on Hans Frei's memorable description of hermeneutics, "that is forever chasing a meaning."[13] In his book *The New Conspirators* the American author and futurist Tom Sine identifies four contemporary streams of Christian "conspirators," each seeking to embrace a radical form of discipleship. He labels them "emerging," "missional," "mosaic," and "monastic," though he acknowledges that "the leaders in each stream don't agree on definitions that describe their movements, because the four streams are dynamic and fluid, and at points flow into each other."[14]

Sine concedes that his four streams are only a rough sketch of the "new conspirators" of contemporary Christianity, but the fluidity to which he alludes suggests that all four streams are perhaps distinctive clusters within the one "emerging church movement": the "emerging church tent" is perhaps much larger than some have supposed. Sine's "missional stream" takes us beyond the essentially contextual character of "emerging," which has much to do with what has been called, particularly in the UK, "fresh expressions" of the church in the community, with its primary emphasis on cultural relevance. Uniquely, the missional stream derives from its focus on the essential nature of God, summed up in the *missio Dei*: in other words the shape of the church emerges out of God's mission in the world. So, as many have observed, the mission has

---

11. Leach, *Liturgy and Liberty*.
12. McLaren, *New Kind of Christianity*, 165.
13. Frei et al., *Types of Christian Theology*, 16.
14. Sine, *New Conspirators*, 33.

a church, rather than the church has a mission. However, we need to be careful not to devalue the currency of "emerging" in the laudable desire to emphasize the primacy of mission. The point that is often made in many commentaries on the proliferation of new forms of church today is that whilst "emerging" and "missional" are not the same, neither are they mutually exclusive. In fact, some of the richest "fresh expressions" within the emerging church movement are strongly missional in their philosophy and practical orientation.[15]

Sine's mosaic stream refers to churches that reflect the diverse cultures in our world: they are essentially multicultural congregations, as for example those populated (but not exclusively) by young African American people from the hip-hop culture, often having a strong missional focus, echoing John's eschatological vision in the book of Revelation of the great multitude from every nation, tribe, people, and language worshipping God. The monastic stream is different from the other three streams: eschewing church planting, which is evident in the other streams, monastic groups, whilst typically evangelical, are "drawn into the richness of the Catholic, Orthodox, Celtic and Anglican monastic traditions,"[16] grounded in an arguably more thought-through theology than the other streams. Many have a special interest in social justice and concern for the poor, whilst others are attracted by the focus on the spiritual disciplines of monastic traditions like the Benedictines and Franciscans.

Sine's distinctive "emerging stream" is characterized by a number of features common to many expressions of that group, such as a preference for narrative rather than propositional truth, an emphasis on relationships and community life, experimentation, experiential worship, missional engagement, whole-of-life discipleship, and a deep concern for justice. DeYoung and Kluck amusingly parody the characteristic and recognizable diversity of the "emerging church movement," listing in a sentence stretching for more than a page a series of cultural, theological, and biblical likes, dislikes, preferences, aspirations, and beliefs, culminating in the statement that "if all or most of this tortuously long sentence describes you, then you might be an emergent Christian."[17] Since the late 1990s, the term "emerging" (or some variant such as "emergent") has become a "catch-all" expression to describe the phenomenon of contextualization,

---

15. For a penetrating analysis and critique of "fresh expressions," see Nelstrop, *Evaluating Fresh Expressions*.

16. Sine, *New Conspirators*, 49.

17. DeYoung and Kluck, *Why We're Not Emergent*, 20–22.

which of course is nothing new in Christendom. Throughout its history, the church has, to a greater or lesser degree, highlighted the importance of communicating the gospel message in such a way that it needs to be *heard* by those to whom it is sent, heard in a language which they can understand, and presented in a way that acknowledges the uniqueness of each specific and concrete time-and-place context. This lies at the heart of the church's participation in the world. Each Christian community, therefore, is a localized congregation of believers called together because of their common allegiance to Christ and their participation in the gracious life of the Trinity, who is working out the divine purpose in a variety of ways precisely because of the variety of local contexts.

Perhaps what makes the "emerging church" significant as a movement is not so much its willingness to embrace new ways and forms of expressing Christian belief and life—which lies at the heart of all contextual theology and ministry—but its origins as a "protest movement," reminiscent of the Protestant Reformation in the sixteenth century. In *Deep Church*, Jim Belcher, a pioneering church planter, identifies the deconstructive processes implicit in emerging criticism, noting importantly that "discovering what someone is *against* is not the same thing as saying what they are *for*, but it does provide a good snapshot of what they care about."[18] He names seven dimensions of emerging church protest: captivity to Enlightenment rationalism, which hinders the church from becoming truly counter-cultural; a narrow view of salvation which focuses on knowing the truth of the gospel at the expense of living the truth, picking up kingdom themes discussed in chapter 4; belief before belonging, so highlighting doctrinal assent as the church gatekeeper; uncontextualized worship, using out-dated and irrelevant music and liturgies; ineffective preaching, which reduces spiritual formation and disciple-making—both of which Belcher cites as the real goal of preaching—to head knowledge; weak ecclesiology, in which form and structure are espoused at the expense of the biblical call to mission; and tribalism, identified as a sectarianism that leads to a critical and disinterested stance towards the world.

Ecclesia Semper Reformanda

It is clear that there is a wide spectrum of new church forms in evidence today, and Belcher's objective in presenting such an array of ecclesiologies

---

18. Belcher, *Deep Church*, 39, author's italics.

is to highlight the importance of one of Luther's key Reformation principles, *ecclesia semper reformanda*—the church is always to be reformed. The real debate has to do, not with the fundamental principle of reformation, but with the degree of reformation that is theologically permissible and culturally appropriate. In his critique of North American Christianity, Ross Douthat describes the growing number of "pseudo-Christianities" springing up all over the nations, examples of what he calls "*bad* religion": "a growing number are inventing their own versions of what Christianity means, abandoning the nuances of traditional authority in favor of religions that stroke their egos and indulge or even celebrate their worst impulses."[19] The result is that "traditional Christian teachings have been warped into justifications for solipsism and anti-intellectualism, jingoism and utopianism, selfishness and greed."[20] Whilst there may be sufficient research findings[21] as well as anecdotal evidence to support such a negative appraisal of some forms of contemporary church life—and Douthat is extremely damning in his assessment of the American context—care needs to be taken to avoid attributing the "heresy" label to every new expression of the Christian faith.

Unfortunately, there has been a tendency on both sides of the ecclesiological debate to stereotype those who hold a different position, thwarting genuine dialogue. The issues have usually been about doctrine, such as the doctrine of the atonement, universalism, and the nature of the gospel, rather than ecclesiology. This, of course, is not surprising, as theological convictions will always inform the way Christians "do church." A grace-filled gospel will shape church practices differently from those that are based on the primacy of human decision. How church and world are perceived in relation to each other will determine the missional stance of the church. Different church structures will be framed around different theologies of vocation and ordination. How we understand worship theologically will influence what happens when we gather together as Christians. Throughout church history, different denominational beliefs have given rise to a rich—some would argue confusing—variety of ecclesial forms and practices.

Whatever position is adopted, the "either-or" mantra too readily raises its ugly head again, as combatants in the emerging and traditional

---

19. Douthat, *Bad Religion*, 4.
20. Ibid., 4.
21. See, for example, Stark, *What Americans Really Believe*.

camps accuse each other of harsh or heretical theology. We do well to reflect on the words of Maurice Wiles, Regius Professor of Divinity at Oxford University: "What is important for the Christian community at large is not that it gets its beliefs absolutely clear and definite; it cannot hope to do that if they are really beliefs about God. It is rather that people within the community go on working at the intellectual problems, questioning, testing, developing, and seeking the practical application of the traditions that we have inherited from the past."[22]

Richard Mouw, the former president of Fuller Theological Seminary in the USA, has written about the lack of what he calls civility, a simple "public politeness" or courtesy towards others. However, this does not mean that we sacrifice convictions: there are times, he insists, when it is appropriate to manifest some very uncivil feelings. Quoting some lines from Yeats' poem *The Second Coming*, Mouw pleads for more "passionate intensity" about our convictions. One example that has created deeply passionate feelings on both sides is the issue of homosexuality, undoubtedly one of the most complex problems confronting the Christian community today. Over the years, the church's traditional response has been pastorally disastrous: as one report concluded, "It may be very theologically correct and proper, but it fails to connect where people really are. In the name of love it can bring exclusion or loneliness; in the name of truth it can bring guilt; in the name of hope it can bring despair and disillusionment."[23] What has been lacking in many cases in the past is a generous and welcoming inclusivity that reflects the hospitable nature of the gospel. One reputable emerging church leader has addressed the issue in his desire to "break the stereotype that the church is homophobic and sexually uptight," arguing that "no matter what the issue is, even if it goes against the grain of culture, *how we say what we believe is critical.*"[24] What is so attractive about Dan Kimball's approach to the issue in his book *They Like Jesus But Not the Church* is not only his irenic manner but also his willingness to stand firm on his position after wrestling with the Scriptures and difficult viewpoints.

---

22. Strudwick, "Towards an Anglican Covenant," para. 26.
23. Gomez, *True Union in the Body?*
24. Kimball, *They Like Jesus*, 161, my italics.

Partners in Dialogue

The "both-and" paradigm espoused in this book is therefore not something to be carelessly trotted out as a convenient postmodern mantra. As I noted in chapter 2, certainty is not to be dismissed. There is a need at times to swing the pendulum away from ambiguity and uncertainty, especially in recognition of postmodernism's epistemological and ethical vacuum, where style has often replaced substance and self-reference is the central creed. Indeed, from a philosophical perspective, postmodernism's fatal flaw may be its lack of commitment to anything at all—except itself! The American political philosopher Allan Bloom insists that "one has to have the experience of really believing before one can have the thrill of liberation,"[25] and it is precisely this need for conviction and commitment that keeps alive the relevance of Christianity, both doctrinally and ethically, providing the critical centre that gives order and shape to the Christian church in the richness of its diversity and pluriformity.

This perspective is precisely what Richard Mouw means when he declares that "the real challenge is to come up with a *convicted civility*,"[26] an ungainly phrase, but one that helpfully expresses the blending of humility and conviction that he seeks to convey. Ultimately, the debate between emerging and traditional is not just about the theological and ecclesiological issues that divide Christians: it has much to do with how willing we are to assume an attitude of humility and charity that sees others as allies rather than adversaries, partners in dialogue rather than enemies of (usually) *my* understanding of the gospel. In a world where public perception of the church is at a very low level, the Christian church needs to be known for its willingness to engage in conversation with those with whom it disagrees, open at least to explore the possibility of the "both-and," rather than allow itself to be torn apart by the "either-or." My plea for convicted civility echoes that of Brian McLaren, who defines "a generous orthodoxy" (the title of one of his books) as "an emerging orthodoxy, never complete until we arrive at our final home in God."[27] For McLaren, the emphasis in his book, and even more in his subsequent writings, is on a spirit of generosity rather than engaging in ongoing debates about right and wrong. His detractors would like him to "come off the fence" and declare his position on certain issues, and it is this evasive-

---

25. Bloom, *Closing of the American Mind*, 44.
26. Mouw, *Uncommon Decency*, 12.
27. McLaren, *A Generous Orthodoxy*, 275.

ness for which McLaren has been most keenly criticized, as well as his tendency to appeal more immediately to the cultural reference point of postmodernism rather than to the biblical text in his understanding of "emerging church."

In the context of the homosexuality issue raised earlier—and cited as a test case on the danger of ambiguity—DeYoung writes: "I'm not impressed with the emergent claim to be a sanctified middle ground between conservative dogmatists and liberal bad guys. The emerging tendency to wind up as the fresh and sane third option between two caricatures is unfair."[28] In fact, as we have already noted, the contemporary ecclesiological debate is typically framed around the two extremes of traditional and emerging rather than the classical conservative-liberal divide. In his attempt to carve a "third way" through the conflict, Belcher traces the contours of what he calls a "deep ecclesiology," embracing the historical anchor of the traditionalists and the culturally-aware perspectives of the emerging churches. His resolution is presented in the form of an equation: Bible + Tradition + Mission = Deep Ecclesiology.

Acknowledging the traditionalists' emphasis on the Bible, and the emergents' emphasis on the Bible + mission, Belcher adds his important third ingredient, "the Great Tradition," which he defines as the classical consensual tradition of the gospel enshrined in the creeds and confessions of the church. As Belcher notes, this is precisely what C. S. Lewis meant by "mere Christianity"—a phrase borrowed from the puritan Richard Baxter, referring to "a standard of plain, central Christianity." In the preface to his classic text of the same name, Lewis describes "mere Christianity" as "more like a hall out of which doors open into several rooms. . . . But it is in the rooms, not in the hall, that there are fires and chairs and meals."[29] The hall is a place from which each person tries the various doors in order to find their own room. Lewis then tellingly continues: "When you have reached your own room, be kind to those who have chosen different doors and to those who are still in the hall. If they are wrong they need your prayers even more; and if they are your enemies, then you are under orders to pray for them."[30]

Here, Lewis is describing the charitable way of life that is the hallmark of Christian living. It is a way that freely recognizes the diversity

---

28. DeYoung and Kluck, *Why We're Not Emergent*, 48.
29. Lewis, *Mere Christianity*, xv.
30. Ibid., xvi.

of expressions that define the Christian church, the richness of denominational variety from which we can all benefit, each drawing from the one common source, which, of course, is ultimately the *person* of Christ rather than the formularies of creeds and confessions that point to him. Earlier in this chapter I recounted my experience of the Spirit revealing this through the different branches of a tree. Much later, in a meeting of church leaders I received what those present acknowledged as a prophetic vision (also recorded in *Dancing in the Dark*). As we were singing together, I was led by the Spirit into a house with several storeys, and I recognized a number of different rooms—a kitchen, a bedroom, a study, a family room. I was taken into each room, where people were engaged in particular activities. In the kitchen, food was being prepared, and the invitation was given to "Come into the kitchen—we've got some good food for you. The door's wide open." In each of the other rooms the scene was similarly busy with people. In the bedroom, the bed was being made and the encouragement was to enter and enjoy the intimacy and closeness that a bedroom offers; the study was lined with books, and people were being invited in to read from the shelves of the library; and so it was in every room. The door was left open and others were being called to "Come into my room . . . ." Then I heard very distinctly what I believed to be the voice of God: "When you begin to walk in each other's rooms, then will I come and visit your house. You do not know when I will come, but it will be as you are willing to walk through your own doors and into the rooms of others."

It was clear to all of us gathered in that room that Christ was amongst us, but in parabolic fashion we were reminded of the urgency to "make every effort to keep the unity of the Spirit" (Eph 4:3). Just as the river in Ezekiel's vision (Ezek 47) flows from the one source in the sanctuary, so the church derives its existence from the one Christological source. The river widens and deepens, but never splits off into different streams: likewise, the church is created as one body with Christ as its head, ever widening and deepening as more are drawn in by the grace of God, yet never dividing: "Christians are one body not because they meet together, but because of divine initiative."[31] This is the mystery of the "one, holy, catholic, and apostolic church," grounded in what Belcher calls "the Great Tradition." And, of course, it is a mystery to be appropriated as well as apprehended.

---

31. Giles, *What on Earth Is the Church?* 103.

Deep Church

In recent years a number of theologians and pastoral practitioners have been exploring a concept called receptive ecumenism, an approach to learning in the church that draws from a willingness to "walk in each other's rooms" rather than adopting a hubristic "come and see what you can learn from us" attitude. Drawing its inspiration from the work of Cardinal Walter Kasper, who has spent many years serving on the Pontifical Council for Promoting Christian Unity in the Catholic Church, receptive ecumenism seeks to reverse the "ecumenical winter" in the church. At a colloquium in Durham in the UK in 2006, marking the award of an honorary Doctor of Divinity to Kasper, 150 leaders from six denominations in ten countries addressed the ecumenical task in a spirit of grace that was applauded as both ground breaking and historic; in the process they acknowledged the need to apply the concept of receptive ecumenism to local church contexts, applying new theoretical insights to the actual practice of ministry "on the ground." Since that gathering a number of others have taken up the receptive ecumenism mantle, and whilst the model of mutual learning is not at all new[32] it is evident that the notion of *listening* to others is very much on the ecumenical agenda today. These ideas will be developed more fully in chapter 9.

Jim Belcher—whose language of "deep church," like that of "mere Christianity," is also borrowed from C. S. Lewis—rightly focuses on the historical tradition of the church. However, his "third way," his "deep" way that veers neither to the extreme left of cultural capitulation nor to the extreme right of conservative traditionalism, lacks a vital perspective if it is to capture the essence of the true nature of God's church. That perspective is eschatology, recapitulating the insight in chapter 4 that the full, "big-picture" gospel to which the church gives witness finds its climax in the new creation of God's promise, a new heaven and new earth. In formulating a theory of "deep church," therefore, it is appropriate to focus more on the "being" of the church—that is, its *identity* within God's salvation history—before we consider what it is called to do (recapitulating the comment made at the end of chapter 4 that we are first called to live as human *beings* rather than human *doings*). This salvation-history approach identifies two fundamental contours of a theology of the church—historical and eschatological.

---

32. Paul Fiddes, for example, cites an early twentieth-century attempt at listening to each other in Fiddes, "Learning from Others."

The church discovers its true life, firstly, whenever it looks back with gratitude and appreciation to where it has come from, grounded in the historical reality of God's covenantal grace, and, secondly, whenever it looks forward simultaneously to its ultimate destiny in the future new creation of God's promise. Both orientations are essential if the church is not to lose its moorings in the midst of the urgent needs of the present moment. Failure to embrace both its theological past and its theological future gives rise to what may be called an "orphan church." Consider the plight of young children who have been tragically caught up in the violence and horrors of the genocide and ethnic warfare endemic in so many parts of the world today. Many of them, traumatized by their experiences, now live in refugee camps or orphanages, cut off from their families, disconnected from their past, their memories numbed. With everything gone, and all their attention focused on survival, they have little or nothing to look forward to. The metaphor is apt: a church that has lost touch with its historic roots and lost sight of its promised future is in danger of becoming a church that struggles to survive. Put differently, a church that chooses to place its primary focus on the present is a church that will sooner or later lose its sense of joy and purpose.

The salvation-historical framework places mission as a vital orientation in the life and purpose of God's church, and within this framework the critical concepts of *covenant* and *promise* are central ecclesiological realities. Indeed, an awareness of our identity as living members of God's church—who we are, where we have come from, and where we are going—has the capacity to energize mission. Covenant points us back to God's eternal purposes in choosing a people for himself. Thomas Torrance, in presenting us with three phases or stages in the life of the church—preparatory, new, and eternal—declares that the church "is grounded in the Being and Life of God."[33] He describes the Israelites under the old covenant as "the Church of God in its preparatory form in the tension and struggle of expectation, unable to be yet what it was destined to be when incarnation and reconciliation were fulfilled," likening them to an expectant mother, "waiting for its new birth in the resurrection and its universalization at Pentecost."[34] The church is who it is because of its covenantal origin in the very life of God himself.

---

33. Torrance, *Theology in Reconstruction*, 192.
34. Ibid., 195.

Eschatological Orientation

The eschatological orientation of the church is well captured in Jürgen Moltmann's phrase "the wayfaring people of God": the church is God's people on the move, a people whose life takes place "in the forum of the future of God and the world."[35] Michael Griffiths once wrote a book called *Cinderella with Amnesia*, reminding us that the church is something beautiful with a glorious future, but sadly it has often forgotten what that future is. And what is that future? It is a future in which God has committed himself to putting everything to rights again, not by demolishing his creation, but by *renewing* it—human and non-human. A vicar in England once told the story of a huge Lego castle that one of his young sons had taken ages to make. He walked in to the room and saw this impressive construction and said to his son, "That's amazing! Did anything go wrong as you were making it?" "Yes, quite a few times," his son replied. "Weren't you tempted to throw the whole thing away?" his father asked. And the boy replied with some indignation that he couldn't do that—it was far too valuable and important to him to give up and dismantle.[36] That's what it's like with God and his world. As we read through the pages of the Bible we discover how, again and again, God was tempted to give up on his people as they rebelled against him, seeking other ways, even other gods. But "How can I give you up, Ephraim? How can I hand you over, Israel? How can I treat you like Admah? How can I make you like Zeboiim? My heart is changed within me; all my compassion is aroused" (Hos 11:8). God will not give up on his ultimate purpose and promise—grounded in his own eternal being—to renew not only his people, but the whole of creation. For God does what he does, and will do what he will do, because *he is who he is*. And it is precisely within this God-honoring, Christ-centred, and Spirit-empowered historical-eschatological framework that the church—in all its richly diverse forms—finds its true identity.

God's redeeming grace has always been at work throughout history bringing this future about, and one way in which we might understand this happening today has to do with what Tom Wright calls four "voices" that echo in the human subconscious: "the longing for justice, the quest for spirituality, the hunger for relationships, and the delight in beauty."[37] Wherever people gather in Jesus' name—honoring him and seeking to

---

35. Moltmann, *Church in Power of Spirit*, 1.
36. The incident is related by the author in Kuhrt, *Tom Wright for Everyone*, 71.
37. Wright, *Simply Christian*, x.

follow him as they live redemptively *in* God's world, looking forward to experiencing it in all its beauty and fullness—there we find an authentic expression of the church. Wherever people gather to sing this gospel song, proclaiming among the homeless and the hungry in both word and deed that Jesus is Lord, seeking justice and equality for all—there we find church. Wherever people gather to sing this gospel song amongst those who say there is no God, witnessing to the truth that we have *experienced* this God in our life together within the trinitarian *perichoresis* of God—there we find church. Wherever people gather to sing this gospel song in the midst of broken fractured lives, proclaiming the power of forgiving love, actualized in the cross and resurrection of Jesus—there we find church. And wherever people gather to sing this gospel song in the good creation of God's love, witnessing to the truth that this is God's world—and he's not going to give up on it!—there we find church.

7

"A communion corresponding to the Trinity"
–Miroslav Volf

Capacity for Relatedness

IN CHAPTER 4 I STATED THAT GOD IS NOT A GOD OF LOVE BECAUSE HE acts towards us in love—he acts towards us in love precisely because he *is* love. This insight is repeated at the end of chapter 6 because it is of fundamental importance in our understanding of the faithfulness of God, who is ever at work in the world that he loves, and who will bring to completion that which he has begun. In his letter to the Christians at Philippi, the apostle Paul expresses his confidence that "he who began a good work in you will carry it on to completion until the day of Christ Jesus" (Phil 1:6). Herein lies our own confidence for the future: the character of God himself. When Moses asked God for his name, the reply he got was "I am who I am" (Exod 3:14). The original Hebrew *Ehyeh asher ehyeh* literally means "I will be who I will be", a translation that conveys the unchangeable faithfulness of God, which is an unbroken golden thread running all the way through the Bible. And the inner being of this God—the God of Abraham, Isaac, and Jacob, the God who is Alpha and Omega—is, as we explored in chapter 3, relationally structured, expressed most emphatically in the trinitarian doctrine of *perichoresis*.

At the beginning of this book, I defined Christian ministry as participation in the relational life of the triune God of grace who is continuously working in his creation through his Spirit to reconcile all things under Christ. However, the starting point for a relational theology of ministry is found in the statement made in the last chapter that if human beings are made in the image of a relational God-in-community, then they are necessarily invested with the same capacity for relatedness, a dynamic that represents the very essence of what it means to be human. Christian ministry as a relational activity is therefore predicated on three interlocking statements:

1. God is a relational being-in-community.
2. Created *imago Dei*, human beings are relational as a matter of ontological necessity.
3. Drawn into God's *perichoresis*, human beings participate in his hospitable, open life in and for the sake of the world.

The logic of this triad is that Christian ministry, at its source, is a relational activity, not a functional one. Again, it is "being" before "doing." However, pursuing the "both-and" paradigm that is an unbroken thread running through this book, the two cannot and must not be separated. It is the sequence that is important: source comes before effect.

It is not the task of the church to decide how and when to make God known: it is the privilege and responsibility of those who confess Christ to discern the will of the Father, and in obedience to respond to the Spirit who ever seeks to glorify Christ in the world. So ministry is not what *we* do, but is "determined and set forth by God's own ministry of revelation and reconciliation in the world, beginning with Israel and culminating in Jesus Christ and the Church."[1] Implicit in this statement is the idea of ministry as *praxis*, a term which Ray Anderson has expanded into "Christopraxis," referring to the reality that "truths of God are discovered through the encounter with Christ in the world by means of ministry."[2] Christian ministry therefore starts and ends with God, who is ever at work throughout his creation and in whose activity Christians are invited—or summoned!—to participate. Unless those who are called to serve in pastoral ministry find their source in what God *is doing* in his world, rather than in what God *has done*—often resulting in efforts to follow or imitate his example or pattern—they will fall into the trap

---

1. Anderson, *Theological Foundations for Ministry*, 7.
2. Anderson, *Soul of Ministry*, 29.

of a dependence on pragmatic methodology, a danger discussed in the opening chapter of this book.

Participants in God's Ministry

In the 1990s a movement gathered pace in America called "WWJD?" = *What Would Jesus Do*? It all started with bracelets with the letters WWJD inscribed for young people to wear, reminding them to continually ask the question "What would Jesus do?" as they journey through life. All kinds of merchandise were offered—and the commercial bandwagon is still rolling today—from mugs to notebooks to T-shirts! Of course, there is something very commendable about encouraging Christians to live a Christ-centred life. However, there is a subtle trap in that message, because taken by itself it could be interpreted as a moral aphorism—"Look at Jesus: he's done it, now it's over to you!" This is what the American theologian Daniel Thimell calls "bootstraps theology!" It's up to you to go out and imitate Christ—reminiscent of the moral influence theory of the atonement. Christian ministry does not belong to the *Do-It-Yourself* bookshelves! We need to offer an alternative slogan: not WWJD, but WIJD?—*What Is Jesus Doing?* And we can only discover that in a relationship with him.

Drawn into the *perichoresis* of the Trinity, we become not *performers* of ministry, which is functional language, but *participants* in God's ministry, which is the language of relationship. In *Dancing in the Dark* I explore this through the lens of three central dimensions of Christian pastoral ministry—worship, mission, and pastoral care. We participate in the worship of Christ, our great High Priest, as he honors the Father, receiving all that we have to offer and incorporating it into the unfolding purposes of God. The Spirit gathers up our flawed and fragile prayers, our weak offerings of love, where they are transformed in Christ. In him our imperfect worship is converted into something beautiful for God. True worship is participation in the worship that takes place unceasingly within the life of God.

We participate in the great mission of God as his Spirit embraces people, whatever their background, color, race, or belief, ever seeking to open their eyes to the truth that they have already been included in God's saving grace! To participate in the continuing mission of Christ in the world is to enter into the reconciling ministry of the Spirit, who is continuously at work in the world. The mission of the church is not defined in terms of mission strategies, however helpful they may be: it is defined as participation in the creative ministry of the Spirit, who choreographs the steps of all who are called into costly identification with a bruised and hurting world. Here we find no deistic God who stands apart from suffering, but a God who is intimately involved in his creation.

And so we participate in the compassionate ministry of the God who will never let us go, who remembers us in our distress and confusion, and who comes alongside us to comfort and restore. This is the essence of the church's ministry of pastoral care. To participate in the compassionate ministry of Christ implies a freedom to respond to the impulse of the Spirit, whose activity in the world reflects the truth that God holds all whom he has created in his memory. In God nothing, no-one, is forgotten. Though distinct from his creation, God holds all things in his memory, acting on behalf of those he loves. The pastoral theologian John Patton quotes the insights of Parker Palmer in an address to the Association for Clinical Pastoral Education in 1987: "Remembered means to re-member. It means to put the body back together. The opposite of remember is not to forget, but to dis-member. And when we forget where we came from . . . we have in fact dis-membered something."[3] To remember someone in this way is to be a part of their healing. We live in a society in which people are being torn apart, dismembered internally as well as from each other. In his grace, God comes to us in Christ and re-members us—puts us back together again. Participating in a ministry described in this way is to acknowledge how fundamentally relational all ministry truly is.

If, as suggested earlier, the mutuality and reciprocity implicit in the inner life of the Trinity is normative as the ontological ground for all human interactions, then clearly relationality lies at the heart of all pastoral activity within the life and ministry of the local church as its members live out their calling as disciples in God's world. Commenting on the unique application of *perichoresis* to divinity, Paul Fiddes is nonetheless keen to maintain the full strength of Christ's prayer in John 17:20-21—"I pray also for those who will believe in me . . . that all of them may be one, Father, just as you are in me and I am in you." Accordingly he suggests that although human *subjects* cannot indwell divine *subjects* in the way that pertains within the inner-trinitarian life of God, they can, in an

---

3. Patton, *Pastoral Care in Context*, 28.

analogous sense, "dwell in the places opened out within the interweaving relationships of God; they dwell, we might say, not in 'spaces of subjectivity' but in 'relational spaces.'"[4] If finite beings like you and me cannot love perichoretically in the exact way that God does within the divine communion, at least we might want to say that "we participate in a sort of availability analogous to that which the trinitarian persons enjoy for one another,"[5] which is, of course, the language of participation.

In *These Three are One*, his insightful study dealing with the practice of trinitarian theology, David Cunningham argues that the doctrine of the Trinity is not just something that Christians think—it is also something they *do*, profoundly shaping the way life should be lived. In a number of places in his *Church Dogmatics*, Karl Barth, whilst acknowledging that the *mysterium trinitatis* must remain a mystery, warns of the danger of irrelevant speculation unless the doctrine of the Trinity is seen as "belonging to the church." A number of well-known trinitarian theologians have also demonstrated, at the least, an awareness of the need to relate the doctrine of the Trinity to Christian life and ministry, including Catherine LaCugna, Leonardo Boff, and Jürgen Moltmann.[6] This chapter is, in part, an attempt to highlight the relevance of trinitarian thinking to pastoral ministry, focusing particularly on the dynamic relationality implicit in the doctrine of *perichoresis*.

Importance of Particularity

There are several ways in which this intrinsic relational core in ministry is played out in the context of local church life, most commonly expressed in the language of "community." Peter Holmes, writing in the context of a particular congregation in the UK that has sought to break new ground in radical, relational community-living, adopts the phrase "theocentric faith community" as one way of defining the perichoretic life of a Christian congregation seeking to reflect the harmony and diversity of the Trinity.[7] Before we examine how such congregational life and ministry might be articulated, it is important that we do not forget the importance of *particularity* in our haste to concentrate on the significance of community

---

4. Fiddes, *Participating in God*, 50.
5. Rogers, "The Stranger as Blessing," 271.
6. See Cunningham, *These Three are One*, 29–30.
7. Holmes, *Trinity in Human Community*.

within the inner life of the Trinity. It is precisely because life is specific and not general, everywhere different, never the same, that Moltmann, taking a pneumatological perspective, can speak of the vitalizing energies of the Spirit that both unite the community of faith and distinguish its members one from the other.[8] The distinctiveness to which Moltmann refers, sharply etched in Cunningham's *These Three Are One*, has nothing to do with the modern cult of individualism, which is grounded in various forms of narcissistic selfism, and everything to do with what Cunningham calls complex webs of mutuality and participation: "because God is Three, particularity is necessarily a trinitarian virtue; and yet, because God is also One, we are called to construe this particularity in an anti-individualistic way."[9]

As noted in the previous chapter, who we are as particular individuals derives from the very interactions in which we are historically and necessarily involved as human beings whose lives are embedded in community. I often ask my students: what is the goal of pastoral ministry? Of course, there are many compelling answers that could be given to that question, but the one that I find most satisfying is that pastoral ministry has to do with enabling each person to live a fully human life, reminiscent of Jesus' words in John 10:10—"I have come that they may have life, and have it to the full." Each person we encounter has his or her own story to tell; each has travelled a particular journey, with unique experiences; there is no "one-size-fits-all" shape to Christian life and growth. The starting point for anyone who is called to Christian leadership is therefore to acknowledge the uniqueness of each person, but to then go on to affirm that each life can only be truly fulfilled in relationship with God and with other people—and not just other Christians! If diversity is one side of the coin of congregational life, then unity, not uniformity, is the other side. Unity and diversity—not "either-or," but 'both-and.' Cunningham illustrates this with reference to his own artistic preferences, shaped and particularized by a range of experiences and exposures throughout his life: "The starkly individualistic claim that 'my tastes are purely my own' can survive only in a radically decontextualized account of my life."[10]

---

8. See Moltmann, *Spirit of Life*, 180.
9. Cunningham, *These Three Are One*, 198.
10. Ibid., 202.

Life of the Minister

In his book, *Ministry in the Image of God*, the American writer and theologian Stephen Seamands argues that the doctrine of the Trinity is far more than singing "Holy, Holy, Holy" or reciting the trinitarian benediction. It is, in his view, "the grammar of the Christian faith"—"the primary purpose of the trinitarian grammar is not comprehension or communication, but communion."[11] Although Seamands' book is ostensibly concerned with ministry, its focus is actually more on the *life* of the minister than the work of ministry: he identifies seven characteristics of trinitarian life that have profound implications for the vocation of ministry, which he then applies in subsequent chapters to the spiritual life of the minister, echoing many of the themes already developed in earlier chapters of this book. In a chapter on "relational personhood," he highlights the importance of relational wholeness—*shalom* would be another appropriate term here—and its outworking in personal and church life, citing four characteristics in particular as necessary for healthy interpersonal relationships, all of which are grounded in the inner life of the Trinity: full equality, glad submission, joyful intimacy, and mutual deference. As a prelude to his exposition, Seamands considers the life of Jesus as a template for the life of the Christian minister. What marks Jesus out as the prototype human being, of course, was his relationship with his Father and with the Holy Spirit.

The British New Testament scholar James D. G. Dunn observes that "a discussion about charismatic and/or enthusiastic phenomena in the ministry of Jesus takes us only so far; they certainly do not bring us to the heart of Jesus' religious experience. For that we have to penetrate rather more deeply."[12] Dunn comes up with two dimensions in the life of Jesus which reflect that heart: his experience of God as Father and his experience of Spirit. In other words, Jesus, the true human being, lived a trinitarian life on earth. He did not just come from the Trinity's life above, but *demonstrated trinitarian life on earth*. During his time on earth, Jesus experienced his Father's presence in a very intimate way: *Abba* is used in every prayer that is attributed to Jesus except one. Dunn declares that *"through this word abba we have touched one of the tap roots of Jesus' authority and power, . . . through this sense of sonship to God, of God as his Father, Jesus drew the convictions which in very large part governed

---

11. Seamands, *Ministry in Image of God*, 205.
12. Dunn, *Unity and Diversity*, 201.

his life and determined his mission."[13] This insight suggests that all who are involved in pastoral work need the same clear sense of identity and deep experience of intimacy if they are to be fully effective in their ministry. Seamands offers the phrase "joyful intimacy" in order to express this characteristic of trinitarian life—it is a life-affirming attribute, grounded in the assurance that we are loved by God *just as we are*.

Ian Pitt-Watson, who taught preaching at Fuller Seminary in the United States for many years, relates a personal story that illustrates this truth. He describes how his exhausted and tearful three-year-old daughter, Rosemary, was handed a rag doll on the family's arrival in Melbourne after the long flight from London. Through the years Rosemary clung to that doll, and it became the most precious thing she possessed: "In time the rag doll became more rag than doll and began to get a bit dirty. The sensible thing to do was to face the fact that the rag doll had never been worth much and was now no more than a bundle of dirty rags that ought to be trashed. But that was unthinkable for anyone who loved my child. If you loved Rosemary you had to love the rag doll. That was part of the package."[14] Rosemary's love for her rag doll was not contingent upon any intrinsic value that it had, a story that reminds us that we are loved because the God who is love chooses to love us. Or, to put it in a nutshell, we are valuable because we are loved—we are not loved because we are valuable. A powerful illustration of this in the life of Jesus is his own baptism, where he experienced the empowering embrace of the Spirit as he heard his Father saying "*You are my Son*, whom I love; with you I am well pleased" (Luke 3:22). Here we note *private* affirmation—Mark records the incident in the same words. But Matthew records it differently: "*This is my Son*, whom I love" declares the Father, "with him I am well pleased" (Matt 3:17). This is *public* affirmation. To know this private and public affirmation at the deepest and most intimate level is the foundation for all ministry—as it was for Jesus, so it is for us.

In *The Lion King*, Simba, the eldest son of the Lion King and Queen Mufasa and Sarabi, is threatened by his uncle Scar, who is out to claim the kingdom for himself. Eventually Scar is killed and Simba takes his rightful place as the Lion King. There is a moment in the story when Rafiki, that strange and lovable baboon, discovers him and says, "You don't even know who you are. But I know who you are. You're Mufasa's boy." And

---

13. Ibid., 203.
14. Pitt-Watson, *Primer for Preachers*, 48.

then later on Simba sees his reflection in a pond and realizes that he really is his father's son and is meant to be the Lion King. The first and greatest secret of Christian life and ministry—and it's an open secret!—is knowing, in the deepest parts of our being, that we are the child of our Father, just as Jesus knew his identity, his sonship, when he was baptized in the River Jordan. As frail and fallible human beings, we may recognize that there are barriers that frustrate such intimacy—Seamands cites childhood wounds and the wounds of ministry—and these will need to be lovingly healed if we are to fully experience the joy and depth of intimacy that is most completely found within the perichoretic life of the Trinity.

Further chapters in Seamands' book emphasize other important aspects of relational life and health such as vulnerable self-giving (echoing God's own *kenosis*), glad submission, and empathic listening.[15] Of interest too in his treatment of the subject—in a chapter entitled "Complex Simplicity"—is his acknowledgment of paradox, mystery, logical contradiction, and ambiguity in the main issues of life and ministry, precisely because God's trinitarian nature is reflected in the world that he has made. The Trinity reminds us that *"nothing is so simple that it's not also complex, and nothing is so complex that it's not also simple. There is a complex simplicity and a simple complexity built into the nature of things."*[16] He teases this out in the context of what Christian Schwarz has called the "bipolar nature of the church," in which the church is paradoxically viewed as both an organism and an organization, paralleling our earlier discussion about the nature of the church with regard to its orientation within the traditional-emerging spectrum. Many ministers, occupying one or other end of the organism-organization spectrum, are uncomfortable with the radical middle where both sides of the paradox are affirmed, reflected in biblical phrases like "living stones" (1 Pet 2:4-8) and "growing into a temple" (Eph 2:19-22). The point here, of course, is that unless we are personally grounded in a trinitarian way of thinking about life and ministry, living that out in the reality of our ministry context, we will probably situate ourselves to the right or to the left, wherever we feel most comfortable, and miss out on experiencing the rich mystery and complexity of situating ourselves in "both-and" territory. In this energizing place we discover the liberty of ministry within a freeing

---

15. Seamands also addresses the notion of trinitarian particularity in a chapter on "gracious self-acceptance." See Seamands, *Ministry in Image of God*, 117–36.

16. Ibid., 112.

theology of participation without dispensing with the necessary practical tools for doing the work of ministry (explored more fully in chapter 8).

In the radical middle those in pastoral leadership discover "a genuine complementarity between an emergent ministerial order and a 'top-down' influence"[17] in which the Spirit is present to facilitate a genuine interdependence in the structures of life and ministry, where "neither ordained nor other ecclesial ministries can be what they are *without the other*."[18] This dimension of the "both-and" paradigm is the particular subject of chapter 9, which delineates the contours of a perichoretic ecclesiology that is essentially charismatic at heart: the community of faith is constituted in its internal ordering as a relational organism by the Spirit of life, who is the agent of diversity.

The Work of Ministry

We now need to consider how the relational core of ministry might be most fruitfully expressed within the Christian pastoral context, focusing in the paragraphs that follow on the *work* of ministry rather than the life of the minister.[19] Here the doctrine of *perichoresis* is highly suggestive in offering a number of valuable insights. If, as we have noted from Fiddes, human beings participate in a sort of availability analogous to that which the trinitarian persons enjoy amongst each another, not an indivisible indwelling but a modified *perichoresis* representing "an indwelling of the Spirit common to everyone that makes the church into a communion corresponding to the Trinity,"[20] perhaps we might want to propose an asymmetrical relationship between God and humanity—but a relationship, nonetheless, which is intensely alive, creatively dynamic and as mutually reciprocal as the divine-human distinction is able to offer. It is in this sense, therefore, that the shape and life of the pastoral community derives from the initiative of the triune God of grace, who has chosen human beings to participate in his dynamic, perichoretic self-giving life of love in the world that he has created.

Implicit in this divine invitation is a way of life that approximates as closely as possible the hospitable life of the Trinity. We noted in chapter

17. Pickard, *Theological Foundations*, 142.
18. Ibid., 154, author's italics.
19. Some of the following material has been drawn from Buxton, *Trinity*, 167–93.
20. Volf, *After Our Likeness*, 213.

4 that the notion of hospitality is a characteristic feature of God, who creates space for human beings to experience in the fullest sense possible what it means to "feel at home." Closely linked to this is the idea of "receptivity," which means that "I invite the other to 'be at home' with me."[21] Neil Pembroke cites the dialogical philosopher Gabriel Marcel: "to provide hospitality is truly to communicate something of oneself to the other,"[22] noting that for Marcel being present for another person is a grace, not a skill to be learned. Within the Christian biblical and historical traditions, hospitality relates most particularly to the welcoming of strangers. For the early Christians, seeking to live out the trinitarian life, hospitality was not so much a gospel command as an expression of what it means to be made *imago Dei*. For the Christian community today, surrounded in the Western world by a culture of individualism and narcissism, the invitation to love from the heart in such a way as to be both attractive to those who belong as well as an authentic reflection of the life of God—and therefore attractive to those as yet outside its boundaries—is as urgent as ever.

Christine Pohl reminds us that hospitality "reflects God's greater hospitality that welcomes the undeserving, provides the lonely with a home, and sets a banquet table for the hungry."[23] Richard Gollings, who was involved for many years in church planting in Mexico City and Tijuana, tells the story of two yearly migrants to the urban construction industry who were welcomed by a local pastor to share his dinner, and given a free room in the *templo* where his family lived. The notion of hospitality is evident here in the missionary heart of the local pastor: likewise, the local church is called into being as a "covenantal community," including and enabling "community obligations to strangers and outsiders."[24] There is a two-way dynamic involved here: strangers are welcomed into the Christian community, which at the same time moves out from its comfortable centre of familiarity and intimacy into costly engagement with others. Ultimately, actions speak louder than words.

Writing of this costly love, Jean Vanier observes that "the more impossible it is in human terms, the more of a sign it is that their love

---

21. Pembroke, *Art of Listening*, 21.
22. Marcel, *Creative Fidelity*, 91.
23. Pohl, *Making Room*, 16.
24. Gollings, "Planting Covenant Communities," 129.

comes from God and that Jesus is living."[25] However, this must not be interpreted as a recipe for passivity in community. Far from it: Christians are called to vibrant participation in the Christian life. This begins in the heart, for "a community is only a community when the majority of its members is making the transition from 'the community for myself' to 'myself for the community.'"[26] And hospitality lies at the heart of this giving of oneself, expressed not only in serving one another *within* the community of faith, but also—and most especially—in welcoming strangers into our churches, into our homes, and to our tables, reflecting the self-giving perichoretic life of the triune God. In his fine exposition of humanity's persistent exclusion of "the other" the Croatian theologian Miroslav Volf argues that Christians are called to distance themselves from their own culture because of their ultimate allegiance to God and his promised future. This *"creates space in us to receive the other,"* because the Spirit "unlatches the doors of my heart saying 'You are not only you; others belong to you too.'"[27] Volf expresses this reorientation towards the other, and especially the stranger—even our enemies—as "the will to embrace": *"the will to give ourselves to others and 'welcome' them, to readjust our identities to make space for them, is prior to any judgment about others, except that of identifying them in our humanity."*[28]

Another word that is helpful in describing the quality of love that the Spirit of God seeks to reproduce in the community of faith is friendship, and it is an intensely practical word. Of particular interest is Moltmann's perspective on *philia*-friendship, grounded in an acceptance of each other's differences: accepted as friends by God, believers discover that "the friendship of the 'Wholly Other' God which comes to meet us makes open friendship with people who are 'other' not merely possible but also interesting, in a profoundly human sense."[29] There is an *ekstatic* dimension to this type of friendship, in which the doors are thrown wide open for others to enter in and participate in the joy of the divine dance. It is an "open friendship," a "vulnerable atmosphere of life," which is based on the virtues of affection and respect: affection, for Moltmann, has to do with liking people for themselves, without making any demands on them,

25. Vanier, *Community and Growth*, 34.
26. Ibid., 22.
27. Volf, *Exclusion and Embrace*, 51, author's italics.
28. Ibid., 29, author's italics.
29. Moltmann, *Spirit of Life*, 259.

whereas respect has to do with their freedom. "Friends throw open the free spaces of life for one another, and accompany one another in sympathy and immense interest."[30] Commenting on this, Joy Ann MacDougall concludes that "open friendship" "leads the believer into the footsteps of Christ—toward imitating the boundless hospitality that Jesus shared with all those he encountered and particularly with those on the margins of society."[31]

The Eucharistic Meal

Perhaps the most powerful expression of perichoretic life in the context of the worshipping life of the community of faith is the communal meal of the Eucharist, a sacrament that resonates strongly with the Christian virtue of hospitality. We noted in chapter 3 that in the Eucharist, the three pastoral dimensions of worship, mission, and compassion (or pastoral care) converge in a powerful way, for there the Christian community participates in a deeply relational way in the history of the triune God—not only with thanksgiving, but also in intercessory identification with the pain and suffering of this world. For David Cunningham, the Eucharist "has become such a ritualized or sentimentalized event that its profundity has evaporated."[32] Theologically, the sacrament represents a powerful appropriation of the saving acts of the triune God as we physically receive the elements of bread and wine into our bodies. In the Eucharist we share in the drama of death and resurrection which is happening in the heart of God, for God still suffers in the midst of all that has gone wrong in this world.

The meal is both communal and eschatological: as the pivotal Christian worship event it reminds us that the church is not a collection of individuals who happen to come together at certain times in a ritual of self-focused pietism, but is "that community within the world which in her worship anticipates the perfect community of the Kingdom, waiting for the marriage feast of the Lamb."[33] In our worship we anticipate the ultimate eschatological community. We do not participate in isolation, but in solidarity with each other, and in communion with the heavenly

---

30. Ibid., 256.
31. McDougall, "Return of Trinitarian Praxis?" 200.
32. Cunningham, *These Three Are One*, 176.
33. Torrance, "Place of Jesus Christ," 358.

company of angels and perfected saints. Our community life on earth, which is at the same time a life of both mutual encouragement and participation in Christ's mission in and for the world, derives from and is in fact an expression of our participation in the worship that characterizes the life of the triune God. In our worship and in our calling to serve God in the world we are a redeemed community, reflecting the loving trinitarian communion into which the Spirit has drawn us. As we go out into the world, strengthened in our faith, renewed by our participation in the worship of Christ, and grasped afresh by the realization of God's love for all that he has made, we summon the world to enter into the gift of life. Commenting on the significance of Andrei Rublev's famous fifteenth-century icon depicting the three angels who visited Abraham near the great tree of Mamre (Gen 18:1–15), traditionally interpreted as an icon of the Trinity, Paul Fromont alludes to Jesus' "Eucharistic action," with his right hand extended over the chalice on the table. We are gathered at the table, fed and filled with God's life and goodness, not as an end in itself but in order that we might be strengthened to serve God in the world: "A Trinitarian spirituality holds in tension both an 'inward' or gathered dimension, and an 'outward' or 'sent' dimension. Both are needful."[34]

The liturgies of the church insist upon this integral link between worship and mission, as expressed in one of the Anglican post-communion prayers:

> Almighty God,
> We thank you for feeding us
> With the body and blood of your Son Jesus Christ.
> Through him we offer you our souls and bodies
> To be a living sacrifice.
> Send us out
> In the power of your Spirit
> To live and work
> To your praise and glory. Amen.[35]

As we participate in God's mission in the world as "living sacrifices," we enter into the reconciling ministry of the Spirit, who is continuously at work in the world in both hidden and improbable ways, with creative innovation and resourceful ingenuity, and with concern for the

---

34. Fromont, "Rublev's Icon," 4.
35. Church of England, *Alternative Service Book 1980*.

particularity of context. Whenever the Christian church ties the Spirit of mission down to its own specific programs, failing to recognize these essential characteristics, it has lost sight of what it means to participate effectively in the *missio Dei*. Mission is, in fact, a defining characteristic of the church, for it expresses the inner impulse of the triune God to reveal himself through his church in the midst of the world. God delights to make himself known, and the church is both a sign of his kingdom, pointing to the reality of his rule of compassionate love, and a sacrament—a dynamic event of grace, in which he is present by his Spirit.

This means that missional ministry is relational first and foremost precisely because it is predicated on the church's participation in the perichoretic life of God, whose impulse is always to welcome others into his life—the God who does not want to be God without us! To be drawn into the depths of his perichoretic life is to be embraced by the same impulse that gives rise to his loving actions in and for the world. Functionally, of course, the community of faith gives form and shape to that impulse under the inspiration of the Spirit through appropriate missionary strategies. Each faith-community is privileged to participate in the mission of Christ in the world in its own unique Spirit-inspired way, but the doing of that mission must never replace—or indeed precede—a profound awareness of our incorporation into the inner-trinitarian life of God himself. In *The Go-Between God*, John Taylor reminds us that

> The primary effect of the pentecostal experience was to fuse the individuals of that company into a fellowship which in the same moment was caught up into the life of the risen Lord. In a new awareness of him and of one another they burst into praise, and the world came running for an explanation. In other words, the gift of the Holy Spirit in the fellowship of the church first enables Christians to *be*, and only as a consequence of that sends them to do and to speak.[36]

In fact, the Brazilian theologian Leonardo Boff—taking the notion of solidarity with the world to its ultimate expression in terms of a preferential option for the poor—points out that the relationship between the being of our life *in* God and the doing of mission with God is a two-way movement: solidarity with the poor and the oppressed, and embracing those who are "strangers," actually helps us in our *understanding* of the

---

36. Taylor, *Go-Between God*, 134.

communion of the Trinity.³⁷ Not only are we motivated to serve the poor, welcome strangers, and offer our lives as a sacrament of grace to a needy world as a *result* of a deepening awareness of who God is, but to live a life of other-centred concern and action in the world is to plumb the depths of trinitarian life, opening our eyes even further to the greatness of God's love and deepening our love for God. As Moltmann puts it, "the more Christians intervene for the life of the hungry, the human rights of the oppressed and the fellowship of the forsaken, *the deeper they will be led into continual prayer*. It sounds paradoxical, but the more their actions are related to this world, and the more passionately they love life, *the more strongly they will believe*, if they want to remain true to the hope which Jesus brought into the world."³⁸ When we are gripped by the truth of our own freedom, when we remember again whose people we are, and dance with the joy of the redeemed, then we will begin to understand in the depths of our being that the liberating feast of the resurrection is not just for ourselves, and there will awaken in us a longing to see others enter the dance.

Pastoral Care

The relational core of ministry is also apparent in the ministry of pastoral care. The framework within which genuine care and compassion can take place may be helpfully illustrated by contrasting two models of offering succor to a person who is struggling. David Benner traces the shift during the twentieth century from the care of souls (*cura animarum*) to the cure of minds, arguing that the rise of modern psychology has been a major contributory factor in the professionalization of therapy, within as well as outside the church.³⁹ The notion of soul care embraces not only nurture and support but also healing and restoration. But the primary thrust in contemporary therapeutic practice has more to do with *clinical* approaches that seek to apply psychological insights than the *pastoral* care of troubled people. The result is that relationally-oriented nurture and support have given way to a greater focus on pragmatic solution-based psycho-therapeutic methods. In a passionate defence of Christian pastoral care, Peterson waxes eloquently against present-day healing and

---

37. Boff, *Trinity and Society*, 13.
38. Moltmann, *Church in Power of Spirit*, 284, my italics.
39. Benner, *Care of Souls*, 35–50.

helping disciplines, which "are like the River Platte as described by Mark Twain, a mile wide and an inch deep."[40]

However, in their desire to help hurting people back into wholeness, those who dispense psychological remedies should not be summarily dismissed as if their insights were inimical to Christian truth. We must beware the "either-or" trap of putting Christianity and psychology into separate boxes, as if they had nothing to do with each other. Nevertheless, the danger of capitulating to the seductive pragmatism of secular therapies remains: as the philosophical theologian James Olthuis declares, the goal of all therapy "is not decisive conclusions or valid interpretation, but transformed connections, changed lives, the surge of mercy, a drawing nearer to each other, and to God. Not: 'Have I mastered the technique?' But: 'Has the person been seen, heard, and blessed?'"[41] This perspective offers a model of pastoral therapy that is perichoretically oriented, based on the notion of two people travelling on a journey together, in which the one offering care and the one in need of care experience the grace of God as they both open themselves up to the Spirit. In this model, the emphasis is on mutual interaction and sharing, in which the space between them is perceived not as something that needs to be bridged by the application of a particular technique or therapeutic strategy that guarantees a solution, but as a risky and unpredictable "dance of blessing," "a sojourning together, a lingering in stages and phases, a sometimes struggle, sometimes dance, always adventure, on the way to renewed and deepened connections and reconnections with self and others."[42]

The metaphor of therapy as a "dance of blessing" corresponds to the perichoretic life of the Trinity in its embodiment of movements of love, a dynamic that is open and caring, always delighting in the other. It is "com-passion" because it is the rhythmic, pulsing surge of God's life within us that is oriented towards wholeness, connecting us back together with God, with each other and with all creation. Human beings participate in the triune life of compassion as they enter into mutually enriching compassionate relationships, characterized by openness, vulnerability, and availability. As a paradigm of pastoral care and compassion, "dancing in the wild spaces of love opens us up to the free play of grace, to the surprises of the spirit, to the indwelling of the Spirit, to the miracles

---

40. Peterson, *Five Smooth Stones*, 3.
41. Olthuis, "Dancing Together," 147.
42. Ibid., 148.

of love,"[43] valuing the spontaneous ministry of the Spirit rather than organized therapeutic programs that are often divorced from the vulnerable real world of hurting people. In its reinforcement of the reciprocity of mutual giving and receiving, and in its enhancement of difference and particularity, the paradigm resonates strongly with the trinitarian concept of *perichoresis*.

We have explored the notion of relational wholeness in the life of the pastoral minster, and identified a number of practical pastoral themes that spring from the perichoretic nature of inner-trinitarian life: vulnerable hospitality, open friendship, eucharistic participation, missional solidarity, and compassionate therapy. In *Mere Christianity*, C. S. Lewis presents God's gracious invitation to fully participate in the relational life of the Trinity in some memorable words that fittingly sum up the relational core of Christian ministry as expounded in this chapter:

> The whole dance, or drama, or pattern of this three-Personal life is to be played out in each one of us: or (putting it the other way round) each one of us has got to enter that pattern, take his place in that dance. There is no other way to the happiness for which we were made. Good things as well as bad, you know, are caught by a kind of infection. If you want to get warm you must stand near the fire: if you want to be wet you must get into the water. If you want joy, power, peace, eternal life, you must get close to, or even into, the thing that has them. They are not a sort of prize which God could, if He chose, just hand out to anyone. They are a great fountain of energy and beauty spurting up at the very centre of reality. If you are close to it, the spray will wet you: if you are not, you will remain dry.[44]

---

43. Olthuis, "Dancing Together," 151.
44. Lewis, *Mere Christianity*, 176.

8

"Nothing astonishes men so much as common sense"
—Ralph Waldo Emerson

Wisdom of the World

Tertullian's oft-quoted question "What is there in common between Athens and Jerusalem?" presents a clear distinction, or opposition, between pagan philosophy and Christian revelation. This dichotomy has led some to hastily reject the insights of management theorists and practitioners in Christian ministry, although I recognize the concern of those who fear we are in danger of burying the gospel message in a misguided pragmatic pursuit of success and achievement, based upon the premise that the end justifies the means.

In Luke's Gospel Jesus relates a parable, in which a dishonest manager, accused by his master of irresponsibly wasting what he had been given to look after, acted in a shrewd, though fraudulent, manner to preserve his own interests (see Luke 16:1-13). In his comment on the parable, Jesus commends the steward not for his fraud nor for his self-centred goals, but specifically for his wisdom and perspicacity: "For the people of this world are more shrewd in dealing with their own kind than are the people of the light" (Luke 6:8). The point of the parable is that those who have been given responsibility in the kingdom of God should be alert to all the resources that may be available to them in the fulfilment of what they are given to do. Whilst Jesus goes on to connect the parable to friendships and the stewardship of money, it is helpful to consider his teaching in the context of opportunities to draw from the wisdom of the world in the affairs of the kingdom of God. May not "the world" have much to teach the "children of light" with regard to intelligence and astuteness?

In fact, the parable suggests that there is more to be said about pragmatism than a simple "ends-means" argument. The Merriam-Webster online dictionary defines pragmatism as "a practical approach to problems and affairs," whilst the American philosophical movement of the same name—originating at the end of the nineteenth century, and with which Charles Peirce and William James are most famously associated—argues that pragmatism, in its narrow sense, means that practical consequences give us the best insight into the truth of a particular notion. Let's take a closer look at William James, an American philosopher who has had a significant impact upon our understanding of pragmatism. Drawing upon his celebrated metaphysical riddle of the man going round the squirrel going round the tree—if a man circles round and round a tree, and a squirrel moves as fast in order to remain on the opposite side of the tree from him, does the man go round the squirrel or not?—James challenges his audience at a lecture series in 1906 to consider the practical meaning of "going round the squirrel." For James, pragmatism demands that we define our language and our terminology clearly, and this is achieved by thinking clearly about the *practical consequences* of alternative ideas. Rather than defining pragmatism in the pejorative sense of a willingness to compromise principles in the search for a solution to a particular problem or issue—the "what-works" scenario—James argues that a pragmatist "turns away from abstraction and insufficiency, from verbal solutions, from bad *a priori* reasons, from fixed principles, closed systems, and pretended absolutes and origins. He turns towards concreteness and adequacy, towards facts, towards action, and towards power."[1]

Practical Consequences

Pragmatism has value precisely because it invites us to think clearly about *practical consequences*: it proposes that a thing is meaningful if it leads to certain practical outcomes that have value, that make a measurable difference, in concrete human experience. Applied to Christian pastoral

---

1. James, *Pragmatism*, 28.

ministry, therefore, pragmatism is not to be automatically disparaged: it suggests that there may well be approaches and methodologies that have value within a theistic worldview. I regularly encounter Christians who have an immediate negative knee-jerk reaction whenever the language of pragmatism enters the conversation. Such a response—understandable in the light of contemporary managerial practices in some Christian church circles—is, however, another example of myopic thinking. As Brian Harris observes, pragmatic leaders "decide on the basis of what they think is most likely to succeed at the time—and clearly this is a dimension of decision-making that cannot be ignored. It is hard to motivate a group of people to do something that you think is unlikely to succeed."[2]

Throughout this book I have been championing the language of "both-and" over "either-or." I have also argued that a *reliance* upon methodology at the expense of mystery is both myopic and ultimately fruitless in the context of the gospel of grace: but that does not mean that methodologies should be dismissed as if they had nothing to offer in the outworking of the gospel in the diverse contexts in which the church finds itself. A management planning model, for example, may be a particularly useful framework for efficient utilization of available resources in order to accomplish desired church goals. Methodology is not to be thrown out of the window because it is capable of being corrupted: God calls his people to wise and efficient stewardship of resources.

The distinction to be made here is between *relying* on what the world has to offer and *plundering* from the world's inventory. An episode from the Old Testament may help us here. When God called Moses to lead the Hebrews out of slavery in Egypt, he added that he would "make the Egyptians favorably disposed towards this people so that when you leave you will not go empty handed" (Exod 3:21). So the Hebrews were enabled by God's grace to plunder, or spoil, the Egyptians of silver and gold and clothing, articles that they would find useful for their journey to the promised land. Likewise, the Christian community may find valuable resources available to them from the world of business management to facilitate their ministry in the world, resources that are not exclusive to those who do not participate explicitly in the life of the church. Plundering is radically different from being seduced by the promises of success offered by extreme proponents of pragmatism. The ultimate idolatry in this regard for those who are charged with pastoral leadership is the

---

2. Harris, *Tortoise Usually Wins*, 35.

espousal of a managerial approach to pastoral ministry that *supplants* the call to participate in the gracious, liberating ministry of the Spirit in mobilizing the community of faith in its witness in and to the world. Methods designed to enhance the health and growth of the church—whatever their source—are therefore not wrong or inappropriate *per se* in the practice of Christian ministry: they have their place alongside a theology of participation in all that God is doing by his Spirit.

William James described himself as a supernaturalist, believing that there is more to reality than the physical, material world around us. His own religious beliefs inclined towards a form of pluralistic "open theism" (see chapter 3), and his pragmatic philosophy led him to subscribe to a belief in a metaphysical spiritual reality that gives rise to practical effects in the sensory world of human experience. His pragmatism is thus idea-generating rather than solution-focused, with an evident practical cash-value. Epistemologically, practical outcomes were, for James, a way into understanding the *truth* of a thing. Understandably, and rightly, Christians will be wary of a philosophical doctrine that sits light on the revelatory truth of the gospel, and to argue that the origin of truth lies in the concrete difference it makes to our lives is clearly subversive. However, one of the great triumphs of the pragmatic method lies in its celebration of "the open air and possibilities of nature, as against dogma, artificiality and the pretence of finality in truth."[3] Here, it is the claim to certainty and finality with regard to truth that unsettles James; granted, his notion of truth as that which is ultimately validated by experience is problematic in its rejection of *a priori* metaphysical truth, but we should welcome his invitation to embrace pragmatism as a way of personal transformation: "Pragmatism unstiffens all our theories, limbers them up and sets each one at work."[4]

Common Sense

Another way of presenting pragmatism as described above is to speak of the currency of "common sense." The virtue of common sense, hinted at above through the conceptual lens of pragmatism and later in this chapter through the methodological lens of Appreciative Inquiry, carries with it a number of meanings. Its more popular interpretation has to do with

---

3. James, *Pragmatism*, 28.
4. Ibid., 28.

what is deemed to be sound judgment based upon an awareness of a situation that does not demand any special sort of knowledge. The essayist Ralph Waldo Emerson once observed that nothing astonishes men so much as common sense. However, the phrase also conveys the idea of a basic perception that most people are expected to have naturally, even if they cannot explain it—in other words, it refers to a sense that is common to most people. This idea also draws in part from the Aristotelian notion that common sense—*sensus communis*—is the integration of all five senses in an overarching perception that simply "makes sense."

One particular area of congregational life that cries out for a common-sense application of prudent practice has to do with the faithful stewardship of resources, an activity requiring careful planning.[5] The idea of planning is not foreign to God. God has a plan for his creation, a plan that is unfolding through history until that time comes when all things in heaven and on earth will be brought together under one head, who is Christ (Eph 1:10). He had a plan for the exiles in Babylon: "For I know the plans I have for you," declares the Lord, "plans to prosper you and not to harm you, to give you a hope and a future" (Jer 29:11). More specifically, God may reveal his plans to his servants in the face of opposition and difficulty, as Jehoshaphat discovered when he prayed to the Lord—"We do not know what to do, but our eyes are upon you" (2 Chr 20:12)—and God's plan gave victory to the Israelites. It is the privilege and responsibility of those in pastoral ministry to discern what is in God's heart as they seek to lead the church as his delegated "managers." Man may propose, but ultimately it is God who disposes: "Many are the plans in a man's heart, but it is the Lord's purpose that prevails" (Prov 19:21). Christian management starts with the recognition that God has plans that need to be prayerfully discerned. It is in the execution of these plans that those in pastoral ministry can most usefully draw from the experience and wisdom of the business world, the arena with which organizational planning is most commonly associated.

Good management theory recommends the adoption of clearly defined objectives. Clear-cut goals present, for all involved in pastoral ministry, great opportunities for focused prayer, enabling a congregation to be specific in its understanding of and commitment to God's purposes. Good planning also requires that a faith-community recognize its own strengths and weaknesses in the light of God's vision for its future. As a

---

5. The following paragraphs on planning and Appreciative Inquiry draw from earlier material in Buxton, *Celebrating Life*, chapter 7.

result, the resources and changes needed to realize the fulfilment of that vision will be more readily discerned. Knowing what exactly is going on *within* the community of faith as well as *externally* within the ministry environment—often referred to as auditing—demands both honesty and perseverance. Business executives ruthlessly assess their internal resources of finance, human personnel, and technology, and their external environment in the form of competitive threats and market opportunities. Likewise, there is value in wisely and carefully discerning the inner strengths and weaknesses of a congregation, as well as appreciating the specific context within which pastoral ministry takes place.

Appreciative Inquiry

A constructive model to help a congregation discover how to prepare for its future by appreciating its strengths is a process called, appropriately, Appreciative Inquiry (AI). AI is an approach that focuses on "the generative and creative images that can be held up, valued, and used as a basis for moving towards the future."[6] In his application of AI to the First Presbyterian Church (historically an ethnically Japanese church), located in Altadena, California, Mark Lau Branson treats the church as an organic, interpretive community, discovering how to draw on its own inner strengths, defined as significant "life forces" that are available in stories and imaginations.[7] As the congregation explores these life forces, new habits and ways of living arise out of the conversations that take place, offering positive scenarios for the future.

Branson argues that Appreciative Inquiry is "more than just a planning method—it is a way of seeing and creating."[8] It "begins with the conviction that organizations are mysteries to be embraced rather than problems to be solved."[9] AI describes a process of congregational reshaping that is grounded in the ongoing life of its members. However, it is not a random exercise. Though it relies critically upon people's self-understanding and memories, it follows a sequence of four steps—Initiate, Inquire, Imagine, and Innovate—within the framework of a clear commitment to positive narratives and images. Branson's study is an excellent

---

6. Watkins and Mohr, *Appreciative Inquiry*, 30.
7. Branson, *Memories, Hopes*.
8. Ibid., 203.
9. Harris, *Tortoise Usually Wins*, 89.

example of how a specific approach that has its origins in the discipline of organizational development[10] can be tailored to a local church, or indeed to any Christian organization.

Since, as we have argued, Christians should not have a knee-jerk reaction against pragmatism, but ever seek to protect or redeem it from ungodly influences, the next step following the auditing process is to explore both prayerfully *and* pragmatically the various options available to fulfil God's vision in the light of what has been discovered. Business executives are accustomed to distinguishing between strategy and tactics, a differentiation picked up in the church growth literature. Strategic planning is broad, whereas tactical planning addresses the details. For example, if a local congregation is convinced of a God-given vision to engage more authentically with the elderly in the community, then it may explore a number of alternative strategies: the provision of a drop-in centre on the church premises; a visiting program involving members of the congregation; special services geared to older folk; a special "Alpha" initiative amongst the elderly; prayer-partnership programs; ministry opportunities in homes for the elderly; the list is endless. These are the strategies that need to be brought before God in prayer as well as before the congregation with regard to practicality.

Of course, the possibility that the Spirit may lead the congregation into new, unexpected opportunities for ministry must never be discounted. In his discussion of Appreciative Inquiry, Branson cites the relevance of insights from chaos theory, a term in the natural sciences that refers not to total disorder, but to unaccountable natural processes in which extraordinarily complex patterns arise unpredictably out of turbulence. He notes:

> In churches, we often attempt to set up some order and purpose only to be repeatedly surprised. A sermon has unintended consequences, one program unexpectedly undercuts another program, or new energy arises when we sense only dissipation. As churches begin to use long-range planning, based on some kind of predictability, we often spend more time adjusting the plan than we did creating it originally. . . . AI theorists hold that by embracing the chaos—gaining new perceptions, imagining new futures—we have a better chance at nurturing the life-giving forces that are available to us.[11]

10. See the "AI Commons" at http://appreciativeinquiry.case.edu/.
11. Branson, *Memories, Hopes*, 234. For a fuller perspective on the contributions

For Branson, applying an Appreciative Inquiry approach to church leadership involves "order at the edge of chaos." He challenges the conventional "business" model for church management, with its reliance upon linear, hierarchical, cause-and-effect systems behavior. Conventional management systems are *not* the stuff of church life, he argues:

> [T]his leads to management by separate functions, applying certain forces, measuring resources and output, maintaining power structures, and making changes by altering a power or a force. . . . In this interpretive approach, the goal of church ministry is to find the staff and develop the programs that can fill the required pews. Business language fits this framework: products and services, marketing and sales, managers and marketers."[12]

What Branson is eschewing here is not management approaches *per se*, but those models that derive from a traditional, *mechanistic* model of business. His application of AI involves processes and sequences that resonate with sound and efficient ways of operating, seeking to obtain the most hopeful scenarios for the future. At the same, time, however, the AI process is thoroughly relational in its orientation, consistent with much contemporary rethinking about management practices. Once the specific strategy or strategies have been discerned, the particular details can be worked out in relation to congregational strengths and weaknesses. This is the "nuts-and-bolts" part of planning, in which every faith-community finds itself involved at different times. At all stages everyone should be offered the opportunity to participate in God's vision for the church in its witness in and to the world. Congregational ownership of the vision, in all its myriad expressions, inevitably encourages the sort of commitment and unity that is sadly lacking in many churches today. The specific example of Appreciative Inquiry discussed above is one approach drawn from the field of management that seeks to promote the best and highest future for the faith community.

The example of planning described above, with specific reference to the Appreciative Inquiry approach to organizational change, is a good example of a "common-sense" approach to congregational management, without ever losing sight of the role of the Spirit in leading the whole process. It is not a question of the leading of the Spirit *or* the leadership

---

of quantum theory, complexity and chaos theory for management, see Wheatley, *Leadership and the New Science*.

12. Branson, *Memories, Hopes*, 31.

of those who have been given the responsibility of managing the AI process: it is "both-and." Human beings have been blessed by God with many gifts, including the faculties of reason and discernment, and overseeing the AI approach to organizational change demands both the application of human aptitude and the discernment of divine direction.

Future Scenarios

Typically, the application of Appreciative Inquiry in a local church will result in the development of a series of future scenarios, presented in the form of "this is what the church will look like if the outcomes of the AI approach were applied over the next few years." The process usually commences with a meeting of members of the leadership team in order to become familiar with Appreciative Inquiry, and to allay fears about its secular origins. It is important at the outset that they acknowledge that the Spirit speaks to God's people in many ways—through the proclamation of his Word, through prayer, as spiritual gifts are exercised, and through other spiritual means. What is sometimes forgotten, however, representing a central insight in AI, is that the Spirit often chooses to reveal himself *through his people* as they recall all that he has done in their lives. To recall the specific acts of God in our lives, and to value them with gratitude is to affirm the reality of "I am the Lord your God...." The reality of God's self-revelation is affirmed *in the context of our human experiences*, in the remembrance of the concrete acts of God in human lives, not as an abstract proposition. In other words, Appreciative Inquiry—used thoughtfully and carefully—does not attempt to replace the person and work of Christ through the Spirit with human stories: rather, it may be a powerful means of affirming Christ's presence amongst us. As church leaders spend time together in thought and prayer, they are encouraged to believe that as Christians share their stories of God's grace at work in their lives, Christ will become known in new and fresh ways in their midst, offering hope and possibility. This, of course, reflects the experience of God's people in the Old Testament—as the Israelites rehearsed the narratives of God's saving actions among them, they discovered fresh hope for the future, especially in the midst of uncertainty and adversity.

As people in a congregation are encouraged to share about what they value most as they reflect on God's presence amongst them over past years, narratives of appreciation rise to the surface. Some of the stories—testimonies of God's goodness—may be personal: healing, strength in adversity, forgiveness, reconciliation. Other stories will be memories of how God has moved amongst the congregation. In addition, the Appreciative Inquiry process invites the faith community to share their hopes and dreams for the church. Thankfulness for God's life amongst his people—past, present, and future—serves to encourage us to look forward with faith and hope to all that he plans to do in the future, both within the life of the church and within the community that we are called to serve. At all times those who are involved in facilitating the Appreciative Inquiry process need both wisdom and sensitivity: wisdom in faithfully interpreting and recording the narratives that are shared, and sensitivity to the guidance and direction of the Holy Spirit. What is important at all times is the need to hear *the people's* stories of Christ's presence and blessing, to hear how God's Word has come alive for them, to discover what they value most about the church as a community of God's people seeking to be his witnesses in the community. As a result of the narration, recording and collation of many memories, hopes, and stories of God at work in a particular local church and in the community surrounding it, a number of key scenarios will emerge, offering positive images for God's future amongst his people at the church.

In one particular congregation known to me they took the following form, shaped (as mentioned earlier) in terms of present experience: living God's truth, celebrating God's life, welcoming change, connecting creatively, applying the Word, responding to the Spirit, and equipping the leaders. Taken together, these proposals represented signposts of what a particular faith community aspired to be and do under the guidance and inspiration of the Holy Spirit, and they were necessarily fleshed out more fully in order to help the congregation determine the specific steps needed to move forward into God's future. Here is an abridged version of those proposals:

1. *Living God's truth.* We are a growing congregation of God's people, young and old, diverse in culture and social background, who seek not just to hear the truth proclaimed, but to live that truth in our common life together and in the way that life is given expression in our neighborhoods, in our workplaces, and in the local community.

2. *Celebrating God's life.* We are a community of faith that recognizes the presence of the kingdom outside the borders of the church, and that God is active in his world by his Spirit; we therefore give regular

opportunities for members of the congregation to share about the things that God is doing in the local community as well as further afield, including overseas.

3. *Welcoming change.* We are a congregation that is open to change, not for its own sake, but in order to reflect the reality that we live in a changing world. Whenever we gather together as God's people we are continually open to the Holy Spirit to inspire us to give creative and imaginative expression to God's life in us, recognizing that we all have gifts and talents to offer.

4. *Connecting creatively.* Because we are a kingdom people, we are continually seeking new ways of communicating God's unchanging Word that resonate with our changing culture, engaging with the local community in ways that respond to significant needs, building bridges and giving fresh expression to what it means to "be church" in the community.

5. *Applying the Word.* As a congregation of people who love and value the Scriptures as God's truth, seeking to live that truth in our daily lives, we are discovering new ways, under the guidance of the Holy Spirit, to take the taught Word and to apply it to our own lives.

6. *Responding to the Spirit.* Whilst the sermon remains central in our teaching and learning, we also value opportunities for new ways of "being church," open to the Spirit to guide us, not only in the way we structure our times together, but also in the rich and surprising ways that he is at work spontaneously amongst us.

7. *Equipping the leaders.* Our leadership structures are flexible and organic in order to help us to respond effectively to the direction in which the Holy Spirit is taking us. Leadership training is an integral part of our internal church ministry, with the goal not only of "equipping God's people for the work of ministry" but also of raising up new leaders who have a heart for God's kingdom.

In a similar Appreciative Inquiry initiative in an Episcopal church in Minnesota, USA, a number of significant themes in its common life and ministry emerged: the importance of food, a deep commitment to hospitality, variety in worship and spiritual practices, the role of the arts in worship, fellowship, and prayer, connecting with the neighborhood, the importance of intergenerational ministry, and welcoming innovation, creativity, and change. The AI model is now widely used in many different denominational churches throughout the world. As evidenced above in the experience of two particular Christian congregations, it is much more than a method of planning an organization's future: rather, it represents a new way of *visualizing*, and then *entering into*, congregational life. When implemented sensitively, graciously, and under the guidance of the Holy Spirit, it offers a compilation of inviting and appealing gospel-affirming scenarios of what God's future truly can be. In the next chapter we shall briefly examine the implications of AI for those who are called to leadership within the life of the church.

Gratitude and Positive Thinking

Appreciative Inquiry has its origins in the 1990s at Case Western Reserve University's Weatherhead School of Management in the United States, but clearly it has great value beyond its initial relevance to business management. If, as argued at the beginning of this chapter, pragmatism's merit is grounded in an event, process, or action that leads to certain practical outcomes that have value, that make a measurable difference, in concrete human experience (following William James' focus on practical consequences), then Appreciative Inquiry has the potential of being an extremely useful pragmatic method for congregational life. Many local churches approach their future by asking questions that address some of the things that are going wrong: the problem-solving approach. Conceptually AI is radically different because it seeks to reveal what is good and right in an organization, not what needs to be fixed. It builds upon the important principles of *gratitude* and *positive thinking*, no strangers to the biblical/Christian frame of reference—in his letters, the apostle Paul often wrote about the importance of thankfulness, and in Phil 4:8 we read his exhortation: "whatever is true, whatever is noble, whatever is right, whatever is pure, whatever is lovely, whatever is admirable—if anything is excellent or praiseworthy—think about such things." This verse alone would serve as an appropriate mantra for AI.

Whenever we import approaches such as AI from business into the community of faith, we need to ask two questions. Firstly, does the methodology serve the ultimate, eschatological, new-creation purposes of God? More specifically, does it serve God's revelation of his will for us, in this place where we now live and have our being? Secondly, if so, is the methodology *in itself* a legitimate expression of the goodness and

9

"I am a bishop for you, I am a Christian with you"
–Augustine of Hippo

Authority of the Spirit

MANY YEARS AGO I ATTENDED A LARGE GATHERING OF CHRISTIANS in the north of England, during which a number of contentious issues were raised by one of the invited speakers from the United States. As we streamed out of the large building in which the convention took place, I spied a friend of mine who had recently left the Anglican church at which I was at that time a lay pastor and evangelist. I scurried over to him, trying not to get too wet in the driving rain, and asked him what he thought of the speaker's address. He mumbled a few words of approval, but I pressed him regarding some of the more provocative elements of the talk. I was expecting at least some reflective response, as my friend had only just become a pastoral leader in one of the newer charismatic "house churches" which had sprung up in the 1970s in England. To my surprise, my friend avoided a direct answer, replying with some ardor that it was up to his senior pastor to give direction on such issues: "After all, he's the one in authority in our church!" I was dismayed by his answer, though I knew where he was coming from. The church to which he belonged espoused a doctrine of ecclesial authority which was at odds with my own understanding at that time of the key Reformation principle of "the priesthood of all believers." Martin Luther's doctrine of the self-authenticating truth of the gospel in the hearts of believers, as revealed by the Spirit of God,

"Nothing astonishes men so much as common sense

righteousness of God? Thus we are to constantly evaluate methodology in the light of theology and God's ministry in the world. Pragmatic methodology drawn from business management is valid if, and only if, it passes through these two filters. Appreciative Inquiry is one organizational model that offers the possibility of points of contact between the business world and Christians who want to become more efficient in the way they engage in ministry in and for the world. Grounded in the virtue of common sense, it represents one constructive example of how the wisdom of the world can usefully inform the practice of Christian ministry.

was lost to my friend in favor of a form of "revelation knowledge" confined to a select band of charismatic leaders who exercised a radical and, at times, extreme form of authority over their flock.

Alister McGrath has summarized the matter admirably: "Who has the authority to speak in the name of God to His people?"[1] Who indeed? In this chapter we will examine this issue with regard to the ministry of leadership, and how that call is interpreted within the community of faith. Here we notice the interplay between leadership and authority in the particular context of Christian congregational life and ministry. In *The Tortoise Usually Wins*, Brian Harris' recent book on what he calls "quiet leadership," the author perceptively observes that leadership "is about helping move individuals and groups towards desired outcomes."[2] If, as Paul teaches in his Corinthian discussion of orderly worship, *everyone* has a part to play in the strengthening of the church (1 Cor 14:26), then it is incumbent upon those who have been given the special responsibility of discerning and, as a consequence, facilitating the Spirit's leading to embrace the contributions of those on whom the authority of the Spirit may rest at any particular time. It is clear that in the Pauline communities charismatic gifts were distributed amongst the congregational members. However, as demonstrated clearly in the Appreciative Inquiry process discussed in chapter 8, we should not limit their participation to *charismata*: everyone has a story to tell, memories to share, hopes to which to aspire, and these all feed into the mix of what the Spirit is saying to the church.

As we will note throughout this chapter, a genuine Spirit-led ecclesiology will therefore comprise those who are leaders precisely because they both value the personal narrative of every member of the congregation and also recognize the unique authority of the Spirit mediated through whomever he chooses, irrespective of their position in the church. At the same time, of course, such leaders will also be recognized by the congregation because of their spiritual discernment and their capacity to inspire church members to embrace "the desired outcomes" that the Spirit is opening up before them. In this connection, the American pastor and theologian Howard Friend proposes three leadership functions—inspiration, consultation, and celebration—at the heart of what he calls *adhocracy*, whereby leaders may be defined as those who "create and nurture a climate of expectancy, of responsibility-taking, of eager lay initiative."[3]

1. McGrath, "A Better Way," 301.
2. Harris, *Tortoise Usually Wins*, 87.
3. Friend, "Leading from the Bottom Up," 50.

Clergy and Laity

My purpose, however, is not to examine the nature and qualities of leadership, Christian or otherwise: much has already been written on that topic. Rather, consistent with my espousal of the "both-and" paradigm, I will argue in this chapter that authority within the life of the church is both a "top-down" and a "bottom-up" phenomenon. McGrath confronts what he describes as the intense authoritarianism found in many expressions of ministry in "modern power evangelicalism," paralleling the sacerdotalism of the medieval priesthood.[4] At root is the relationship between what we may call here "professional ministers of the gospel" and all other "lay" Christian people. Luther, of course, challenged the very notion of a distinction, at least ontologically, between clergy and laity, insisting that the only difference is one of function. However, in our eagerness to promote the priesthood of all believers and the creative ministry of the Spirit at work in all Christians, we must be careful not to dismiss the notion of ordination, even though we may choose not to adopt that term. In his 1976 Grove Booklet, *Authority and Ministry*, John Goldingay argues that there is no valid theology of ordination, and therefore "the emperor has no clothes!"[5] Whilst Goldingay rightly challenges the notion of authority being vested in a single person—usually male—at the top, perhaps a more generous "both-and" case may be made for clothing the emperor as well as his subjects!

In chapter 7 we noted Stephen Pickard's advocacy of what we might describe as a "both-and" leadership paradigm, where neither ordained nor other ecclesial ministries can be what they are *without the other*, indicative of what he calls a genuine Spirit-inspired complementarity between an emergent ministerial order and a "top-down" influence. Speaking on the anniversary of his ordination, the great early Christian theologian and bishop Augustine of Hippo draws these two dimensions together in an exquisite tension in these famous words: "But if you would sustain me, that we may bear our burdens for each other according to the precept of the Apostle, then thus we will together and for each other be fulfilling the law of Christ.... In the times when I am frightened that I am *for* you, I am then consoled that I am *with* you.... I am a bishop *for* you, I am a Christian *with* you."[6] So how might we see this tension played

---

4. McGrath, "A Better Way."
5. Goldingay, *Authority and Ministry*, 24.
6. Augustine, *Works of Saint Augustine*, 292.

out in the context of local church leadership? Given the strength of feeling on both sides—amongst those who endorse the primacy of ordained ministry over "the priesthood of all believers," and congregationalists for whom "the ministry of the entire church is associated with that of Christ, through the Holy Spirit"[7]—are there any fruitful models to which we might turn in order to support a "both-and" leadership paradigm?

Pickard's reflections on this issue, drawing from his own scientific insights, are a useful starting point in our discussion of the nature and function of leadership and the attendant tensions between hierarchical and collaborative approaches to pastoral leadership. Taking his cue from the Anglican threefold order of bishops, priests, and deacons and the vocation and ministry of *all the faithful* (lay and ordained), Pickard asks: "is there a way of understanding the inner relations between the ministries of the church that justifies genuine collaboration and confers enriched ministerial capacities on all ministries?"[8] Pickard is a realist with regard to how human beings behave in community, recognizing the reality of conflict and disharmony in human relationships. Accordingly, his ecclesiology seeks to avoid what he describes as "an idealized vision of human society generated from an abstracted theory of Divine operations."[9]

Truncated Ecclesiology

In this connection, Pickard rightly notes that contemporary trinitarian thinking has not been as productive as it might have promised in this area: he specifically critiques the way the doctrine of *perichoresis* has been inadequately translated into the church context, leading to what he calls a "truncated ecclesiology." In a similar vein, in her critique of the way that *perichoresis* has been interpreted as a negation of "the eternal order of Father begetting Son and 'spirating' the Spirit," Edith Humphrey argues that mutuality and asymmetry seem to cohere in the trinitarian mystery.[10] She challenges those who postulate that some form of hierarchical order is a sign of discord or misconduct within inner-trinitarian relations: "Only in the Godhead do we see the answer to the dichotomy that we tend to

---

7. Greenwood, *Transforming Priesthood*, 142.
8. Pickard, *Theological Foundations*, 123.
9. Pickard, *Seeking the Church*, 104.
10. Humphrey, "Gift of the Father," especially 94–102.

make, both intellectually and in our lives, between mutuality and order. ... In the wisdom of the Holy Spirit, we have come to understand that hierarchy and mutuality are not at odds in the triune God, but an ineffable mystery."[11] The Trinity, she maintains, presents us with a paradox that confronts our rational, democratic ideologies, and this is a particularly important observation in our attempts to translate our understanding of trinitarian relations to an ecclesial context.

A number of recent trinitarian theologians—such as Catherine LaCugna, Paul Fiddes, Miroslav Volf, and Colin Gunton—have argued that the mutuality and reciprocity implicit in the intradivine life is normative as the ontological ground for all human interactions (see chapter 3), but for Pickard there are some underlying problems in seeking a correspondence between divine and ecclesial *perichoresis*. These have to do with what he perceives as the doctrine's failure to attend to conflict and tension (noted above), the tendency for it to be restricted to "the community of the redeemed" disconnected from the wider society, and its lack of depth and reach, unable to "embrace the dynamic ways in which God's transformative work occurs throughout creation."[12] In response, I would agree that we must not ask of *perichoresis* what it cannot deliver, precisely because it essentially expresses that which ultimately is not achievable amongst human beings: the indwelling of other persons is an exclusive prerogative of God. Human beings participate in the perichoretic life of God in a distinctively *different* way to that which reflects the interiority of trinitarian divine life: the Spirit indwells human persons, but humans do not indwell the *person* of the Spirit in the same way that the Father and Son indwell him in divine *perichoresis*. Therefore, as Volf points out, "it is not the mutual perichoresis of human beings, but rather the indwelling of the Spirit common to everyone that makes the church into a communion corresponding to the Trinity."[13] Citing Fiddes, we noted in chapter 7 that human beings can, in an analogous sense, "dwell in the places opened out within the interweaving relationships of God; they dwell, we might say, not in 'spaces of subjectivity' but in 'relational spaces.'"[14] So we do need care, and perhaps some restraint, in the way we make trinitarian connections between the human and the divine. This is why Pickard rightly

---

11. Humphrey, "Gift of the Father," 98–99.
12. Pickard, *Seeking the Church*, 107.
13. Volf, *After Our Likeness*, 213.
14. Fiddes, *Participating in God*, 50.

insists that the key to the life of the church is the dynamic energy of the Holy Spirit, ever seeking to lead it more deeply into the life of God as well as into the life of the world, "patterning the life of Jesus."[15]

Pickard similarly notes the limitations of trinitarian thinking with regard to the reciprocal nature of lay and ordained ministries, leading him to explore the notion of order and the specific contribution of the physical sciences in his search for a resolution. Noting the rise of Darwinian evolutionary thinking in the nineteenth century, he acknowledges science's uncovering of "the richly dynamic implicate order of the world and human life,"[16] in which order emerges *from below*, rather than as a "top-down" phenomenon. In developing his thesis, Pickard turns to the science of *emergence*, a term that describes what happens when an interconnected system of relatively simple elements self-organizes to form more intelligent, more adaptive, and complex higher-level behavior.[17] At the most basic level of understanding, emergence may be described as a "bottom-up" process that represents "a movement from low-level rules to higher-level sophistication."[18] Michael Fuller offers three simple scientific examples in which emergent properties arise: water, a cell, and a human brain. Water molecules are not in themselves wet, yet combined with many others they produce "wetness"; proteins, nucleic acids, and other chemicals are themselves not alive, but combined into a cell they become a living organism; finally, a neuron is not conscious, but acting together with other neurons it produces consciousness.[19]

Closely related to the concept of emergence are the notions of *complexity* and *chaos*. When scientists talk about complexity, they refer to intricate self-organizing patterns of cells, organisms, neural networks in the brain, ecosystems . . . indeed the whole cosmos. Chaos theory refers not to total disorder, but to unaccountable natural processes in which extraordinarily complex patterns arise unpredictably out of turbulence. This occurs when the heat is turned on under a pan of soup: molecules move around all over the place in a dramatic frenzy of activity, and then, when the conditions are right, hexagonally shaped convection cells form as the liquid gets hotter. This is a classic example of "bottom-up"

15. Pickard, *Seeking the Church*, 115.
16. Pickard, *Theological Foundations*, 133.
17. For a helpful non-scientific introduction to the concept of emergence, see Johnson, *Emergence*.
18. Ibid., 18.
19. Fuller, *Atoms and Icons*, 32.

emergence, a higher-level order arising out of disorder. Other common examples include the sudden appearance of a vortex in the disordered turbulence of a flowing river, and the remarkable emergence of six-sided crystalline snowflakes from randomly moving water vapor molecules. In his discussion of emergence, Steven Johnson refers to the behavior of ant colonies: remarkably, there is no command structure telling the ant what to do. In a quite extraordinary way ants participate in the life of the colony in a coordinated fashion not because they are carrying out orders from a leader, but because they respond at the immediate, local level to all that is going on around them. They do not have a "big picture" available in order to determine their behavior.[20]

Open Systems

What has all this to do with church leadership? Well, quite a lot. In applying the new insights of quantum theory, complexity, and chaos theory to the field of human organization and management, Margaret Wheatley—whose book *Leadership and the New Science* is credited with establishing a fundamentally new approach to how we think about organizations—describes life as "open systems that engage with their environment and continue to grow and evolve."[21] She suggests that organizations that regard themselves as open systems, adapting to their environments in fluid, flexible ways and avoiding the rigidity that accompanies an over-reliance upon structures, are more likely to sustain themselves. Pickard affirms the rich correspondence between the multi-layered, complex, and graduated ordering of physical reality, permitting—even *requiring*—some form of hierarchical structuring, and the nature of institutional life. Acknowledging the modern antipathy towards order *per se*, he proposes a conceptual understanding of order as a "mode of togetherness," a constructive term that focuses on mutually supportive and creative relations. In the same way that the science of emergence presents us with an ordering of the world that relies upon layered orders and hierarchy, so in the life of the church ministries at all levels "are co-related, integrally and dynamically linked and in this way truly establish one another."[22] The integrating "mechanism" or instrument in the life of the church enabling

---

20. For a biblical insight on this, see Prov 6:9.
21. Wheatley, *Leadership and the New Science*, 77.
22. Pickard, *Theological Foundations*, 142.

this to happen is the activity of the Holy Spirit: "the transcendent agency of the Spirit is immanent within the natural ecclesial system generating a cruciform pattern of order."[23]

The model presented here, grounded theologically in the life-giving presence of the Spirit in creation, is one that involves the exercise of authority *within* the community of the church, mediated by the Spirit, who is ever at work in life-affirming ways to proclaim the mystery of God's ways. So the Spirit directed the leaders at Antioch to set apart Barnabas and Paul for apostolic ministry (Acts 13:1–3), and in many and various ways he led the early church in its ministry in the world. Today the Christian church is privileged to have the Bible as its agreed measure of orthodoxy, by which the inspired direction of the Spirit may be tested. But this must never be interpreted as giving Scripture authority over the Spirit, who is, of course, the Spirit of Christ.

In *Dancing in the Dark* I cite an incident that is particularly appropriate in the light of the above.[24] In 1966 Michael Harper, seeking material for a book on the charismatic movement within the churches in the United States, travelled to the Episcopal Church of the Redeemer in Houston, Texas, and discovered a remarkable work of the Spirit amongst the people there, shaping them into a compassionate, charismatic community of faith reaching out to society. What particularly struck Harper in the incident he records was how authority was expressed in a number of complementary and mutually reinforcing ways. The minister knew the inward call of God on his life, yet he was also aware of the need to submit himself to those whom he was called to serve. Direction came through the Spirit's ministry amongst the people of God, yet the mantle of leadership was not lifted from his shoulders. Charismatic gifting was evident in a prophetic word submitted by a member of the congregation: such manifestations of *charismata* were not uncommon in the everyday life of the church community. Within the tradition of the church in question, a joyful atmosphere of worship was evident, enhanced through liturgy and sacraments. At the same time, there was a high respect for the Scriptures, as Harper's account demonstrates.[25]

There is a noticeable correspondence between the experience of the Pauline churches in their mediation of the authority of God and that of

---

23. Ibid., 142.
24. Buxton, *Dancing*, 146–47.
25. Harper, *New Way of Living*, 20–21.

the Houston community quoted above. As Robert Banks reminds us, authority in the local church in Paul's day "resides not only in the most prominent members but in everyone without exception": each Pauline community was "a *participatory* society in which authority is dispersed throughout the whole membership."[26] Undoubtedly, there is risk in not toeing a strictly traditional or ecclesiastical line, and being willing to be open to the leading of the Spirit. Misinterpretation of God's word may occur, perhaps through immaturity or human fallibility; even worse, mischievous, even heretical, leaders may manipulate whole congregations. But the risk of *not* being open to the Spirit is perhaps even greater. Where adequate safeguards are introduced, the spontaneous and Spirit-inspired exercise of authority within the dynamic life of the Christian community can be a powerful demonstration of the life and joy of God.

In similar vein, Jürgen Moltmann, in *The Church in the Power of the Spirit*, discusses the relationship between the "assignments," or callings, of individual people and the calling of the community as a whole. Commenting on those who function in the church in their assigned tasks, he points out that their commission "does not separate them from the people and *does not set them above the people either*, for it is exercised in fellowship with and by commission of the whole people and in the name of that people's commissioning. But the thing for which the people are commissioned does not come from them themselves; it comes from their God, in whose name they speak and act."[27] What Moltmann is emphasizing here is a simultaneous outworking of divine authority through the gathered community and through individuals, which he defines as a *genetic connection*. "The Spirit leads men and women into the fellowship of the messianic people, at the same time giving everyone his own place and his particular charge."[28]

Moltmann's interpretation of authority exercised within the charismatic community is specifically pneumatological. The Spirit must be given full freedom to reign within the community of the church, distributing his authority through the individual and through the community as a whole. Consequently, there can be no fixed pattern by which the will of God is accomplished within each community. This does not mean, of course, that there are no norms for community life: Moltmann specifically

---

26. Banks, *Paul's Idea of Community*, 170, author's italics.
27. Moltmann, *Church in the Power of Spirit*, 303, my italics.
28. Ibid., 306.

identifies *kerygma*, *koinonia*, and *diakonia* as essential elements of all that the church is called to be. But in the performance of these essential "commissions of the community," we must acknowledge the inventiveness and ingenuity of the Spirit, who alone "constitutes" the church, to use the terminology of John Zizioulas, for whom "pneumatology does not refer to the well-being but to the very being of the Church."[29]

This simultaneous exercise of authority can only take place if all members of the community recognise their dependence not only on one another but also on the Holy Spirit. Only the Spirit has the wisdom and power to orchestrate a community of individuals in such a way as to mediate divine authority in the service of the kingdom of God. Only the Spirit can enable congregational members to "be like-minded, having the same love, being one in spirit and purpose" (Phil 2:2). Tradition, party spirit, and prejudice may all contribute to a false, even destructive, exercise of authority, but where there is genuine humility and an openness to listen to the voice of the Spirit, the church will challenge the world's perception of authority and present a way of life that reflects the true diaconal nature of authority. This has been likened by Tickle to what mathematicians and physicists call "network theory," in which every part contributes to the whole in a self-organizing system of relations in a dynamic and evolving structure: "The duty, the challenge, the joy and excitement of the Church and for the Christians who compose her, then, is in discovering what it means to believe that the kingdom of God is within one, and in understanding that one is thereby a pulsating, vibrant bit in a much grander network."[30]

Listening Leadership

In an earlier discussion of what has come to be known as "receptive ecumenism" (chapter 6) I commented that the notion of *listening* to others is very much on the ecumenical agenda today. Before exploring receptive ecumenism further, along with another innovative concept in practical theology known as "ordinary theology" and some further more specific reflections on the role of leadership in Appreciative Inquiry, a few words on listening are in order. A few years ago I planned to write a book with the title *Listening Leadership*, highlighting leaders as those who not only

---

29. Zizioulas, *Being as Communion*, 132.
30. Tickle, *Great Emergence*, 152–53.

listen to God (a given, one would hope!) but who also listen to their congregation, or other community group, whatever that might be—unfortunately I have never managed to find the time to develop my ideas on the subject. In my working framework I identified a number of critical dimensions of "listening leadership," focusing specifically on a leader who is *discerning* (a key aspect of listening), *decisive* (good at making decisions), and good at *delegating* (so critically involving others, discerning how they might be inspired and drawn in). Spiritual discernment, decisiveness, and the ability to delegate are, I suggest, critical attributes of a leader who seeks to operate within the sort of communal "participatory society" that I am advocating. My emphasis was therefore going to be on leaders who are recognized because they actually listen with discernment both to God in their personal lives, and also to the revelations of the Spirit amongst the people. Then, with decisiveness, they draw people into the outworking of that which has been discerned (the delegation part).

The point I am making here is that the willingness and capacity to listen is a key attribute of leadership and cannot be underestimated. The Appreciative Inquiry (AI) model of change and growth discussed earlier in the context of congregational life is itself grounded in empathic listening, representing perhaps the most critical dimension of what Gil Rendle and Alice Mann call 'holy conversations.' These are conversations structured around "what a group of people believe God calls them to be or to do,"[31] thus honoring the insights and wisdom of congregational members. Wise leadership understands Appreciative Inquiry as a *congregational* process that seeks to listen to the voice of the community of God's people as a means of discerning God's direction. If the church is to draw its identity and shape from the Trinity, seeking to image the communion life of God in its structure and practices, then ecclesial leadership structures will necessarily be shaped by inclusiveness, interdependence, and cooperation. Using a cosmic analogy, Leonardo Boff suggests that the "solar mystery of perichoretic communion in the Trinity sheds light on the lunar mystery of the church."[32] His "communion-perichoresis" vision of the Trinity leads to "a vision of a church that is more communion than hierarchy, more service than power, more circular than pyramidal, more loving embrace than bending the knee before authority."[33]

---

31. Rendle and Mann, *Holy Conversations*, 3.
32. Boff, *Trinity and Society*, 153.
33. Ibid., 154.

Human beings are often inclined to frame things in terms of hierarchy: instead of viewing A in *relation* to B, our natural preference is to view A in *comparison* to B, from which perspective we derive description, direction, and purpose. We therefore find ourselves attributing greater value to some ministries than others, which can easily lead to the devaluation of some people, whilst others are given an exalted status.[34] What is needed is a theology of the body of Christ, as spelled out by Paul in 1 Cor 12:12–26, in which we value the "least" member, and encourage all parts to work together. In this respect, Appreciative Inquiry values the stories, memories, and hopes of *everyone* in the body of Christ, and leadership's role is to facilitate the art of listening in order to draw out these stories, valuing them as critical to the health of the whole body. This way of thinking *does not eliminate hierarchy*—indeed, as suggested earlier in this chapter, hierarchy is integral to the ordering of physical and social reality. Specifically, in local church life *all* ministries, including the ministry of leadership, "inhere in each other, emerge out of each other, generate new ecclesial order and enable transformation in social practice. The critical element in this transformative work is the role of human agency seeking to participate in the work of the Spirit."[35]

We noted earlier that the Spirit is—or, rather, should be!—the creative power and life-energy in all ecclesial structures. As we yield the AI process to the Holy Spirit, we should expect to discern the Spirit's voice amongst God's people. This calls for wisdom in leadership, as there is a creative tension in Appreciative Inquiry between the Spirit's agenda (expressed in terms of revelation) and human agendas. How can we be sure that we are hearing the voice of the Spirit amidst the myriad human voices contributing to AI's "holy conversations"? From a philosophical perspective, social constructionism, an underlying theoretical premise undergirding AI, argues that social reality is constructed out of different human contexts. Social constructionists would say, for example, that reality arises "from below," rejecting the notion that reality is objectively determined and independent of human influence. At first glance this would seem to conflict with the notion of the authority of the Spirit within a Christian understanding of reality. However, Christians can, up to a certain point, have their constructionist cake and eat it too, because constructionism has to do with *our perception* of reality, rather than its

34. I am grateful for this insight to Elizabeth Smith, a graduate student in my Summer 2003 class at Fuller Theological Seminary.

35. Pickard, *Seeking the Church*, 164.

objective, ontological being. As Branson notes, the "focus here is epistemology (how do we know), not ontology (the nature of reality as studied in metaphysics)."[36] The key here is *language*: "We live our lives within a construct—a world created in our minds through language. . . . We use discourse—ongoing, thorough conversation—to make social meaning out of our pasts, to imagine possible futures, and to form cooperative practices."[37]

In our finitude, we are limited in our knowledge and understanding. We all use symbols, metaphors, and stories in order to communicate our understanding of what we see around us, and one of leadership's roles in congregational life is, through sensitive and careful listening, to discover meaning through the *language* that people use to express that understanding. Wise leadership will recognize that personal narratives occur within specific settings, thus giving contextual shape to what is shared, and that these narratives need to be filtered through a process of spiritual discernment, listening for "the still small voice that beckons us onward, quietly revealing what we are here on earth to do and to become."[38] The Spirit authenticates the will and presence of God not in a one-size-fits-all toolkit for congregational action, but in unique church contexts that enable us all to bring to the table our own longings, hopes, and desires: we are invited to offer our stories as spiritual gifts for the benefit of the whole community. Through this listening process, leadership's role is to reconnect us thankfully to God's narrative of grace amongst us, generating hope for the future.

Receptive Ecumenism

In chapter 6 I observed that the notion of listening to others is very much on the ecumenical agenda today. As Paul Fiddes remarked in a paper delivered in the UK in 2007, the point of what has come to be known as "receptive ecumenism" is "to allow 'learning' to take precedence over 'teaching,' to move from an attitude of defensiveness to . . . attention to the other."[39] In the words of Paul Murray: "What can we learn, or receive, with integrity from our various others in order to facilitate our own

---

36. Branson, *Memories*, 37.
37. Ibid., 37.
38. Rendle and Mann, *Holy Conversations*, 139.
39. Fiddes, "Learning from Others," 54.

growth together into deepened communion in Christ and the Spirit?"[40] It would seem that the primary goal of receptive ecumenism as elucidated in a number of conferences and discussions around the world is to facilitate a greater awareness of the need to listen to one another within the framework of national or denominational church structures. And that perhaps is where the primary effort amongst Christian leaders may be focused in the future. However, receptive ecumenism may prove to offer useful contributions to the issue of leadership in *local congregations*. Geoff Moore, a professor of business ethics at Durham University, UK (where much work is being done in the field of receptive ecumenism studies) is a member of the "Receptive Ecumenism and Local Church" research project in the north of England. One of the research areas in which he is involved is "leadership and ministry," which is looking at the role of ordained ministers—their leadership styles and how appropriate they are for the different denominations. A "learning and formation" group was set up to address issues such as the formation of laity and ordained in congregational life, including ministerial training. It is already clear from the work of the research team that because of financial pressures on local churches more and more lay people are becoming involved in church leadership and ministry. This is being worked out in different ways in the different denominational settings being studied. So key questions arise: what can each denomination learn from other denominations, and what can individual local churches learn from other churches grappling with similar problems? In Moore's view, if receptive ecumenism fails to have an impact on local church life, the project will have failed.[41]

Receptive ecumenism's promise is grounded in a willingness to listen to those who may have something to offer regarding how we "do church." In the context of the present chapter, it suggests that those who are involved in specific leadership roles may find resources to help them as they seek to encourage and enable the local congregation of God's people to live out its calling in the local community of which it is a part. "Whoever has ears to hear, let them hear" (Mark 4:9). In chapter 6, I recounted my experience of walking along a country lane in England, disturbed by a claim made by one particular denominational group that they were the "new breed" of Christians through whom God would fulfil his eschatological purposes in the world. As I stood under a large tree

---

40. Murray, "Receptive Ecumenism," 279–80.
41. Moore, "A Fuller Unity."

with spreading branches, I was heartened by the realization that each branch was different, yet the same sap was flowing through each one, eventually to turn bud into leaf. So God delights to express himself in glorious diversity in the life of his church, with each local church having the potential to offer a gift to the whole church. In God's kingdom there is no place for the arrogant for whom listening is a wasted exercise because they have a monopoly on discerning how God has spoken. The simple truth is that we all need to listen to one another, an insight that may be likened to the giving and receiving of pieces of a jigsaw puzzle, as suggested by the rabbi Lawrence Kushner:

> Each lifetime is the pieces of a jigsaw puzzle.
> For some there are more pieces.
> For others the puzzle is more difficult to assemble.
> Some seem to be born with a nearly completed puzzle . . .
> . . . But know this. No one has within themselves
> All the pieces to their puzzle . . .
> . . . Everyone carries with them at least one and probably
> Many pieces to someone else's puzzle.
> Sometimes they know it.
> Sometimes they don't.
> And when you present your piece . . .
> . . . To another, whether you know it or not,
> Whether they know it or not,
> You are a messenger from the Most High.[42]

"No one has within themselves all the pieces to their puzzle." This is a refrain that lies at the heart of all church life, and, if the truth be known, local church life *is* a puzzle—frustratingly, perplexingly, and at times gloriously so! The lesson of this chapter is that congregational life is necessarily fluid and adaptive if it is to accommodate to the surprising initiatives of the Spirit, whose voice both lay and ordained seek to discern as they listen to one another.

---

42. Kushner, *Honey from the Rock*, 69–70.

Ordinary Theology

"Ordinary theology" has been defined as "the theology and theologising of those who speak of God reflectively, but who have received little or no theological education of a scholarly, academic or systematic kind."[43] In his earlier pioneering development of the concept, Jeff Astley, who coined the phrase, describes it as "the theological beliefs and processes of believing that find expression in the God-talk of those believers who have received no scholarly theological education."[44] Ordinary theology takes seriously the voice of the people, a voice that is not easily discernible because the reality in which many people live out their faith is an ambiguous one, containing many themes, ideas, and concepts that jostle alongside each other, often in contradictory ways. How, then, can we penetrate this hybrid "polydox" nature of religious belief and experience? The obvious answer is that we need to listen more attentively to the reflective God-talk that is going on around us all the time; as Astley points out in *Exploring Ordinary Theology*, normal pastoral conversations and alert, empathetic, and intelligent observations can already tell us a great deal about what people believe—about salvation, eschatology, the meaning of sin, and the nature of the church, for example.[45] Astley's conviction is that if we truly listen to what ordinary theologians are saying—"listening up" and listening in depth—and follow this with probing questions, seeking to understand the connections they are making in their "God-talk," then it will be possible to propose a "theology of ordinary theology," in which the claims of "ordinary theology" are challenged, the norms of academic theology enriched, and its own assumptions perhaps similarly challenged.

Clearly, there are points of convergence between Appreciate Inquiry and ordinary theology as both approaches value listening to those whose voice is often submerged beneath the multiple voices of leaders, scholars, and teachers who are frequently regarded as the experts on matters of faith and belief, whether in the local church context or in the wider Christian community. Again, the mantra of "both-and" needs to be emphasized here, ensuring that in our haste to acknowledge the legitimacy of "people's often halting, unsystematic, and poorly-expressed words

---

43. Christie and Astley, "Ordinary Soteriology," 177.
44. Astley, *Ordinary Theology*, 1.
45. Astley and Francis, *Exploring Ordinary Theology*, especially chapter 1.

about their faith"[46] we do not downgrade the contribution of those whose scholarly or leadership gifts have much to offer for the enrichment of congregational life.

---

46. Francis et al., *Empirical Theology*, 179.

10

"What indeed has Athens to do with Jerusalem?"
—Tertullian

The Grandeur of God

ONE OF MY CENTRAL CONVICTIONS IS THAT GOD IS NOT IN THE business of abolishing creation, but redeeming it, a perspective that challenges the narrow and unhealthy sacred-secular divide that surprisingly afflicts a good number of Christians today. I say "surprisingly" because the world in which we live today is gloriously rich and abundant in its provision for every human need, despite the inequalities between rich and poor that confront us daily in the media, if not in or nearby the neighborhoods in which we live. Recent studies reveal that the world has the capacity to produce enough food to feed everyone on the planet:[1] the reality is that hunger is caused by poverty and inequality, not scarcity. Human beings have been blessed not only "in the heavenly realms with every spiritual blessing in Christ" (Eph 1:3), but also in the earthly realms with every physical blessing! In Gen 1 we are reminded again and again that when he created the earth "God saw that it was good." The world is charged with the grandeur of God, writes the poet Gerard Manly Hopkins, but when we gather to worship God we may sometimes find ourselves singing a different song. In her hymn *The Heavenly Vision*, the refrain of which begins with the words "Turn your eyes upon Jesus," the

---
1. Ramankutty et al., "Comparing the Yields," 229–32.

American hymn writer Helen Howarth Lemmel wrote that "the things of earth will grow strangely dim." Now this rightly directs our attention to the glory of God "above," but it should never be *at the expense of the glory of creation all around us*!

In chapter 3 I argued that this sort of dualistic thinking fails to appreciate the inherent goodness in all that God had created, leading to (as well as arising from) mistaken and false ideas not only about the nature of God, but also about the nature of creation and salvation. Too often dualism has suggested that at death Christian "souls" will be liberated from this earthly existence to the safe haven of a type of ghostly heaven. Nothing could be further from the truth. We are both spiritual creatures and physical creatures, and we shall *always* be both, though our future postmortem physicality will be of a different order entirely from that which we know now on this present earth. Jesus appeared suddenly in his resurrection body to his disciples even though the door to the room in which they were standing was locked. He then said to them: "Look at my hands and my feet. It is I myself! Touch me and see; a ghost does not have flesh and bones, as you see I have" (Luke 24:39). Just as there is both continuity and discontinuity between God's original creation and his promised new creation, so we might want to propose both continuity and discontinuity when we talk about the distinction between our physical bodies now on earth and when they are resurrected. Tom Wright sums up the matter admirably: "God's plan is not to abandon this world, the world which he said was 'very good.' Rather, he intends to remake it. And when he does he will raise all his people to new bodily life to live in it. That is the promise of the Christian gospel."[2] Our calling as Christians is to live redemptively *in* the world because we are looking forward to experiencing it in all its glorious physicality, beauty and fullness in the new creation of God's promise. This is how redemptive grace is played out in creation—we are privileged to partner the triune God, Father, Son, and Spirit, as they sing their song in the world, always pointing forward to what is yet to come, yet always grounded in the concrete realities of human culture and society.

---

2. Wright, *Simply Christian*, 186.

Culture and Creation

My purpose in this chapter is to demolish the myth that Christians should put a wedge between the church and the world. I would like to examine this in subsequent chapters with respect to two particular dimensions of the world in which we are privileged to live—the social concept of culture, and the natural world around us. My argument is that our humanity is intrinsically and necessarily tied up with both culture and creation: indeed, I will argue that our spirituality is defined by how human we allow ourselves to be, and that humanity is shaped by the extent to which we embrace both engagement in (not withdrawal from) our cultural environment, and immersion in (not escape from) the natural world.

In his fine historical study of the ambiguity of the church's response to nature,[3] the American ecological theologian Paul Santmire invites us to imagine that we are climbing a mountain. There are two alternatives that we are asked to consider as we make our way up the mountain: either we keep our gaze firmly fixed upwards, unaware of all around us as we journey towards the transcendent light above; on the other hand, we may choose to look around us as we make the journey, our eyes drinking in the beauty and glory of the mountain scenery. The first perspective—what Santmire calls the metaphor of ascent—is predicated on a form of spirituality that takes us not just towards God, but *away from* nature. The second metaphor, that of fecundity, invites us into an awareness and appreciation of the rich goodness of creation, which Santmire couples with his metaphor of migration to a good land, an eschatological vision of promise that offers inspiration and hope *in the midst of nature*. As Elaine Wainwright reminds us, the promise of a restored humanity in Isa 35:5–6 is framed by the promise of a restored world, in which the desert will rejoice as it blossoms like the crocus, the burning sand will become a pool and the thirsty ground bubbling springs: then will the blind see and the deaf hear—the two promises are inextricably linked and are not to be pulled apart.[4] Both-and, not either-or: as it will be in God's new creation, so it is now in the genius and goodness of God's fecund creation.

Similarly, Christian wholeness is measured by the extent to which believers engage in the culture around them. Hoebel defines culture as "the integrated system of learned behavior patterns which are characteristic of the members of a society and which are not the result of biological

---

3. Santmire, *Travail of Nature*.
4. On this, see Wainwright, "A Transformative Struggle."

inheritance."⁵ So culture is a *social* concept, reflecting patterns and rules that arrive through consensus over a period of time. Walsh and Middleton argue that when we look at culture, we are looking at the pieces of a puzzle, reflecting the full range of human activity: "We can see the functioning of assorted institutions, like the family, government, schools, cultic institutions (churches, temples, synagogues, and so on) and businesses. We can observe different modes of recreation, different sports, transportation and eating habits. Each culture develops a unique artistic and musical life. All these cultural activities are pieces of a puzzle."⁶ However, not only is culture the product of human beings . . . human beings are the product of culture. Each of us develops throughout life within the context of our own culture. We make decisions that, more often than not, reflect the norms of our culture, and dress, speak, and eat according to cultural expectations and norms that have been established over many years. Rodney Clapp argues that, for this reason, we are all sectarians, because "whatever we may consider the core of our identity, all of us learn that identity through the language and practices of one or another culture."⁷ These cultural norms are strengthened in the media, particularly through television, film, video, and popular journals and magazines, all of which not only convey powerful messages that reflect the prevailing culture, but also—by their very power—help to influence and therefore *shape* contemporary culture.

Platonic Dualism

Before examining the importance of engaging in culture and creation and their formative shaping of our humanity we need in this chapter to consider the pervasive influence of dualism in society today.⁸ The term "dualism" can be most easily understood with reference to the metaphysical ideas of Plato, the great Greek philosopher who was born into an upper class family in Athens in 427 BCE. During the early years of his life he became very much aware of the reality of political and civil strife in Greece, particularly between the two important cities of Athens and Sparta, and also within the cities themselves. He reacted strongly against

---

5. Quoted in Kraft, *Christianity in Culture*, 46.
6. Walsh and Middleton, *Transforming Vision*, 18.
7. Clapp, *A Peculiar People*, 140.
8. Much of the rest of this chapter draws from Buxton, *Celebrating Life*, 13–22.

the tyrannical rule of Athens over her subjects, and he eventually saw the decline of the Athenian empire. Plato was also deeply troubled by the moral relativism prevailing in Greece, summed up in Protagoras' famous statement: "A man is a measure of all things: of what is, that it is, and of what is not, that it is not." The idea of "each man for himself" hardly encouraged people to live together in harmony and unity! So both politically and personally life in Greece was not something to be admired, leading the philosophers of the day, especially Socrates—Plato's mentor—to ask: how then do we know what is "good"? How can we achieve the highest good, or *summum bonum*? What are the virtues that will enable people to live together without strife?

Plato was not an activist—he was a thinker. One of his major goals in his philosophical thinking was to try and articulate a system, or theory, which would contribute to the achievement of good government, which is the primary thrust of *The Republic*.[9] But to do that he had to come to grips with the nature of reality and truth, which is the essence of metaphysics. This was, for Plato, the highest form of inquiry. Plato's own ideas about God were confusing—sometimes he seemed to be monotheistic, at other times polytheistic, even pantheistic. What really interested him was the nature of ultimate reality that was, as for Greek philosophy generally, *impersonal* rather than personal, a concept of pure "perfection" that was far removed from the reality of the known physical world.

In the sixth century BCE, the philosopher Thales, who lived on the eastern shore of the Aegean Sea, suggested that all reality consisted of water. What he was trying to do was to identify the one unifying metaphysical principle that held everything together. The modern philosopher R. M. Hare writes: "We find in these early thinkers the beginnings of the urge to reconcile the 'One' and the 'Many,' which is a recurring theme throughout Greek philosophy, above all in Plato. There confronts us a multitude of phenomena in the world as it presents itself to our senses; cannot some unifying principle be found to bring order into this chaos?"[10] In other words, is there some constant, unchanging principle, above and beyond the material world, which gives some sort of order and meaning to the changing restlessness of the known world around us? Here we have to probe a little more deeply into the background to Plato's thought. Two philosophers who influenced Plato greatly in his search for a solution

9. Plato, *The Republic*.

10. Hare, *Plato*. Some of the insights on Plato in this chapter are drawn from Hare's brief but helpful text.

to this problem were Parmenides and Heraclitus. Parmenides taught a *universal unity of being*: Being alone exists, eternal and unchangeable. As you look around, you may see everything changing and in a state of flux, but that is not as it really is, for that is only as it *appears*. On the other side, we have Heraclitus, the "philosopher of *eternal change*," who expressed his idea of eternal change in analogical terms as the continuous flow of a river which always renews itself. So, on the one side, we have a philosophical system that is grounded in the unity of *being* (and the denial of the reality of change), and on the other side a system that focuses on a multitude of phenomena in a state of *becoming* (with a denial of the reality of a unity of being). It is the known as the classic dualism between the "One" and the "Many."

To the logical philosophy of Parmenides Plato added strains of mystical thought drawn from Pythagoras and from the "mystery religion" known as Orphism, which was current in Greece at the time. This mystical strain was dualistic in presenting a separation between mind/soul and body, and would therefore have been influential in Plato's attempt to resolve the tension between the idea of reality as unchangeably one and the eclectic, many-sided, changing world of appearances. The point is that Plato accepted this idea of a split world, and much of his philosophical energy was devoted to achieving some sort of synthesis between these two worlds, the "One" and the "Many," between the constant and the changing, between being and becoming. "He found it . . . by postulating two worlds, a world of sense, always in flux, and a unified world of Ideas, not available to our senses but only to thought, which alone are fully knowable."[11] In *The Republic* these two worlds are defined in terms of the higher world of knowledge, on the one hand, and the lower world of opinion on the other. In Plato's thinking, the dimension of knowledge is subdivided into pure thought or intelligence and mathematical reasoning, which alone are capable of apprehending the intelligible world of Forms; the dimension of opinion is subdivided into belief and illusion, which reflect the nature of the physical world in which we live.

In order to explain this, Plato presents us with his famous *simile of the cave*. The simile may be summarized simply as follows. Imagine a cave, running a long way underground, in which there are prisoners, who have been bound since they were children in such a way that they can only look directly ahead at a wall in front of them. Behind them a fire

---

11. Hare, *Plato*, 9.

casts shadows of objects that are paraded behind them—and invisible to them because they cannot turn their heads. For these bound people, reality is represented by the shadows on the wall rather than the actual objects themselves. Ian Bruce helpfully summarizes what has come to be known as Plato's "Theory of Forms" as follows:

> The theory basically postulates the existence of a level of reality or "world" inhabited by the ideal or archetypal forms of all things and concepts. Thus a form exists for objects like tables and rocks, and for concepts such as beauty and justice. . . . The forms are eternal and changeless, but enter into a partnership with changeable matter, to produce the objects and examples of concepts, we perceive in the temporal world. These are always in a state of becoming, and may participate in a succession of forms. The ever-changing temporal world can thus, only be the source of opinion. Plato likens the opinions derived from our senses, to the perception of shadows of real objects, cast upon the wall of a cave.[12] True knowledge however, is the perception of the archetypal forms themselves, which are real, eternal, and unchanging. Whilst the forms are invisible to the eye, our souls have participated in the eternal world of forms prior to being incarnate in a physical body, and retain a memory of them. . . . All learning, Plato maintains, is but recollection of what our soul already knows.[13]

At the human or anthropological level, the dualism between body and soul is fundamental to Plato's philosophy. Essentially the soul or mind belongs to the higher pure realm, and the body belongs to the lower realm of nature, a divide that anticipates—though not with any precise correspondence—the sacred-secular divide that was to pervade much of Western thought post-Plato. Prior to modernity, which eschews the religious dimension, this divide reflected Christendom's distinction between a "sacred" realm, identified with the church, and a non-church "secular" realm, which was nevertheless infused with the divine. Modernity, however, evicted God from the secular stage, giving rise to a sacred-secular divide that pitted the religious against the non-religious.

But what of the religious dimensions in Plato's philosophical thinking? Firstly, Plato's "Good" is located within his higher realm of Ideas

12. See Plato, *The Republic*: 514a–520b.

13. Bruce, *Plato's Theory of Forms*, n.p. Remember that Plato is only speaking here about learning about the forms, not learning about the changing world we see around us. We obviously can learn new things about *that*.

or Forms. Some people think that he equates the "Good" with deity, but Plato is not at all clear in his definition of God. Plato's God is the "Demiurge" (the Craftsman), who molded pre-existent matter into the world as we know it—a being totally dependent upon the "Good," which is itself utterly self-sufficient and perfect. However, some have suggested that the Demiurge cannot really be identified with God as such, since he is inferior to Ideas. For Plato, the Demiurge is eternal alongside both the "Good" and physical matter.

Sanders suggests that Plato "distinguished between a personal God (the Demiurge) and an impersonal principle (the Good) and then elevated the principle above the personal in the order of being."[14] This would certainly be in keeping with the rational elements of Greek philosophy.

In summary, Plato's religious understanding is ambiguous and confusing! Whatever our understanding here, the important point to derive from all this is that Plato's system of philosophy led to a way of thinking which interpreted creaturely life in the lower world as inferior—Greek philosophers talked about the body as the "prison house of the soul," and in *Phaedo* Plato viewed the body as that which defiles the soul and impedes the soul's knowledge of the divine. The higher world (the world of Ideas) was perfect, pure, and the goal of human attainment.

It is worth noting here that Greek philosophy emphasized the superiority of *unchanging, timeless, unfeeling* reality. Changeableness, temporality, and emotion were considered to be the characteristic features—negative ones, too—of the lower physical world, the world of creatures, of you and me. Plato's idea of God—whatever that was—corresponded to the superior, higher world with the inevitable implications of a God who is unchanging, timeless, and unfeeling. To argue for any other sort of God was—for the Greeks, and for others in subsequent centuries, including many influential Christian thinkers—to argue for a God who is no longer perfect, and therefore no longer God.

Hebrew Worldview

The *biblical* presentation of reality is totally at odds with the Greek ideas associated with Plato—indeed the Hebrew worldview is much more robust and holistic than anything that the Greeks had to offer us. Nancy

---

14. Sanders, "Historical Considerations," 62.

Scott reminds us that the Hebrew mindset was quite different from the Greek mindset:

> The Hebrew view of the world was grounded in the earthy, material reality in which they lived, and yet it was overshadowed at every point with spiritual truth. In contrast to the Greek view that the highest human experience was knowledge, to a Hebrew scholar like Paul, moral beauty and righteousness was the highest human experience. There was no need to separate experience into spiritual and material, as everything they did or thought, from their perspective, included both. The process of broken humans being transformed into the glory of holiness, to which we would ultimately be completely conformed in the Kingdom, was the hope of Paul's gospel.[15]

The implications of this Pauline perspective are profound:

> Perhaps we can reclaim in the arts and sciences the beauty of creative expression for which God created us. We can cease to frame everything as either/or, and enjoy the many gifts God has given us in our earthly, material world. Perhaps we will value more firmly the creation itself, and become better stewards of the natural resources God has given. We can better see that the material world is imbued with the splendour and majesty of its Creator, and we can rejoice in His presence in all these things. But most of all, perhaps we can have a voice to communicate the relevance of the gospel to this dying generation.[16]

The Jews have always maintained a robust affirmation of the created world. Indeed, as Walter Brueggemann has argued, the Old Testament has as a central theme the importance to God of the land. McAfee Brown comments: "The affirmation of God as Creator is a late development in Jewish reflection about God, but it is an affirmation that has persisted, centrally and powerfully, ever since."[17] But this is not how the Christian church viewed reality over the centuries. The primary culprit is Augustine, notwithstanding all the good and noble things that he contributed to Christian theology, and we will be looking at him shortly.

---

15. Scott, "Dueling with Dualism," para. 1.
16. Ibid.
17. Brown, *Spirituality and Liberation*, 74.

Historical Developments

The great Jewish thinker Philo tried to reconcile biblical teaching with Greek philosophical ideas. He adopted a hierarchical cosmology with three levels: the unknowable, transcendent God at the top; then a knowable realm, full of knowable intermediaries; and at the bottom the knowable realm of matter. Whilst not as speculative as Plato in his ontological scheme, Philo's legacy was still strongly philosophical, even though he accepted that God could have an effect upon his creation, a creation which he actually brought into being (as distinct from Plato's belief in matter as eternal). Tertullian sought to break the hold of Greek philosophy on the development of Christian theology, especially in his insistence that God was not an abstract deity, distant from his creation, but one who interacted with his world. Hence his famous triple question, "What indeed has Athens to do with Jerusalem? What concord is there between the Academy and the church? What between heretics and Christians?" To which he replied: "Our instruction comes from 'the porch of Solomon,' who had himself taught that 'the Lord should be sought in simplicity of heart.' Away with all attempts to produce a mottled Christianity of Stoic, Platonic, and dialectic composition! We want no curious disputation after possessing Christ Jesus, no inquisition after enjoying the gospel! With our faith, we desire no further belief."[18] Whilst his concern here had to do with the influence of worldly *philosophy* on Christian belief, he was equally troubled by the extent to which Christians were conforming to the culture of the day. Christianity was, for him, "basically a counter-cultural movement, which refused to allow itself to be contaminated in any way by the mental or moral environment in which it took root."[19] Origen taught the immutability of God and, in contrast to Tertullian, partially accommodated to the Hellenistic worldview. His view of the incarnation reflected others before him: only the human side of Jesus suffered; his divinity remained untouched. Other biblical references to the passion of God are explained by Origen as anthropomorphisms and were not to be taken literally.

So the early church's understanding of the relationship between God and creation was, in Sanders' words, a mixed bag of Greek metaphysics and biblical faith. Whilst early church prayers and liturgies expressed the relationship between God and his people, more abstract notions of God

---

18. Tertullian, *Tertullian on Testimony of Soul*, chapter 7.
19. McGrath, *Scientific Theology Vol. 1*, 13.

began to inform the thinking of the Christian church. It is here that we need to turn to Augustine (354-430 CE) who followed Manicheism[20] for nine years before becoming interested in Neo-Platonism under the influence of Plotinus (204-70 CE). However, Augustine began to distrust their claim to access Absolute Truth by rational means and in 384 CE went to Rome where he came under the influence of Bishop Ambrose (339-97 CE). It was here that Augustine accepted the Christian faith (and church) as that for which he had been searching.

Augustine held that inner reflection/contemplation was greater than pursuing sensual gain. In fact, his ascetic denial of his sensual instincts may have come largely as result of his conversion experience and regret at his past life (he was an incorrigible womanizer, and fathered a child out of marriage). Yet ascetic denial would also continue to recur in his thinking and form a major part of his theological worldview. After his common-law wife's death he returned to Africa in 388 CE where he was coerced into eventually becoming Bishop of Hippo. Augustine's "otherworldly" focus prioritized the spiritual over the physical: in *The City of God* he spoke of the rational soul "inhabiting" the body,[21] though, as Margaret Miles has shown, his thinking on physicality was uncertain, betraying what she calls "ambivalence and incomplete integration."[22] "The most perceptive of Augustinian scholars agree that his theory of sensation is riddled with inconsistencies and difficulties."[23] By primarily focussing on the spiritual realm he reinforced in the Christian church a negative view of human sexuality and an unhealthy contempt for the body. Following Augustine, the shape of Christian theology was typically characterized by a worldview that distinguished between the spiritual and the physical, and the Christian church was set on a course which posited the church *over and above* the world. The church as an ecclesiastical institution was seen as the repository of grace, and all of nature was excluded from the realm of grace. The picture we have here is that of grace *versus* nature: "The spiritual realm of ecclesiastical affairs was regarded as superior to the natural world and was thus more highly valued. This elevation of one

---

20. Manichaeism was a Christianized form of Gnostic religion that held to a radical dualism between good and evil.
21. Augustine, *City of God*, 22.24.
22. Miles, *Augustine and the Body*, 8.
23. Ibid., 9.

dimension of creaturely life at the neglect and expense of the other was, in effect, a form of idolatry."[24]

This distinction between nature and grace was critical because it opened up the way for the secular, natural realm to assume dominance in the later period of Enlightenment thinking and modernity in Western culture. Pit grace *against* nature, and sooner or later nature was going to climb into the driving seat. In other words, the dualism that pervaded the life of the church "opened the door to the triumph of secularism as the guiding spirit of Western culture."[25] The tables were turned. This had implications for the way the created world was viewed. Instead of the world, and created matter, being relegated to an inferior role in the order of reality (as in earlier Platonic dualistic thinking), the growth in humanism and the scientific world view gave creation a place centre-stage. The world was no longer something to be avoided but to be embraced. Creation was seen as something significant, but—and this, of course, is the legacy of modernity—its significance was grounded in its being viewed as a world to be mastered and exploited rather than appreciated as God's good creation. This left the church out on a limb. Humanism pushed it out on the margins, where it was left, hopefully, to disappear from the scene of life as an irrelevancy in a world that had now come of age.

Theology of Creation

But, as Tom Wright asks, "Is the church to sit on the margins of the world, offering a salvation that is an escape, which seems to leave the world to go its own way?"[26] Is that the biblical view? There are some who think precisely this, arguing that the church offers a safe haven from the corruptions of the world. This, of course, buys heavily into the dualistic paradigm we have been talking about. Wright offers another scenario. If we *do* feel that we, as Christians, have something to say, how are we to say it? "Are we to leap with both feet into the political pit of snakes, issuing denunciations to the left and (more likely) right, and getting ourselves a bad name for mingling religion and politics . . . ?"[27] Wright's response is helpful. Rather than going down the road of personal piety (the way of

---

24. Walsh and Middleton, *Transforming Vision*, 114.
25. Ibid., 115.
26. Wright, *Bringing the Church*, 19.
27. Ibid., 19.

escape) or political activism, our approach must be based on a realistic understanding of the way the world really is. He suggests that there are two options that most people follow. Either they go down the dualist path, "cutting the world in half," or they try to put everything back together again, and become monists. We have already looked at some of the problems associated with dualism. What about monism? That way, too, is unbiblical. The monist either sees the world as one big materialistic "machine" to be analyzed and dissected scientifically, or treats the cosmos as one great integrated mystery, identified with God himself. No dualism here, separating the spiritual and the physical, because all is one in the new pantheistic worldview. The Bible, however, presents us not only with a view of creation that is far richer and far more wonderful and mysterious than merely the sum of its parts, but also with a theology of creation that makes a clear distinction between God and the created order. There is plainly no room for monism here.

So what path are we to follow? Wright's answer is radical. The church needs to repent of the narrow dualism that avoids any form of genuine contact with the world, a suffocating dualism that treats God's creation as intrinsically contaminating rather than intrinsically wholesome and good; and it needs to repent of a monism that fails to clearly differentiate between God and his world, and between good and evil. If the world is as bad as some say it is, then the sooner we get back to the good old dualist days, the better! This dualism could be one of two varieties: on the one hand, we may adopt a dry, dusty form of dualism, preaching good old evangelistic sermons, and avoiding any contaminating contact with such topics as politics or sex. The overriding concern in this form of dualism is to ensure that everything done is kept under control within clear and narrow guidelines. As an alternative to this over-cerebral, intellectual, and wordy "dry" dualism, Tom Wright offers what he calls "wet" dualism (borrowing some terminology from *The Pilgrim's Regress* by C. S. Lewis), which presents us with an over-simplified black-and-white sort of world. In this world the *true* church consists of the children of light, and the rest of the world lies in thick darkness, in which demons abound and are in an incessant war with angels![28]

And if dualism is not a very good option, then monism doesn't offer anything much better. In monism, God and the world get all confused to the point where the difference between good and evil is denied. This is

---

28. For a fuller account of these two representative positions, see ibid., 116.

the "if you can't beat them, join them" approach! It is the way of *assimilation*. Now that is the danger into which many Christians fall—if we agree that cutting ourselves off from the world is not the right way to go, then let's swing the pendulum in the other direction and go out and enjoy all that God's good creation has to offer us. Let's celebrate! Where is the danger? Well, the danger is that you fail to offer any theological critique: the church "is so concerned to be *like* the world that it ends up having nothing to say *to* the world."[29] However, as God's kingdom people who are summoned to witness to God's redemptive grace, we dare not succumb to the world's agenda, however attractive that may be. God has called his church to be a *prophetic* voice in the world, communicating a vision of the kingdom of God that challenges the norms and patterns of behavior that characterize contemporary society. Michael Wittmer points out that Christians are, in fact, metaphysical dualists, but only in the sense that they believe in a *horizontal* distinction between God and his creation. There is an ontological chasm between the infinite Creator and his finite creation: God is God and his creation is not. However, many draw their line in the wrong place, living "as if there is a vertical line separating two contrasting parts of God's creation."[30] This "either-or" mentality has for too long and in too many ways squeezed the juice of gospel life out of many parts of God's church.

Two-way Traffic

I quoted earlier the words of Jürgen Moltmann:

> The more Christians intervene for the life of the hungry, the human rights of the oppressed and the fellowship of the forsaken, the deeper they will be led into continual prayer. It sounds paradoxical, but *the more their actions are related to this world*, and the more passionately they love life, the more strongly they will believe, if they want to remain true to the hope which Jesus brought into the world.[31]

For Moltmann, there is no conflict between the "vertical" dimension of faith and the "horizontal" dimension of love: they are two sides of the Christian way of life. They converge not only in the political struggle for

---

29. Ibid., 113, author's italics.
30. Wittmer, *Heaven Is a Place on Earth*, 42.
31. Moltmann, *Church in Power of Spirit*, 284.

justice, equality, and liberation, but also in the celebration of God's creation and the myriad diverse expressions of cultural life that characterize human creativity, intellectual endeavor, and organizational behavior. Of course, human beings may take God's many gifts and talents and distort or abuse them so that they no longer give glory to him. But that should not lead us to distance ourselves from them because they are capable of corruption. For it is not just in his church, but also in and through human culture and in his creation that God is pleased to reveal and glorify himself—and where he might be found for those who have ears to hear and eyes to see. Culture and creation will therefore be the subject of the next two chapters. There is much in the world that is good and holy and beautiful, which Christians can appreciate and from which they can learn. In other words, the traffic between church and world is *two-way*, not one-way. We need to recognize both the freedom of the gospel as gift to all people, manifested and transmitted through the church, and the joy of life and living which is also God's gift to all people (see John 10:10), present and available in many dimensions of what has too often been disparaged as "secular life."

11

"A wager on transcendence"
–George Steiner

Celebration and Solution

In this chapter we consider the role of faith in two very different dimensions of contemporary culture—the realm of literature and the arts, and the political realm, with particular reference to the biblical concern for social justice. Throughout this book I have insisted that Christians do not live in the safe haven called "church"—in a very real way they are called to partner with the community of which they are a part in the solution of its problems as well as in the celebration of its life, recognizing God's presence in the midst of the diverse cultures that constitute human society. And these two dimensions—celebration and solution—often go together.

The American theologian Kevin Vanhoozer suggests that many Christians are guilty of what he calls the "Great Omission," which he describes as the failure to interpret the signs of the times, specifically the inability to both "read" and "write" culture. "Cultural literacy," he argues, has to do with both cultural engagement ("reading" culture) and making our own mark in the everyday world ("writing culture").[1] Thus there should be no wedge between the church and the world, for the cultural environment that surrounds us—the soup in which we swim—is precisely where I meet my neighbor whom I am summoned by the gospel

---

1. Vanhoozer, "What is Everyday Theology?"

of grace to love and serve. And how can I serve my neighbor if I do not understand the context in which she lives? What is needed in Christian ministry is honest, critical, contextual engagement, not culture-denying ministry, but culturally *aware* ministry.

In his ministry on earth, Jesus called people to repent of their self-centred ways and to embrace the kingdom of God, personified in himself. As the Word made flesh, he was uncompromising in his radical pronouncements. Many people felt uncomfortable in his presence. Yet, equally, others felt wonderfully comforted, accepted, and restored because he gave of himself to them. As the Word made flesh, he entered into the pain and reality of ordinary human experiences, mixing with outcasts, prostitutes, and all manner of needy people: in doing so, he continually crossed the accepted boundaries of his day. In his humanity he identified with others around him in his Jewish cultural surroundings—he was shaped by that culture as a Jew, but he wasn't bound by it. In his divinity as *autobasileia*—the reign of God personified in himself— he proclaimed the culture of the kingdom of God. As God incarnate he inhabited two worlds—the world of his Father and the world of human beings—and with deep joy he celebrated the fullness of God's life in the goodness of God's creation.

In the same way, the church is called to celebrate the reality of God in our midst in a world that is searching for answers to the alienation, confusion, and brokenness that permeate human lives and social structures. God is at work in his world and always has been; it is time, therefore, for the church to take the incarnation seriously on the grounds not that we are different from other people, but precisely the opposite . . . because we are *no* different from them.[2] This is true worship: celebrating God in the world in which he has placed us, and getting involved in his world precisely because that is where he is involved. I wrote *Celebrating Life* a few years ago because I wanted to affirm the goodness of God's creation and of human life, including the myriad different ways in which human beings express that life in contemporary society, whether in poetry and politics, in movies and management, or in sculpture and science. In that book I wanted to do more than nod in the direction of contemporary culture. And so I argued for a genuine engagement between church and world, so that the traffic between gospel and culture is not one-way but two-way, fleshed out in five chapters that look at literature, the creative

---

2. A theme developed in Drane, *Cultural Change*.

arts, politics, the world of business, and science. In this chapter we will reflect on the first three areas,³ and then consider the relationship between faith and science in chapter 12, with special reference to the need for Christians to connect with and care for God's good creation.

Sacred-Secular Divide

I have come to realize in recent years how much Christians have to learn from those who live outside the borders of the church. We need the wisdom to discern where the Spirit is at work, often in the unlikeliest places and in the most improbable ways. Grenz and Franke express this well with respect to the construction of human artefacts:

> Because the life-giving Creator Spirit is present wherever life flourishes, the Spirit's voice can conceivably resound through many media, including the media of human culture. Because Spirit-induced human flourishing evokes cultural expression, we can anticipate in such expressions traces of the Creator Spirit's presence. Consequently, we should listen intently for the voice of the Spirit, who is present in all life and therefore who "precedes" us into the world, bubbling to the surface through the artefacts and symbols humans construct . . . but always a voice that does not contradict the voice of Christian Scripture.⁴

Sadly, however—as explored more fully in the previous chapter—the lives of many are characterized by what has commonly been referred to as the "sacred-secular divide syndrome," in which a wedge is placed between the church and the world. The result is that the Christian life is often portrayed as being *above* the world, rather than *within* the world, an unholy and unwholesome dualism that not only robs Christians of the abundance of life that God has given to them (see John 10:10), but also causes others who might otherwise be attracted to Christianity to switch off completely. If Christians, renewed and transformed by the Spirit of God, are unable to demonstrate what it means to be fully human, both contributing to and responding to the culture in which they live, where is their witness to God's abundant life? Living a Christian life does not "de-contextualize" believers, extracting them from their native culture

---

3. Condensed from material in Buxton, *Celebrating Life*. The "business" area is partially addressed in chapter 8.

4. Grenz and Franke, *Beyond Foundationalism*, 162.

and inserting them into a "Christian culture": rather, the reverse is true—we become more alive in the culture we inhabit, as demonstrated most completely in Jesus Christ's incarnate life in Palestine. In his book on a Christian theology of religions, *Beyond the Impasse*, Amos Yong, a leading Pentecostal theologian, amusingly recalls a conversation he had with his parents shortly after the family had emigrated to the United States from Malaysia, where he was born. Responding to his uncertainty about which culture he belonged to—American, Chinese, Malaysian—his parents said, "None of those—we're Christians!"[5] However, Paul's statement in Col 1:13 about being transferred, or translated, into the kingdom of God's beloved Son implies deliverance from our old self-centred way of life, *not* from our cultural heritage. We are not "either-or" but "both-and" citizens—citizens of two worlds. The incarnational character of Christianity proclaims the truth that God has chosen to make himself known as a human being in human culture and in the midst of the structures of society. God is not distant from human culture but understands us and sympathizes with us as *cultural* beings. This means that we should expect him to be revealed in the many diverse cultural expressions that make up a particular culture or society. Let's see how this insight might be played out in the spheres of literature and the creative arts.

A Good Bookshelf

Many years ago I was one amongst several Christians asked by a pastor to name an author whose writing we were enjoying most at the time, along with a specific title. All those who responded before me referred to a Christian book that had overt religious or spiritual themes . . . until I mentioned a book by the Australian author Morris West. There was a pregnant pause, as if I had said something heretical! The irony is that West, who was a superb storyteller, wrote about the human condition from the perspective of a deep, though not always explicit, Catholic faith. There are some Christians whose library consists of nothing else but Christian books—testimonies (lots of these), devotional classics, Christian biographies, and the like . . . perhaps even some fiction written by Christian authors. I am not against Christian books *per se*, and there are many fine volumes that fall squarely within this category. But compared with the wealth of literature available today, embracing both the classics

---

5. Yong, *Beyond the Impasse*, 9.

and contemporary writings, they do not sufficiently represent, as a single category, the contents of what may be described as a "good bookshelf."

In *An Experiment in Criticism*, C. S. Lewis writes that literature "admits us to experiences other than our own."[6] Good books—whether novels, essays, or poetry—give us windows into other worlds. In John Keating's memorable words in *Dead Poets Society*, we read and write poetry because we are members of the human race, and maturity in this regard is measured by our willingness and capacity to see beyond ourselves. As we explore the worlds in which others live out their lives, as we enter their feelings, their joys and sorrows, their hopes and fears, we ourselves are enriched as human beings. Indeed, it may well be that the primary goal of literature is to make us more human. Lewis goes on to say that through literature we become "a thousand men" and yet remain ourselves. So our *humanity* is enhanced as we read: we become more fully human as we enter the worlds of others, more human in the sense that we do not allow ourselves to be stifled by a narrow parochialism that limits our awareness of the lives and circumstances of those who may be very different from us. Reading involves "transcending our own competitive particularity."[7]

Of course, literature also exists for the joy of the reader: God has given all good things for our enjoyment, including good literature, which has intrinsic power to please. I was teaching on this once at a theological seminary in California, and it was clear that many of the students in the class simply had not come across much good literature. I was asked to provide them with a list of books that I thought might help them to widen their horizons. Later on, one of them told me that his life had been transformed—his being had been enlarged. I am convinced that one of the problems we face in our contemporary world is *a*literacy, not *i*lliteracy. Most people either choose not to read or simply concede defeat in the face of the ever-increasing march of the electronic revolution, where social networking and imprisonment to mobile phone technology has replaced the sheer pleasure of what John Milton once described as the benefit of books "promiscuously read." The transmission of truncated text-messages, in which emasculated language masquerades as authentic communication, further erodes the beauty and richness of human vocabulary. In a phrase, language needs to be redeemed. In saying this, I do not want to minimize the importance of understanding the technology

---

6. Lewis, *Experiment in Criticism*, 139.
7. Ibid., 138.

through which much of our communication occurs. Again, the "both-and" mantra reappears. If Christians are to have a realistic impact upon today's e-generations, then it is appropriate to discern how the church might respond sympathetically to the opportunities presented by the revolution in electronic communication. However, the benefits of the Internet age should not blind us to its obvious disadvantages: web users typically browse, or sample, cyberdata. They demand hard information, readily accessible, and requiring minimum evaluative effort. Language is sacrificed in the cause of efficiency. Words are no longer gifts to be savored, but tools to get results . . . and Christians are not exempt from this temptation to degrade language. If the community of faith is to have an influence for good in the world, then it must adopt a positive and welcoming attitude towards the contribution of the literary disciplines, placing itself in the vanguard in the redemption of language.

The more good books we read, then, the better. This, of course, raises the question: what is a "good" book? There is no obvious answer, and definitions are inevitably very subjective. Perhaps one measure of whether a book is good or not is to ask if it treats someone as a "reader" or a "consumer." Veith claims that "modern bookstores are filled with shallow, salacious, badly written books that are travesties of true literary art."[8] We might also ask if there is such a thing as "Christian literature," and whether or not the elusive quality of "goodness" has something to do with its explicit Christian nature. The twentieth-century English poet W. H. Auden once commented that there can no more be something described as Christian art than there can be a Christian diet. This is certainly true with respect to an author's "quality of writing": how a poem or novel is written—its structure, characterization, and use of various literary devices—has nothing to do with it being Christian or not. If I have a raging toothache, I do not demand that I go to a "Christian dentist"; more important is that I go to a *good* dentist, meaning one who has a reputation for good dentistry!

I suggest that a piece of literature may be described as "Christian" insofar as it connects in some way with the Christian worldview as presented in the Bible, and specifically in the New Testament. It is perfectly possible for a Christian to write about such topics as pornography and profligacy, but it is how they are treated that defines how Christian the material is. Leland Ryken, a professor of English, suggests that it is useful

---

8. Veith, *Reading between the Lines*, 29.

to speak of the ways in which a work of art *intersects* with Christianity.[9] In the same way that some theologians talk about the creation exhibiting signs of the Trinity (*vestigia trinitatis*)—in other words, we can discern the marks or imprints of God in the created order, because this universe in which we live is God's creation—it may be helpful for us to speak of a work being Christian to the extent that one is able to discern distinctly Christian themes such as forgiveness, grace, wholeness, community life, and redemption. In that sense, we may be close to coming to some understanding of "goodness" in terms of a work's correspondence to the goodness inherent in the Christian worldview. For example, George Eliot's novel *Silas Marner* is a story replete with religious themes, such as the loss and rediscovery of faith, the tenderness of family life, and the interconnectedness between community and faith. Eliot's treatment of human nature is reflected in her portrayal of Silas as a gentle, kind, and honest man, in contrast to the two disreputable sons of prosperous Squire Cass. He displays a capacity for love and goodness, and the novel highlights the themes of hope and redemption in the midst of great personal loss and isolation. Whilst not explicitly a Christian book *Silas Marner* clearly intersects powerfully with the Christian faith.

Reading Stories

Eugene Peterson insists that reading novels is one of the more serious activities in which a Christian pastor should be engaged. Novels, he claims, are fine ways to get across to busy pastors the importance of the particularities of story, person, and place.[10] Peterson's assertion applies not just to those who are engaged in pastoral ministry—it is relevant for all Christians. Our beings are enlarged, our horizons broadened. And there is an apologetic dividend to all this: as we read, we are encouraged, even inspired, to open our minds to the contributions of poets and writers who "work away day after day, year after year, . . . showing the story-shape of all existence, insisting on the irreducible identity of each person, and the glory of this piece of geography."[11] If we are willing to take the time, we will come to realize that each place we enter through prose or poetry is a particular place, shaped by its own local features, and we will discover

---

9. Ryken, *The Liberated Imagination*, 199.
10. Peterson, "Pastors and Novels."
11. Ibid., 186.

the value of treating each person we encounter—imaginary or real—as a distinct human being. We discover afresh the value of communicating the gospel in a way that pays attention to detail. Good literature has the capacity to open our eyes to the essential particularity of human and physical life—this is especially so of poetry because of its powerful use of imagery. Stephen Spender claims that the poet's primary task is to "think out the logic of images."[12] The result is that we, the readers, are enriched in our awareness of what the medieval theologian Duns Scotus called the "thisness," or unique feature, of individual things. Poetry is particularly rich in its ability to accomplish this in the experience of the reader.

This emphasis on uniqueness and detail should not surprise us—indeed, particularity fleshed out in the stories of ordinary people lies at the heart of the Christian gospel. Whenever we present the *grand récit* of the gospel we are confronted with the temptation to strip it of its narrative dimension in our desire to communicate the essentials of the Christian message. Yet the gospel is not a set of propositional dot points, but a *story*—the multi-faceted story of God and his creation, and of a world made new through redeeming grace. And this story is played out in particular places amongst particular people. Whenever we read the Bible we are confronted with people with whom God deals in different ways—patiently, graciously, miraculously, and sometimes in anger and judgment. We should not come to the biblical text ignoring such literary features as characterization and plot in a determined effort to keep our noses to the theological grindstone. Quite the reverse, in fact. It is only as we engage with the circumstances of life recounted in the Bible that we discover not only how God works in human life, but how different we are from each other.

Girl with a Pearl Earring is the title of Tracy Chevalier's imaginary account of the circumstances leading to the creation of the famous masterpiece of the same name by the seventeenth-century Dutch painter Johannes Vermeer. A young Protestant servant girl named Griet is allowed into the artist's studio. She soon displays an intuitive appreciation of Vermeer's craft, and begins to offer him advice and help as he paints. On one occasion Griet asks Vermeer, who converted to Catholicism at the age of twenty-one, why there are paintings in Catholic churches. Vermeer responds: "A painting in a church is like a candle in a dark room—we use it to see better. It is a bridge between ourselves and God. But it is not a

---

12. Spender, *Making of a Poem*, 54.

Protestant candle or a Catholic candle. It is simply a candle." Griet counters that she doesn't need such things to help her to see God: "We have his Word and that is enough." Vermeer then goes on to say that Protestants, like Catholics, see God everywhere, in everything: "By painting everyday things—tables and chairs, bowls and pitchers, soldiers and maids—are they not celebrating God's creation as well?"[13]

The Creative Arts

This celebration of God's creation in human artistic endeavor needs further exploration and affirmation with regard to the creative arts. There is a powerful myth prevailing in many church circles that maintains that Christians are inevitably engaged in a form of "cultural warfare" with mainstream popular arts, especially the visual and audiovisual arts, reflecting the dualistic paradigm discussed in chapter 10. Steve Turner, an English poet and writer, records his early experiences of the tension amongst Christians about how enlightened we should allow ourselves to be as far as the entertainment world goes, based on the reasoning that "most art was created by unbelievers and could therefore damage our spiritual health."[14] It was okay to get involved in the arts, so long as the end goal was outreach: "Thus we had movies with tissue thin characters and threadbare plots that moved inexorably toward climactic conversions."[15]

But engagement with art is surely to be applauded because, in the same way as literature works, our beings are enlarged as we are exposed to the creative arts: we become more fully human in the sense that we encounter, in some mysterious sense, what George Steiner calls the "real presence" of God. For Steiner, experiencing the aesthetic, whether in poetry, painting, music, or any other artistic endeavor, is what he calls "a wager on transcendence," because of his passionate belief that a transcendent reality grounds all genuine art.[16] Some art, of course—and the same point applies to literature—is so trivial and banal, so commercialized in its intent, that it rightly earns Steiner's label of "the pornography of insignificance." Whilst Christians are called to be vigilant and discerning in the light of the contemporary consumerist culture, they would do well

13. Chevalier, *Girl with a Pearl Earring*, 148–49.
14. Turner, *Imagine*, 16.
15. Ibid., 17.
16. Steiner, *Real Presences*, 4.

to acknowledge Madeleine L'Engle's observation that great artists "keep us from frozenness, from smugness, from thinking that the truth is in us rather than in God, in Christ our Lord."[17] L'Engle goes on to suggest that exposure to art helps us in our quest for truth: might we often be closer to God when we are beset by doubt than when we enclose ourselves in rigid certainties?

In our search for meaning expressed through art, we need to remember that contemporary hermeneutical theory attributes increasing importance to the role of the reader or viewer in the interpretive task. Confronted by a stone sculpture we might reasonably ask ourselves, what does this work of art do *for me*? But that should not be the end of our questioning. In 1953 M. H. Abrams wrote a book called *The Mirror and the Lamp*, in which he analyzed the literary criticism of the Romantic period.[18] He suggests that the literary critic—and here we might extend that to refer to all artistic criticism—needs to take into account the relation of art to four objects: the artist, external reality, the audience, and the internal characteristics of the work itself. These four coordinates translate into his classical model of the four major approaches to critical theory. The sculptor doubtless has a message to convey, encouraging us to discover what we can about the intention behind the work. Furthermore, we might want to enquire whether or not the artwork expresses some truth about the world in which we live. Finally, might there possibly be something intrinsic to the sculpture that is embedded in the work itself, such that the stone contains an inner reality that says something to us irrespective of the intention of the sculptor or the referential field of the viewer? The clever use of materials in a sculpture or the vivid application of colors in a painting may appeal to us aesthetically without our having to probe for a meaning that may not be there!

However, art does not merely describe *what is*: "through the artist's imagination, it adjusts and manipulates a portion of the world, to allow its mystery to be unlocked."[19] Artists are not obliged to mirror reality in a simplistic way. The abstract imagery of a Kandinsky painting has the power to communicate the elemental themes of life and death in a way that other more realistic compositions are frequently unable to accomplish. Though a visual distortion of reality, Edvard Munch's well-

---

17. L'Engle, *Walking on Water*, 155–56.
18. Abrams, *Mirror and the Lamp*.
19. Deeks, *Pastoral Theology*, 44.

known expressionist painting *The Scream* is nonetheless "true" insofar as it imaginatively witnesses to the actuality of deep human emotion. The Spanish cubist painter Pablo Picasso once said that "art is a lie that makes us realize the truth." Abstraction, novelty, and exaggeration, even distortion, are all grist to the artist's creative mill. Imagination and creativity—even the grotesque—play an important part in the truthfulness of art. It is the Spirit's privilege to unveil the kingdom of God, and he will accomplish this in ways that resonate with the culture of the day, immersing himself in whatever cultural "texts" offer the best vehicles for communication.

Music and movies are two other significant vehicles of contemporary culture through which the Spirit of God may speak into our lives. Consider two ends of the music spectrum—classical and heavy metal. Karl Barth, one of the Christian world's greatest theologians, once paid homage to Mozart in a forty-minute lecture at the University of Geneva, testifying to the reality and the peace that he experienced in an art that embraces nature, humanity, and God. If Mozart's music has universal accessibility and acceptance, the same cannot be said about heavy metal, a musical genre that has had an enduring place within many different youth sub-cultures over the last three or four decades. The hostility displayed by many heavy metal bands should not mask the fact that some are communicating, in the midst of their aggressive protests against injustice and hypocrisy, a profound derision for a form of Christianity that obscures the radical mutiny of Jesus against the social order. Listening with open, yet discerning, hearts to the culture of heavy metal brings the promise of transformation, not only to those who espouse that culture, but to those of us within the Christian community whose first instinct may be to run as far as possible from that culture—with hands clasped firmly over our ears!

In the early days of Hollywood, however, it was the eyes, not the ears, which needed to be covered up! "Picture houses" were regarded as sinister assaults on the purity of the Christian faith, with very little attention paid to the way movies might offer us a window into the way things are. This does not mean, of course, that movies are above reproach—far from it. Like literature and other art forms discussed previously, there are good movies and there are bad movies, judged according to such criteria as technical or production quality and moral content. Movies, then, mirror life and also offer us a window into life. Space does not permit further discussion here, but it is worth mentioning two films that highlight the contrast between religion and life, between a *graceless* Christianity and a *grace-full* Christianity, between a spirituality that denies our humanity and a spirituality that rejoices in our humanity: *Chocolat* and *Babette's Feast*. They are a testament to the power of movies, as for all forms of art, to speak in an appealing and imaginative way to the truth that we live in a world in which there is no room for the legalistic split-vision worldview that can rob us of the abundant life that Jesus came to give us.

Intimations of God's truth can penetrate us—even transform us—as we open ourselves to the creative endeavors of painters and poets, musicians and movie makers. We begin to see new things that speak to us of the truth of a God who is freedom, love, and grace . . . and a God who knows and understands the realities of the human condition. So pain, suffering, doubt, fear, love, joy, and despair are played out in the images before us, and we discover the truth about ourselves. All artists have this great privilege of participating in God's creative energies, whether they realize it or not. As our hearts and minds are blessed or disturbed by the creative gifts of the artistic community, we may, in the words of the late Irish poet Seamus Heaney, hear "a music we would never have known to listen for."

Politics and Faith

We now turn briefly to the world of politics, with particular reference to the longing for a more just society. Not too many people today would openly argue that politics and faith have nothing to do with each other. They converge precisely because both have to do with making a difference in this world. Both are concerned with creating conditions that enable people to realize what Aristotle once called *summum bonum*, the "good life." The important questions today have less to do with whether or not faith and politics mix, but what sort of mix we should advocate. In his book *Spirituality and Liberation*, Robert McAfee Brown reminds us of that well-known verse Mic 6:8:

> He has showed you, O man, what is good.
> And what does the Lord require of you?
> To act justly and to love mercy and to walk humbly with your God.

In a precise and clear exposition, Brown argues that in this verse "[w]e do not have *three different assertions* being made, but one assertion being made in *three different ways.*" So we "cannot talk compellingly about any one of the three phrases until we have talked about all three of them."[20] He expresses the logic of his case persuasively in the form of three equations: to *act justly* means to love tenderly and to walk humbly with God; to *love tenderly* means to walk humbly with God and to act justly; to *walk humbly with God* means to act justly and to love tenderly. So you cannot divorce spirituality from issues of social justice and compassion and care for the needy. True worship has to do with how we live the *whole* of our lives, not just that part which we take along to church on Sundays. Worship has to do with getting involved in God's world precisely because that is where he is involved.

Paul reminds us in Rom 1 that our worship is reflected in the offering of our bodies as living sacrifices, holy and pleasing to God. Christians are politically most powerful when they live and act in society in ways that reflect the ethics of the kingdom of God. Politics and Christian faith converge precisely because Christians are members of the human race, along with everybody else, whatever their creed or color. However, such a view should not be taken as a denial of the potential impact of political pressure groups, lobbying for changes in such areas as education policy, human welfare, and social injustice. In many countries throughout the world the impact of initiatives at both local and national levels is evidence enough of the transformation that committed individuals and groups can achieve in alleviating poverty, encouraging community, providing basic essentials, and fostering healing. These initiatives are essential in complementing the social welfare support available through government funding. Political engagement has to do with how Christians might exercise power in such a way as to avoid the corrupting temptations so eloquently identified by Lord Acton, who once famously observed that power tends to corrupt, and absolute power corrupts absolutely. The language of power in the Christian context derives from and is predicated on the reality that Christians are privileged to participate in the powerful work of the Holy Spirit who is ever at work in the world, seeking to bring about healing and reconciliation from the vantage point of the gospel.

---

20. Brown, *Spirituality and Liberation*, 70.

"A wager on transcendence" 169

Subversive Infiltration

How, then, might Christians most effectively participate in the political process in such a way as to make a stand on key issues of the day, such as justice for the homeless and the poor? Arguing from the basis that Hellenism infiltrated the embryonic Christian world through Gnostic ideas, the German theologian Helmut Thielicke asks whether a similar process might not apply with regard to the Christian church's influence upon the world. He presents his law of subversive infiltration not as a pragmatic attempt to master the world—as apparent, for example, in some conversionist agendas in America—but as "a law of action which is grounded in the nature of the Christian message itself."[21] The example he gives comes from Paul's letter to Philemon, in which he offers a response to the vexed question concerning the New Testament's silence about a social order that tolerates slavery. By sending Onesimus, a slave, back to his master as a Christian brother, which is precisely what Paul does in writing to Philemon, he does something that is radically new. Paul's action presents "a way that is diametrically opposed to that of slavery morality . . . at this point at least the order of slavery will have been shattered from within . . . this particular structure of society will have been undermined. *The changing of persons will necessarily mean the changing of the order.*"[22] The transformation of the social order is, for Thielicke, only an incidental by-product of the changing of lives. Political action by the church is therefore indirect: "it does not debate *things*; it aims at the conversion of *persons*."[23]

The same point is made by Miroslav Volf in his important distinction between *social arrangements* and *social agents*. In the development of his central argument regarding human identity in *Exclusion and Embrace* he proposes the priority of personal transformation over social reorganization, without diminishing in any way the need to tackle social arrangements. To fully be ourselves, he contends, is to be rooted in the self-giving love of the triune God, in whom the theology of embrace is most completely fulfilled in the self-surrender of Christ on the cross. And only in embrace can true justice be found. Volf spells out the relationship between justice and embrace as follows: "Embrace is part and parcel of the very *definition* of justice. I am not talking about soft mercy tampering

---

21. Thielicke, *Theological Ethics, Volume 2*, 642.
22. Ibid., my italics.
23. Ibid., author's italics.

harsh justice, but about *love* shaping the very content of justice."[24] So justice for others—a central concern and goal of the political process—is a relational reality, not an abstract concept, precisely because it is situated within the embracing love of the triune God, in whom we ourselves are situated. It is a justice that transcends *my* interpretation of what justice is. Because all human beings belong to the one God, I cannot simply insist on my own personal ethic: I must take the plank out of my own eye (Matt 7:3-5) before passing judgment on another. This does not mean that I agree with the actions or viewpoints of others, especially in the light of the biblically-attested preferential option for the poor and the powerless. As Volf asks in rhetorical fashion, "Is wrath against injustice appropriate? Yes! Must the perpetrator be restrained? By all means! Is punishment for the violation necessary? Probably." But it is his next sentence that carries the weight of his polemic: "But all these indispensable actions against injustice must be situated in the framework of the will to embrace the unjust. For only in our mutual embrace within the embrace of the triune God can we find redemption and experience perfect justice."[25] And how might this be achieved? The temptation for us is to plead helplessness and appeal to eschatology, but Volf appeals to the empowering grace of the Holy Spirit who "pours energies into the margins, opens the eyes of small people to see what no one has seen before, puts the creative words of prophecy into their mouths, and empowers them to be the agents of God's reign."[26] Accordingly, "theologians should concentrate less on social arrangements and more on *fostering the kind of social agents capable of envisioning and creating just, truthful, and peaceful societies, and on shaping a cultural climate in which such agents will thrive.*"[27]

In Col 3:12 the apostle Paul writes: "Therefore, as God's chosen people, holy and dearly loved, clothe yourselves with compassion, kindness, humility, gentleness, and patience." Christians are called to live by the Spirit, manifesting fruit that includes such attributes as patience, kindness, and gentleness. At times, our struggles against injustice and oppression will give rise to anger and rage, but it is only as we enlarge our vision in such a way that we see things from the perspective of others, even those who are our enemies, that we can be the sort of social agents

---

24. Volf, *Exclusion and Embrace*, 220.
25. Ibid., 224–25.
26. Ibid., 228.
27. Ibid., 21, author's italics.

capable of participating in the Spirit's work of bringing justice and mercy to the nations (Mic 6:8). Embracing this double vision[28]—seeing things from our own perspective *and*, crucially, from the perspective of others—is challenging and costly, but it is probably the vision we need to practice if we are to be "where we will be when the home of God is established among mortals."[29]

More Said than Done

The reality is that, when confronted with views different from their own, Christians will usually display one of three different responses. Some will shake their heads in despair, bewailing the state of the world, and retreat into their private, comfortable faith-spaces, lacking the courage of their convictions. The "will to embrace," using Volf's language, is sacrificed on the altar of self-interest. At the other end of the spectrum, there may be those who, in the words of the Christian philosopher and ethicist Richard Mouw, contribute more to the problem than the solution: "Well-known clergy tell their followers that the time has come for a 'battle' against the forces of unbelief. The TV cameras show Christians on the picket lines, angrily shaking their fists at their opponents."[30] What Mouw is concerned about in this second response is the lack of what he calls civility, a simple "public politeness" or courtesy towards others. However, this does not mean that we sacrifice convictions: there are times, he insists, when it is appropriate to manifest some very uncivil feelings. Quoting some lines from Yeats' poem "The Second Coming," Mouw pleads for more "passionate intensity" about our convictions. "The real challenge," he argues, "is to come up with a *convicted civility,*" a phrase we noted in chapter 6 in the context of church disputes. It is this course of action that represents a viable third way for all Christians, who are called to live as salt and light in the community.

Political action can be accomplished in any number of ways—getting informed about important issues, sharing in public debate, lobbying MPs, voting in elections, and taking part in demonstrations. But always done with civility as well as conviction. There is no "either-or" option available to Christians: faith and politics are inextricably entwined. In

---

28. Volf's phrase: see ibid., 213.
29. Ibid., 231.
30. Mouw, *Uncommon Decency*, 11.

fact, individual Christians and local faith communities are privileged to influence contemporary society through their political activities. Politics has to do with making a difference in this world: it is a "doing" word. The tragedy is that when all is said and done, there is often more said than done. At the beginning of this chapter I observed that Christians need to take the incarnation seriously on the grounds not that we are different from other people, but precisely the opposite . . . because we are *no* different from them. When we identify in radical solidarity with others in the misery and confusion of life—as well as in its more positive and hopeful expressions—the gospel is truly heard as *theologia crucis*, and the church becomes a prophetic voice. However, as Karl Barth rightly reminds us, the church's motto must be "solidarity with the world, not conformity to it!"[31] An approach that substitutes conformity for solidarity trivializes the gospel—it is the danger of assimilation that we discussed in chapter 10. We can only summon others to embrace the kingdom of God if we ourselves live under the shadow of the cross.

---

31. Barth, *CD Vol. 4, Part 3.2*, 773.

12

"Earth's crammed with heaven"
–Elizabeth Barrett Browning

God's "Creation-Community"

IN CHAPTER 1 I QUOTED SOME LINES FROM *AURORA LEIGH*, ELIZABETH Barrett Browning's nineteenth-century verse-novel of contemporary early Victorian life in England, highlighting the role of the imagination in helping us to see things that we might otherwise overlook in our recurring human tendency to focus on the self-evident:

> . . . Earth's crammed with heaven,
> And every common bush afire with God:
> But only he who sees, takes off his shoes,
> The rest sit round it, and pluck blackberries . . .[1]

Of course, Browning's key point in these lines is that God is immanent in his creation, and, more deeply than we realize, we are part of God's "creation-community," a community of both creatures and environments contributing to a "web of life on earth." In fact, to live fully human lives means that we are privileged to experience—at a deeply personal level— our own interconnectedness with all of creation. The Spirit who brings us to new life in Christ, transforming us into his likeness with ever-increasing glory (2 Cor 3:18), is the same Spirit who breathed life into creation *ex nihilo*, sustains all created things and pervades every corner of

---

1. Browning, *Aurora Leigh*, 265.

the cosmos. He is the creative and re-creative Spirit, the vitalizing Spirit, active from the moment of the big bang, releasing life and possibility as creation unfolds and reaches towards its intended goal. The activity of the Spirit may therefore be described as the eschatological power of God at work in all creation, enabling all that exists to fully and finally become itself in the freedom of divine love. All humanity is caught up in this eschatological drive towards fulfilment in God, who, as trinitarian love, welcomes and draws all creation—human and non-human—to himself through his Spirit.

Earth is Our Home

Any dualistic talk of distancing God from his creation, presenting him as some sort of deistic being who somehow keeps things going "from a distance," is, as we have already seen in chapter 3, inconsistent with an understanding of the triune God who has made space for creation within himself. Throughout this book, we have been drawing attention to the paradigm of "both-and" rather than "either-or" and in this chapter we focus attention on the fact that the planet earth is our home and we have been summoned by God to care for it precisely because it has integrity in itself as the creation of God. Furthermore, Christians are not those who have somehow been "caught up" by the Spirit, and transported out of this world and into some mystical, spiritual reality that has no bearing on the created order. We are grounded, landed creatures, created to live in this good earth. The name Adam probably comes from the Hebrew word ʻ*adam* meaning "to be red," perhaps referring to the reddish color of human skin, and Gen 2:7 points to an intriguing word play on ʻ*adamah*, which means earth: "the Lord God formed man from the dust of the ground." And, as we have already seen in earlier chapters, one day we shall all rejoice in our physicality in the glory of God's new creation. In this life as well as in the next, as Ricki Watts declares, "you can't get away from physicality."[2] He asks the question, "what does it mean to be saved?" to which he replies that you cannot really talk about salvation until you talk about creation, because to be saved is to live out the love of God concretely with real people in this life in the creation that he has brought into being. Salvation *and* creation . . . "both-and", not "either-or." How Christians respond to this topic influences the way they approach issues

---

2. Watts, "What Does It Mean to be Saved?"

"Earth's crammed with heaven" 175

such as the care of the environment, the nature of being human, and what our future hope might look like.

There is an amusing but sobering reminder of the indifference that some Christians display towards God's creation in a popular cartoon that identifies "just three awful reasons why stewardship of the creation is a non-issue for many Christians":

1. "I believe that soon God is gonna burn it all up. So it'd be a waste of all our time and effort."
2. "It is a 'secondary' issue. Our primary task is to preach Jesus to the unwashed of the world."
3. "My cool 4x4 and the many flights abroad each year are a real sign of God's blessing on me."

One Christian pastor speaking at a major conference in America collapsed the first and third responses above into a statement that it's perfectly OK for him to drive his SUV (a 4x4 sport utility vehicle) because Jesus is going to burn up the earth when he returns. This announcement, which led to some people walking out of the room, reflects both moral insensitivity and theological myopia. Moral insensitivity, not because SUVs are in themselves scandalous—there may be good reasons why some people need to drive a SUV, though it is difficult to sustain the practice in urban areas—but because that pastor didn't seem to be concerned about care for creation nor did he make the critical connection between environmental pollution and issues of human justice. When we pump carbon into the atmosphere, and when we degrade and deforest the land and pollute the water for commercial gain, we often rob the poorest people of their subsistence: God cares deeply for the poorest and most vulnerable people in society and arrogant indifference towards the environment has a profound and lasting impact on the poor and the marginalized. Theological myopia because, as we have already noted earlier, God has committed himself to putting everything to rights again, not by demolishing his creation, but by *renewing* it . . . and this applies not only to humanity, but also to his physical non-human creation. God's promise of a new creation is replete with references in the biblical text to a redeemed humanity participating with joy in the renewed physical creation . . . not apart from it, but intimately in communion with it.

The second response above echoes Paul Santmire's "metaphor of ascent" discussed in chapter 10, which refers to a form of spirituality that takes us not just towards God, but *away from* nature. In his book *The Travail of Nature*, Santmire traces what he calls "the ambiguous ecological promise of Christian theology," applauding the stance of theologians like Irenaeus, the later Augustine, and, of course, the medieval figure of St. Francis of Assisi, for whom the "metaphor of fecundity" found expression in his care for all of God's creatures. Other theologians throughout the history of the church have both shaped and been shaped by the dominant "spiritual motif," giving rise to a measure of indifference towards nature in Christian theology.[3] In 1966, Lynn White, a professor of medieval history in the United States, delivered a lecture tracing the roots of the existing ecological crisis, and he laid the blame not only at the door of secular progress in the form of the industrial revolution, but also at the door of Judeo-Christian theology.[4] White's central thesis with regard to Christianity is summed up in one of his concluding statements: "we shall continue to have a worsening ecologic crisis until we reject the Christian axiom that nature has no reason for existence save to serve man." For White, Christianity was an anthropocentric religion, serving the needs of human beings at the expense of nature, arising out of and contributing to dualistic thinking about the relationship between human beings and the natural world.

Faith and Science

Before addressing White's thesis in more detail, especially with regard to our responsibility to care for God's creation, we need to consider the issue of faith and ecology in the wider context of the relationship between faith and science. The dualistic undercurrents in the contemporary debate concerning Christianity and the environment can, in part, be traced to the history of the science-religion relationship over the past 150 years. I suggest that there are four compelling reasons why those who are involved in pastoral ministry need to address the science-faith relationship. Firstly, there is a growing awareness within the Christian community of the impact of science and technology on contemporary life, ranging from advances in medical science to the global telecommunications revolution. Recent developments in the contentious area of embryonic stem

3. Santmire, *Travail of Nature*, 176–83, for a summary of the historical perspective.

4. White, "The Historical Roots," 1203–7.

cell research have generated the most vocal opposition, and the pastoral responsibilities of the Christian community obligate it to engage with the scientific agenda more urgently than ever before. What science can do—and what scientists *say* science can do—is very much part of the debate.

Secondly, the media are doing a good job promoting the idea that science and religion really have very little to do with each other, and in fact sit on opposite sides of the fence. And there are some—like the "new atheists"—who know how to use the media to good effect. Whilst it is certainly true, taking a historical perspective, that religion and science haven't always got along well together, they haven't actually been as hostile towards each other as some have supposed. In fact, Christians have played a significant role over the last four or five centuries in the development of a whole range of scientific discoveries, inventions, and insights.

Thirdly, taking an apologetic perspective, those who are engaged in Christian ministry need to be properly informed about the culture in which they are embedded, a culture in which the scientific worldview is a dominant feature. We need to take time to educate ourselves about the issues that inform the lives of our church members. And, of course, the same injunction applies to scientists when they make pronouncements about faith. A critic of Richard Dawkins' book *The God Delusion*, wrote these stinging words: "Imagine someone holding forth on biology whose only knowledge of the subject is the Book of British Birds, and you have a rough idea of what it feels like to read Richard Dawkins on theology"![5]

Finally, Christians need to re-connect with God's creation if they are to discover what it means to live fully human lives. We are all part of the created order, and are meant to live in communion with creation, not over and above it. The privileged relationship that we are invited to experience not only with the God of creation but also with the creation of God draws us directly into the interface between science and faith. The grandeur of God lies not only in his sovereign glory as the Creator of all things, but also in the extraordinary diversity of his creation, unfolding over time in the human, animal, and natural realms. It is this rich and wonderfully complex creation that science is in the business of probing, investigating, describing, and seeking to understand. The myth that we have to make a simplistic choice between science and faith is wheeled out either by people who fear science, thinking that it has the potential to shipwreck faith, or by those who scorn faith, thinking that it has nothing

---

5. Eagleton, "Lunging, Flailing, Mispunching."

to do with science, or is inferior to science, even anti-science. Others are simply confused by the whole issue. Still others don't know what the fuss is about.

In the science-and-faith resource series called *Test of Faith*, produced by the Faraday Institute for Science and Religion in Cambridge, UK, the stories of ten contemporary scientists are presented, offering a number of reasons undergirding their conviction that science and faith really do have something to say to each other.[6] Three main reasons are cited: the rationality of the Christian faith, an awareness of beauty and order in creation, and the limitations of science with the consequent need for humility in the face of questions that take us to the very limit of what science can tell us. These reasons, amongst others raised in the book, help to dispel the myth that science and faith are incompatible. Science is not a worldview in the way that the Christian faith is: its power lies in its ability to explain *mechanism* rather than *meaning*: push it beyond the limits of mechanism, and it begins to operate in alien territory. There are many things science can't explain, like the "moral law" that helps us to distinguish between right and wrong, our awareness of beauty in the universe, and why we have an inner desire to worship a transcendent being.

The process of evolution, for example, is a theory that explains very well why some organisms survive and others don't. It is a mechanism that explains the "how" but it doesn't take us very far along the "meaning" path. Problems arise when we ask of evolution questions that it was never intended to answer. Whilst the process creates novelty and variety in creation, it doesn't address the ultimate questions of purpose and meaning. And, of course, evolutionary biologists are the first to admit that they do not have the whole process worked out. Scientists are still working on it . . . but it does make a lot of sense amongst those who are working in the fields of biology, geology, and paleontology. But problems also arise when we ask of the Bible questions it was never meant to answer. Some scientists—and Christians too!—need to recognize the limitations of the Bible with regard to scientific insights, as well as the purpose for which it was written: as Galileo once famously quipped, "The Bible was written to show us how to go to heaven, not how the heavens go."

In the matter of science and faith, then, we recognize that the paradigm of "both-and" makes a lot more sense than "either-or." Unfortunately the relationship between science and faith has—at least in the

---

6. Bancewicz, *Test of Faith*.

public arena—been characterized by too much talking and not enough listening. Two monologues don't make a dialogue, and there are many Christians and scientists who have spoken wisely about the need for dialogue as we seek a way forward in what can sometimes be a very heated debate. One Christian molecular biologist has written a book the title of which directly challenges the "either-or" perspective too frequently attributed to the conversation between the two, focusing on the issue that is often cited as the litmus test for Christian orthodoxy: *Creation or Evolution: Do We Have to Choose?*[7] In similar vein, Pope John Paul II once declared: "Science can purify religion from error and superstition; religion can purify science from idolatry and false absolutes. Each can draw the other into a wider world, a world in which both can flourish."[8]

Enlightenment Thinking

With this background of the interface between science and faith, we now return to the issue of the Christian concern for God's creation, revisiting Lynn White's comments in his 1966 lecture. Many Christians have expressed indignation at White's remarks, including his judgment that "modern technology is at least partly to be explained as an Occidental, voluntarist realization of the Christian dogma of man's transcendence of, and rightful master over, nature."[9] He presents the Christian stance towards nature as one of superiority and contempt, "willing to use it for our slightest whim." His solution? Either find a new religion or rethink the old one. In the light of Paul Santmire's assessment of Christian theology's historical preference for the "metaphor of ascent" in its attitude and response towards nature, it is tempting to uncritically accept White's thesis. But this would be a hasty judgment, not least because, as Santmire points out, the Western classical theological tradition has included a corrective "ecological motif" at different points in its historical development (in this regard, Lynn White invokes St. Francis of Assisi as "the greatest radical in Christian history since Christ"). Whilst the Christian church, particularly in the West, cannot be absolved from its failure to adopt a more welcoming and holistic vision of creation in its theological formu-

---

7. Alexander, *Creation or Evolution*.

8. On the relationship between science and faith see Giberson and Collins, *Language of Science and Faith*; Buxton et al., *God and Science*.

9. White, "The Historical Roots," 1206.

lations, the responsibility cannot be laid exclusively at its feet. Deeper forces have been at work in Western culture, especially over the last few centuries of human history, as Enlightenment thinking ushered in the supremacy of human reason and progress, with its attendant anthropocentric emphasis on the instrumental value of nature. In other words, so the argument goes, this planet on which we live offers us all the resources that we need in order to prosper and achieve the "good life," and so we are entitled to use it in whatever way we like in order to realize this goal of human happiness, which in today's materialistic age finds expression in humanity's "frenzied grasping for stuff."[10] And in some (mainly evangelical) Christian circles utilitarianism has been justified with reference to the biblical command given to Adam to exercise dominion over the created order. In this regard, Christianity's weakness has been not only its failure to present a much-needed prophetic challenge to secular humanism's hubristic exploitation of nature, but also its slowness in elucidating and championing the Bible's ecological wisdom grounded in a carefully-articulated and informed biblical hermeneutic. Ultimately, the crucial error in Lynn White's thesis is his own misrepresentation of the biblical text, to which we will turn towards the end of this chapter. Thankfully, the ecotheological vacuum is now being filled with a number of texts addressing the themes of creation care, ecological hermeneutics and environmental ethics along with volumes providing pastoral resources for Christian ministry.[11]

The central tension in Santmire's thesis is, as we have seen, that a person's "identity as a human being may be essentially rooted in the world of nature (the metaphor of fecundity) or it may not be (the metaphor of ascent)."[12] His affirmation of the metaphor of fecundity as a mark of what it means to be made *imago Dei* is reinforced by his statement that we are all essentially "landed creatures": indeed, to be disconnected from the world of nature is to violate our identity as human beings. Not only do we—as created beings—"live and move and have our being" within the world of nature, but spiritual experience is itself located within the ecological context. To pull spirituality and ecology apart is to do violence

---

10. See Roberts, "Our Materialism."

11. See, for example, Horrell et al., *Ecological Hermeneutics*; Horrell, *Bible and Environment*; Snyder and Scandrett, *Salvation Means Creation Healed*; Habel et al., *Season of Creation*.

12. Santmire, *Travail of Nature*: 25. The discussion in some of the paragraphs that follow first appeared in Buxton, *Trinity*, chapter 6.

to the very fabric of creation as God's gift of self-communicating love. Spirituality and ecology are intimately connected within a "both-and" paradigm that invites us to *embrace* the physical creation as an expression of our God-given humanity, a creation that displays extraordinary diversity unfolding over time in the human, animal, and natural realms. Biologists teach us that there is an amazing branching network in the "tree of life." The millions of species that exist on planet earth are not a haphazard jumble of animals and plants and other natural phenomena—rather, they share a nested relationship in the "tree of life," each contributing to and drawing from unique ecosystems that are themselves interdependent. For Jürgen Moltmann, for example, space, as created reality, is primarily *living space* for the richness and variety of different forms of life. His ecological thinking is summed up in his assertion that "living spaces belong to life."[13]

However, if creation is treated as an object to dominate, the particular environments created by God for the nourishment of unique living things are destroyed in the drive to create a homogeneous environment amenable to humanity's desire to dominate all things. The drive for uniformity (especially in today's highly globalized culture) weakens and destabilizes the rich diversity of God's creation. Everything becomes "McDonaldized" in our contemporary consumer-driven culture. Things are valued for their usefulness to humanity rather than for what they are *as creations of God*. Douglas John Hall echoes Santmire's critique of the metaphor of ascent when he states that imaging God "is not rising above the earth, as if we were pure spirit . . . we are bodies, and our imaging of God is inseparable from our imaging of the earth."[14] He suggests that human pride—a refusal to acknowledge our basic creaturehood—is responsible for our desire to rise above "this affinity with our earthly source and matrix."[15]

The "Loving Eye"

The English mystic, Evelyn Underhill, writing at the beginning of the twentieth century, described many Christians as "deaf people at a concert": "They study the program carefully, believe every statement in

13. See Moltmann, "God and Space," 111–26.
14. Hall, *Imaging God*, 179.
15. Ibid., 180.

it, speak respectfully of the quality of the music, but only really hear a phrase now and again. So they have no notion at all of the mighty symphony which fills the universe, to which our lives are destined to make their tiny contribution, and which is the self-expression of the Eternal God."[16] The "mighty symphony" to which Underhill alludes may be interpreted as the symphony of a creation that is replete with biological diversity and fecundity, which is itself "the dynamic, exuberant overflow of the fecundity of trinitarian life."[17] The implications of this are spelled out further by Denis Edwards: "the rain forest of the Amazon is to be understood as the self-expression of the divine Trinity. It is a sacrament of God's presence. Its vitality and exuberance spring from the immanent presence of the Spirit, the giver of life. They express the trinitarian love of life. The rain forest, in its form, function and beauty as a harmonious biotic community is the work of art of divine Wisdom."[18] Whereas Ps 104 presents us with a picture of God delighting in his creation (culminating in verse 31: "May the Lord rejoice in his works"), in Ps 148 we see the converse—all creation joins in worshipping God.

Richard Bauckham interprets Ps 148 as a "cosmic choir" or orchestra, with each created being contributing in their own distinctive way to a symphony of praise to God simply by being themselves and fulfilling their divinely-ordained role in creation. For Bauckham, "the most profound and life-changing way in which we can recover our place in the world as creatures alongside our fellow-creatures is through the biblical theme of the worship all creation offers to God."[19] To experience nature in this sacramental way is to experience transformation as we discover afresh our basic humanity in solidarity with God's created order. Bauckham follows Moltmann in his endorsement of the image of a community of creation as the most helpful way to express the interconnectedness that all creatures, including human beings, share with each other within the divine community of the triune God. This "creation-community" framework resonates with Sallie McFague's focus on an incarnational love of nature that involves paying attention to "what is," highlighted in the earlier-quoted lines of Browning from *Aurora Leigh*. Interpreting this "paying attention" as an awareness, even a celebration, of *difference*, she

16. From the first of four broadcast talks by the English mystic Evelyn Underhill, subsequently published under the title *The Spiritual Life*.

17. Edwards, *Jesus the Wisdom of God*, 116.

18. Ibid., 117.

19. Bauckham, *Bible and Ecology*, 76.

admits to the difficulty of really learning to see what is different to ourselves: "We can acknowledge a thing in its difference if it is important to us or useful to us, but realizing that something other than oneself is real, in itself, for itself, is difficult."[20] Citing Emily Dickinson's insight that "we cannot love what we do not know," McFague contrasts two ways of seeing. The first—what Marilyn Frye calls the "loving eye"[21]—is an attention to detail that exalts "the specialness, the difference, the intricacy, the 'unutterable particularity' of each creature, event, or aspect of nature that calls forth wonder and delight—a knowing that calls forth love and a love that wants to know more."[22]

The second, and inferior, way of seeing—the "arrogant eye"—is epitomized in the popular NASA poster of planet earth as a swirling blue and white colored marble floating in black space. McFague acknowledges that such an image has immediate cosmetic and popular appeal, finding it a useful image to raise consciousness about the fragility of the planet; it also evokes a sense of wonder in calling to mind the inhospitable environments of all other planets known to humankind, reinforcing God's special creation of earth, unique and "fine-tuned" to provide just the right conditions for life to be sustained for billions of years. But her key criticism is that it utterly fails to convey the rape and pillage, the environmental pollution, and violence that take place on a daily basis in every part of the planet. As an image, it is remote and ultimately meaningless precisely because it fails to acknowledge and respect earth as *subject*. As an alternative to the dominant "subject-object" model, she proposes an ecological "subject-subjects" model, on the analogy of friendship, which is predicated on the language of relationships: "respect, reciprocity, interest in the particular, openness, paying attention, care, concern."[23] As we have seen, Moltmann expresses this friendship in terms of community: "if nature and humanity are to survive on this earth, they must find the way to a new community with each other. Human beings must integrate themselves once more into the earth's cosmic setting."[24]

The new discipline of ecotheology is burgeoning today as the result of a growing awareness of humanity's failure to look after God's good gift

---

20. McFague, *Super, Natural Christians*, 28.
21. See Frye, "In and Out of Harm's Way, " especially 72-76.
22. McFague, *Super, Natural Christians*, 31.
23. Ibid., 37.
24. Moltmann, "From the Closed World," 168–69.

of creation. To live responsibly as human beings within the created order is to move beyond a purely utilitarian ethic and to embrace a spirituality that acknowledges the wonder and mystery of creation as "sacramental reality." However, jostling alongside concerned Christians are many others, amongst whom are those whose interest in the environment stems from neopagan roots, including a fascination with nature mysticism. This has been stimulated in part by the failure of the Christian church to demonstrate respect for and concerned involvement in nature, a neglect over the years that has prompted Sallie McFague to insert what she calls a "deeply subversive" comma between "super" and "natural." Her writings express a passionate desire to see Christians live not just "supernatural" lives, but "super, natural" lives, living "*in* the earth, and *for* the earth . . . understanding ourselves as excessively, superlatively concerned with nature and its well-being."[25]

Our discussion has an important bearing on Christian pastoral ministry. Enthused by "the Spirit of adventure," who animates the human spirit, we are encouraged to discover our place in God's creation, and to enter into a new awareness of our identity in relationship with created matter. Such symbiosis with nature is in stark contrast to the person who is so "caught up in the idolatries of tyrannical professionalism, and such pragmatism of spirit, that instead of seeing creation with a childlike and overwhelming delight" he or she sees it "only as data for the intellect, and as resources for consumption."[26] The Spirit of adventure leads us into an attentiveness to *everything* that God has made precisely because we are constrained by an ethic of love that respects the richness of God's creation as the self-expression of God's fecundity.

The Biblical Text

In his introduction to the first volume of the ground-breaking Earth Bible series, Norman Habel argues that many Christian traditions, especially in the West, have interpreted the biblical text in such a way as to devalue earth.[27] The purpose of the Earth Bible Project is to promote a renewed interest in creation as a central theological theme, not as a topic in the biblical text, nor as backdrop to human history, but critically concerned

---

25. McFague, *Super, Natural Christians*, 5–6.
26. Houston, *I Believe in the Creator*, 215.
27. Habel, *Readings from Perspective of Earth*, 25–37.

with "listening to Earth as a subject in the text." Habel and his fellow-contributors argue that the thrust of biblical interpretation in the Western tradition has tended towards anthropocentrism, androcentrism, and patriarchy, based on a reading of Gen 1:26-28 that emphasizes God's explicit directive to rule over every living thing and subdue the earth. The members of the Earth Bible team make a powerful plea for ecojustice in humanity's relationship to planet earth. Eschewing Western, hierarchical, dualistic thinking that places human beings *above* nature, they advocate a policy of partnership that resists the violation and exploitation of nature.

Accordingly, six "ecojustice principles" undergird the Earth Bible Project endeavor: they are the principles of intrinsic worth, interconnectedness, voice, purpose, mutual custodianship, and resistance. Each of these principles is addressed in the Earth Bible series. For example, in a study of Gen 6:11-13, Anne Gardner interprets the biblical text as a failure of God's creatures to respect the intrinsic worth of each other and of the earth.[28] Duncan Reid, in his exegesis of Rev 21:1—22:5, identifies John's evident allusions to the "this-worldly" vision in Isa 65: here we have no "earth-despising gnosticism"—in fact, heaven comes down to earth, not the reverse! So the earth, "turned into a place of God's absence by godless human beings, is to become once more the dwelling place of God."[29] Earth, once shamed and denuded, is replete with the glory of God. And from Genesis through to Revelation, the biblical text is perceived by the Earth Bible team as active subject rather than passive object: planet earth has a voice to be heard, not silenced; it functions according to an in-built purpose; and it exists—human and non-human—as a complex and mutually-supportive community of interconnected living things. In his commentary on Rom 8:18-22, the Jesuit New Testament scholar Brendan Byrne offers an ecojustice hermeneutic, arguing that the passage conveys "a strong sense of solidarity in both suffering and hope between non-human creation and the human world."[30]

In his quest for a radical re-enchantment of nature, David Tacey argues that there needs to be a moral and ethical revolution in our hearts if we are to arrest the impoverishment of the earth caused by our exploitative abuse. Treating God's universe as a "creation-community" may take us part of the way along the road. But there is a second revolution that

---

28. See Gardner, "Ecojustice."
29. See Reid, "Setting Aside the Ladder to Heaven."
30. See Byrne, "Creation Groaning."

Tacey insists must be experienced, a spiritual revolution that percolates deep within the human psyche: "The truly ecological task is to repair not just our damage in the outer world but also the deep splits in our psychological make-up and dualistic world view."[31] Pride—the arrogant Babel-like lust for power and quest for "pseudotranscendence"[32]—has turned us away from our God-ordained "ontology of communion" with nature. Indeed, as Moltmann points out, to speak of nature in terms of *our* environment is already to diminish nature's integrity by making it part of the human world. Nature will not—cannot—be saved that way.[33] Nor can human redemption be achieved by returning to nature, as some contemporary spiritual gurus maintain. What is needed is the recognition that "transcendence is immanent in every natural being": when we name the reality in which we live "creation," we are expressing in the strongest possible way "resistance to the transformation of nature into *human environment*."[34]

A central thesis throughout this chapter is that human beings have been placed by God *within* the community of creation, not above it, a proposal that has good biblical support. Richard Bauckham interprets the Gen 1 account of creation as an "ecological" rather than a "dominion" text: the scheme of creation is primarily spatial rather than an ordered progression that builds towards a culmination: "Humans, the last creatures to be created, have a unique role within creation, but they do not come last because they are the climax of an ascending scale."[35] A key insight here is that the dominion granted by God "presupposes that humans bear the divine image, so that God can authorize them to use their superior power *in a way that reflects God's own rule over his creation.*"[36] Care and compassion, rather than violence and force, are therefore the more likely implications of the Hebrew word *radah* ("rule") in Gen 1:26-28. Humanity's image-bearing status is similarly noted by Liederbach and Bible: "Recognizing this vital element of human nature is crucial to our discussion on creation care because of the special place

---

31. Tacey, *Re-Enchantment*, 177.

32. A term used by Hall, *Imaging God*, 179-80; "pseudo" because this desire does not properly belong to our essential, created being.

33. See Moltmann, *Source of Life*, 118-21.

34. Ibid. My italics.

35. Bauckham, *Bible and Ecology*, 14.

36. Ibid., 18, my italics.

humans are granted within the created order."[37] In God's good creation other creatures find their own ecological "living space" under human beings' benevolent care, delegated to them by God.

Bauckham also makes the point that God's covenant in Gen 9:8-17 never to flood the earth again is made not just with Noah and his family, but with "every living creature that was with you" (v. 10). In fact, it is noticeable how many times the inclusion of all creatures is repeated in this one single passage—five times, with three further references to "all life." And in verse 13 God declares that the rainbow will serve as "a covenant between me and the earth." Planet earth is home for *all* that God has created, a "creation-community" of all creatures and environments residing within the perichoretic life of God. In the book of Job, we find the longest passage in the Bible about the non-human creation, chapters 38-39. Job and his so-called "comforters" have been debating with each other about how God orders his world. In anguish, Job questions God, and eventually, having listened patiently to Job and his friends, God responds by inviting Job to consider the immensity of his creation, with the implied question: "Who, then, do you think *you* are?" In this appeal to cosmic humility, Bauckham observes: "We need the humility to recognize that our place in the world is a limited one. . . . We need the humility to recognize the unforeseeable risks of technology before we ruin the world in pursuit of technological fixes to all our problems."[38]

Human Hubris

Human hubris is most particularly evident in the claim that we have within our power the capacity to harness nature and bring it under control. Indeed, taming nature has often been considered as one of the great Western dreams, reminiscent of Sir Francis Bacon's seventeenth-century utopian vision of a mythical land called Bensalem, whose inhabitants fully embrace the sciences as a means of ultimately achieving control over nature in order to satisfy every human desire.[39] Whilst science must rightly continue to seek to alleviate human suffering and misery, it is important to understand that human beings live in a world that is good, but not perfect. God's evaluation of his creation in Gen 1-2 as "good" "carries

---

37. Liederbach and Bible, *True North*, 56.
38. Bauckham, *Bible and Ecology*, 46.
39. Bacon, *The New Atlantis*.

the sense of corresponding to the divine intention, including elements of beauty, purposefulness, and praiseworthiness."[40] Perfection—which is a measure of what *we* think the world should be like—is clearly not an appropriate way to describe creation, given the presence of catastrophes like earthquakes, tsunamis, volcanoes, wildfires, and hurricanes, to name just a few of the extreme weather events that afflict our planet on a regular basis. Whilst climate change is increasingly recognized today as something to which *human* activity has contributed through sinful behavior, including personal and political greed and indifference to the plight of others, and poor management of the earth's resources, natural disasters are built into the very fabric of creation and reflect God's continuing activity in his unfolding creation.

Certainly there is much that governments can do to reverse the gross injustices caused by environmentally irresponsible practices. As Sir John Houghton, former co-chair of the Intergovernmental Panel on Climate Change, observes, "there is a very strong moral imperative for rich nations to lead in the necessary reductions in emissions and to use their wealth and skills to help poorer nations develop sustainably."[41] But alongside this obvious call to action at the human level, a coherent "theology of nature" makes room for the wisdom of a God who has set in motion a process with a general direction and goal, the realization of which is left not only to the operation of the laws of nature but also to free choices, random events, and other unpredictable interactions within nature itself. Perhaps we need to acknowledge that we live in a universe that exists, in the words of Keith Ward, "by opposition." The continent of Australia, which is now my home, regularly experiences devastating bushfires, during which vast tracts of forest are consumed by fire. Bushfires, though they can lead to the tragic loss of life and property, are all part of the natural processes. Whilst human neglect and sinfulness repeatedly contribute to increased fire risk, bushfires are essential to clear areas and allow new growth, and this process is critical to ecological health. Ward writes:

> It is of the nature of the energy of which [the material universe] is constituted to destroy as well as to create, to renew itself precisely by destruction, and so generate the new by its own continual perishing. . . . Its vast energies continually interact and annihilate one another, yet generate new properties in the process. In such a world-system of many delicately balanced

40. Fretheim, *Creation Untamed*, 13.
41. Houghton, "Dried Up, Drowned Out," 3.

energies, held in an elegant mathematical web of rational principle, capable of generating emergent properties, including all the mental properties involved in the existence of a community of free rational wills, the creative originating Will can act to form and realize the structures of the physical order and bring its diversity into final unity with itself.[42]

It is worth reminding ourselves, therefore, that we are called to live in communion with creation, not over and above it, and so we need to learn to respect creation in all its beauty, diversity, complexity, mystery, raw power, and energy. And that respect embraces not only the imperative to care for creation—which critically involves acting responsibly so that the poor are not marginalized through environmentally reckless practices—but also the wisdom to respect the natural forces that shape the unfolding evolution of our planet and acknowledge that perhaps we are not as smart as we sometimes think we are.

The Wonder of Nature

Throughout this chapter we have acknowledged the physical as an intimation of the divine. Sacramental reality is expressed in the glory of natural forms, proclaimed in their particularity, their diversity, their thickness—in their unique "*it*ness." Sally McFague calls this "horizontal Christian sacramentalism," focusing on the things themselves rather than their divine message.[43] In this view, nature is enchanted precisely because it is the creation of God, not because it points to the God of creation. This perspective takes us further than McGrath's observation that nature, "when rightly understood, points beyond itself, to a 'yonder' we shall one day know and inhabit."[44] Nature, then, is to be treasured *for what it is*, rather than just for what it does; it has integrity and is therefore to be respected, cared for, and cherished precisely because it is God's creation ever before it is our environment. In his remarkable first book entitled *The Immense Journey*, the American scholar and scientist Loren Eiseley writes with reverence and lyricism about the wonders of the universe, imagining himself at different stages and in different places in the unfolding journey of the universe through time and space. The book is a remark-

---

42. Ward, *Divine Action*, 65.
43. McFague, *Super, Natural Christians*, 172–75.
44. McGrath, *Re-enchantment of Nature*, 188.

able narrative of life unfolding through time, a delightfully imaginative and sensuous voyage through history in which the storyteller invites the reader into a rich tapestry of experiences and events that reflect Eiseley's own sense of awe at the mystery and wonder of creation.

One incident that he recounts has come to be known as "the judgment of the birds." In a sunlit glade a sleek black raven gulps down a squirming nestling, indifferent to the helpless outrage of the little bird's parents. Then into the glade flutter a few other birds, then many others, until in the hush the crystal note of a song sparrow is picked up. Soon the whole glade is filled with the joyous sound of birdsong. In Eiseley's account, they sang "because life is sweet and sunlight beautiful. They sang under the brooding shadow of the raven. In simple truth they had forgotten the raven, for they were the singers of life, and not of death."[45] Commenting on this poignant incident, Douglas John Hall observes that "human spirituality is cheapened when it fastens on the divine in such a way as to exclude nature and even history from the realm of transcendent wonder."[46] Again and again throughout the Bible, those who love God are summoned to "sing a new song" (see, for example, Pss 33:3; 96:1; 98:1; 149:1; Isa 42:10; Rev 14:3), and for those who have ears to hear, creation teaches us how to sing the song that God has put in our hearts. John Muir, the pioneer conservationist and "Father of the National Parks" in America, once said, "I only went out for a walk and finally concluded to stay out till sundown, for going out, I found, was really going in."[47]

The life of Henry Thoreau, another "imaginative naturalist," was infused with a rich and profound sense of wonder. He was a "complete human being" who had discovered how to live fully *imago Dei* with his fellow beings and with nature, and with a God who was, for him a "Benefactor and Intelligence that stands over" nature, as he once wrote in *Walden* (which describes the simple life he led at Walden Pond for over two years). "His delicious prose and his descriptions of his interactions with nature testify to his firm belief that there is an unseen power just beyond the veil of the visible. . . . It is only through developing a proper relationship with nature that individuals and communities can

---

45. Eiseley, *Immense Journey*, 175.
46. Hall, *Imaging God*, 138.
47. Muir, *John of the Mountains*, 427.

achieve true fulfilment."[48] The following is an example of Thoreau's prose in *Walden: The Pond in Winter*:

> Standing on the snow-covered plain, as if in a pasture amid the hills, I cut my way first through a foot of snow, and then a foot of ice, and open a window under my feet, where, kneeling to drink, I look down into the quiet parlor of the fishes, pervaded by a softened light as through a window of ground glass, with its bright sanded floor the same as in summer; there a perennial waveless serenity reigns as in the amber twilight sky, corresponding to the cool and even temperament of the inhabitants. Heaven is under our feet as well as over our heads.[49]

There is no doubt that, like many today who seek to relate to nature, Thoreau's understanding of God was eclectic, with discernible traces of nature mysticism, but this should not discourage us from seeing in his life an example of a person who was convinced of the interconnectedness between all things in creation. In particular, he insisted that human beings have a responsibility to care for creation in order to allow the natural world to be free to express itself in all its beauty and wonder . . . and, at times, uncontrollable ferocity and violence. When we live on this planet imbued with a desire to care for it and do what we can to live in an ethical and sustainable way, caring for *all* of God's creation—other people, all animals, birds and fish, and the inanimate world of plants and land and water—then not only is creation more free to express its potential as "good," but those of us who name Christ as Lord will discover a new freedom to live "super, natural" lives—*both* super *and* natural, not "either-or."

---

48. McGrath, *Re-Enchantment of Nature*, 136.
49. Thoreau, *Walden*, 275.

13

"For anything to be real it must be local"
–G. K. Chesterton

Universalizing of Culture

IF THE LANGUAGE WE USE REFLECTS IN PART THE SOCIAL CONDITIONS of the day, then the creation of many new words over the last few decades testifies to the rapid development of information technology in our modern world. The "Internet," for example, an abbreviation of Internetworking, which is itself a combination of the words *inter* ("between") and *networking*, has now become a standard term in our vocabulary. Today's technophile—there's another neologism!—uses vocabulary that is at times far removed from the language of earlier generations. One neologism that is gaining increasing currency is the word "glocal" and its associated term "glocalization," which is a newly coined amalgam of "globalization" and "localization." We live today in a culture that is often described as globalized, referring to the complex interconnectedness of politics, economics, science, technology, culture, and religion. As a direct result of the telecommunications revolution and vast improvements in international transportation infrastructures, the world is "shrinking": "different institutions function as parts of one system and distant peoples share a common understanding of living together on one planet."[1] Global interests and concerns proliferate, giving rise to a wide range

---

1. Boli and Lechner, "General Introduction" to *The Globalization Reader*, xvii.

of cross-border systems and networks such as the United Nations, the International Monetary Fund, the Intergovernmental Panel on Climate Change, the United Nations High Commissioner for Refugees, The World Trade Organization, Al-Qaeda ... and the Internet!

These networks operate both formally and informally to bring about desired goals, sometimes in imaginative and innovative ways. US President Barack Obama cited the role of technology in the 2011 Egyptian uprising, praising those who used their creativity, talent, and technology through the Facebook and Twitter social networking sites to help to topple the government of Hosni Mubarak. Multinational corporations with budgets bigger than many national economies conduct business on a global scale, but, as Harold Netland points out, the capitalist system on which these companies thrive invites wildly different assessments: "it has not alleviated the poverty of much of the world's population; indeed, the gap between the rich and poor widens, and many contend that the great wealth of some has come at the expense of deepening poverty of the many."[2] Perhaps the most significant visible consequence of the "global revolution" over the past twenty or thirty years is what we might call the "universalizing of culture," flattening distinctives in such a way as to generate a homogenized culture in which there is a McDonald's in every major city in the world, where English is the *lingua franca*, and where the Internet connects everybody with everyone else.

The Gift of Place

However, it would be hasty to minimize the importance of the local in the midst of the global revolution. Indeed, to champion globalization at the expense of the local is to fall into the trap of denying the rich texture of local communities and the contribution that the local context makes to people's lives. G. K. Chesterton once remarked that "for anything to be real it must be local," reflecting what Eugene Peterson calls "the gift of place" which "locates us on the earth where we become oriented, find work, experience freedom in obedience, and find companionship in a community of others."[3] The danger of losing touch with our local "home" is that we end up becoming rootless nomads, always looking for new experiences beyond our borders. For Christians this might translate into

---

2. Netland, "Introduction: Globalization," 20–21.
3. Peterson, *Christ Plays*, 72.

hopping from one church to another in order to find our "spiritual home" instead of contributing to the life of our local congregation because that's where we are *situated*.

Peterson's interpretation of the first two chapters of Genesis is particularly instructive as we grapple with the idea of the interaction between global and local. As Old Testament scholars have pointed out, the opening two chapters of the Bible provide us with two creation accounts which, for Peterson, are primarily texts for living in the time and place in which we find ourselves when we wake up each morning. Time and place—these are what make us truly human. Genesis 1 is characterized by a recurring structure, so offering us a framework for entering into the rhythms of creation time, enabling us to internalize "a creation sense of orderliness and connectedness and resonance that is very much like what we get from music."[4] So Gen 1 helps us to "keep time," encouraging us to enter into the "large, encompassing rhythms" of God's creation, immersed in the liturgical cadences of life. But in today's busy world, rush has replaced rest as the primary shaping mechanism of our lives. Carl Jung is once reported as saying that hurry is not *of* the devil; it *is* the devil! Many Christians can testify to the reality of pressure and busyness in their lives—and that is even before they get involved in church activities! James Gleick has written a book called *Faster*, subtitled *The Acceleration of Just About Everything*. In a racy style, his critique of contemporary society—"While you wait, you look at your watch. It's a habit"[5]—dissects our struggle to squeeze as much as we can into every 1,440 minutes of each day. Nowhere is this more evident than in the way we eat . . . or don't eat: not many families sit round a table these days and enjoy a meal *together*. The ubiquitous McDonald's, the quintessential global purveyor of fast food, has changed our eating habits forever.

If *time* is the integrating motif in Gen 1, *place* serves that role in Gen 2. The opening creation account in Gen 1 lays out a theology of belonging as we discover God's invitation to us to participate in his creational work. But Gen 2 shifts the focus from theology to geography: "The first account is comprehensive, the entire cosmos and everything in it. The second account zooms in on earth and then on one place on earth."[6] And place is where we are called to live out our human existence. In chapter 3 I

---

4. Ibid., 67.
5. Gleick, *Faster*, 31.
6. Peterson, *Christ Plays*, 72.

recounted an incident in which a foul-mouthed neighbor in an inner-city London parish to which I had been called suffered a debilitating stroke shortly after my wife and I had prayed earnestly to God to either move him or shut him up. As he recovered, we began to develop a new, open relationship with him, in which God revealed himself to us as the hospitable triune God who welcomes all people into his life. That experience taught us not only to be careful about what we pray for (!), but much about the importance of geography, of grounding our life in the local community rather than seeking greener pastures elsewhere. "Theology divorced from geography gets us into nothing but trouble."[7] In our home at the time we had a poster in one of the rooms of a small primrose with yellow flowers that had pushed itself up in a dark corner of a garden, above which were the words, "Bloom where you are planted." As Peterson rightly observes, "It is so easy to get excited and enthusiastic about the gospel outside our gardens. But it is in our gardens that we have been placed."[8]

This pattern is, of course, discernible in the Bible. Throughout the Old Testament we notice that God's dealings with human beings are localized in the unfolding drama of his relationship with his people Israel. The stories of prophets, priests, kings, and the many other people who make up the rich fabric of life in those days are set in a small strip of land bordering the Mediterranean Sea in the Middle East. And in Jesus' life on earth, we see God involved in particular lives: celebrating with the happy couple at their wedding in Cana in Galilee, healing the paralytic man at Capernaum, responding to the faith of the Syrian Phoenician woman whose daughter was possessed by an evil spirit, and lovingly welcoming those who were looked down upon by the religious authorities of his day. Jesus loved, laughed, played, wept, and cared, and in so doing he healed and transformed the lives of particular people in particular places. What we learn from our understanding of the time and place significance of Gen 1 and 2, echoed throughout the biblical text, is the importance of holding the two accounts in tension, the immediacy of place within the overarching rhythms of time. The specific events recorded in the Bible are narratives that find their meaning and purpose within the wider narrative of God's saving work in history. In their discussion of the way narrative works in the Bible, Fee and Stuart helpfully distinguish between three levels in the Old Testament, which together comprise a hierarchy of

7. Ibid., 77.
8. Ibid., 73.

narratives.[9] Individual narratives represent the first level, embracing, for example, stories about the great heroes of faith in Israelite history; these stories fit into the second narrative level, which has to do with God's special relationship with Israel with its repeating cycle of obedience, rebellion, punishment, and deliverance. This middle level is in turn a part of the ultimate narrative of salvation history, or *Heilsgeschichte*—the whole universal plan of God worked out in creation and redemption. The particular finds its real meaning within the ultimate.

"Glocal" Faith Perspectives

In Gen 1–2 the particular work to which Adam and Eve are called finds localized expression within the more globally comprehensive and expansive sweep of God's creating—and creative—genius. Both are necessary, the universal and the particular, the global and the local, to give full meaning to what is meant to take place within the Garden of Eden. So it is today within our globalized culture: the expression of faith in a particular vicinity draws not only from the exigencies of a unique local context, but also from an awareness of the need to participate in and learn from insights and trends that inform the catholicity of the wider church. The key question is how the two actually relate to one another: what specifically are the marks of a "glocal" faith perspective, and how does "glocalization" work out in practice? Various alternative paradigms present themselves and they can be represented in the simple form of: the impact of the global on the local; the impact of the local on the global; and the extent to which global and local inform each other.

Over the past few years a number of congregations in different parts of the world have experienced both challenge and opportunity in their ministry as refugees and asylum seekers from different countries have made their spiritual home in their midst, with a good number of them converting to Christ and being baptized. In one local church known to me in Australia, a group of Iranians has become part of the congregation, and sermons have been translated into Farsi, with Farsi translations of Scripture passages accompanying the English-language texts projected onto the wall. Congregational members are beginning to learn new ways of being hospitable and welcoming, following the lead of many of the Iranians themselves. No one planned this, or even anticipated it, and it

---

9. Fee and Stuart, *How to Read the Bible*, 74–75.

is unclear what the future will hold. One woman just happened to visit a nearby detention centre where many Iranians were being held, and her concern and care for them encouraged some of them to attend the church. Their presence in the church is the outcome of a tragic situation in one particular country (amongst many others, of course) whose inhabitants feel that they are unable to stay any longer in their own nation for fear of being persecuted or because of the struggles they are experiencing in trying to live freely in their own land. The plight of many of them does not match the severe condition of those whose lives have been devastated by war and violence, social upheavals or natural disasters like earthquakes and tsunamis, who are now in refugee camps or in some other form of protective care. The aim of agencies like the UNHCR is to help these desperate refugees find lasting solutions to their plight, repatriating some voluntarily to their homeland, integrating others in countries of asylum or resettling in third countries.

However, there are many people who do not fall within the status of "refugee" who choose to follow a more dangerous and risky course, following the earlier example of the so-called "Vietnamese boat people" in the late 1970s, who were themselves refugees following the fall of Saigon in 1975. Recent years have seen an increase in the number of people fleeing from Iran, Iraq, Afghanistan, Sri Lanka, and Sudan to Indonesia, where they are often kept in detention centres while their claim for refugee status is processed by the UNHCR. In some cases, this has led to the charge that those who are not strictly "refugees" are "queue-jumping," a controversial claim that has given rise to much debate and misunderstanding. Whilst there, some fall prey to illegal "people smugglers" who charge exorbitant fees to get them onto boats, often in a very unseaworthy condition, bound for Australia. In some cases, lives have been lost at sea in the dangerous waters. As illustrated above, many have been finding their way to local churches, with the result that congregations are becoming increasingly aware of their responsibility to engage in the wider issues that have given rise to the problem in the first place. The presence of asylum seekers has opened up a new way of thinking about the meaning of church, such that "what was once known as the local is itself an aspect of the global in the same way that a quark or electron is part of the entire universe."[10] Not only are local churches discovering new insights about what it means to be a welcoming community, but they are being forced to

---

10. Van Engen, "The Glocal Church," 160.

think deeply about how they might be more fully committed to becoming what Miroslav Volf calls "*social agents capable of envisioning and creating just, truthful, and peaceful societies.*"[11] For Amos Yong, such "congregational hospitality involves at least the following elements: a visible and welcoming public face, a dialogical posture, and a commitment to public servanthood. These are minimal aspects of a congregational ministry oriented towards welcoming, including, and reconciling strangers."[12] Such are the challenges that a number of local faith communities are beginning to face as asylum seekers come amongst them.

More broadly, the resurgence of Christianity in such regions as the Asia-Pacific region, especially South Korea, Latin America, and sub-Saharan Africa, coupled with the decline of Christianity in the West and the increasing threat of Islamic religious fundamentalism, have radically transformed the worldwide Christian landscape. It is not easy trying to forecast the impact that these global trends might have on local church life. Perhaps one of the greatest changes will be in the area of mission, where the ideal trajectory is "not in a straight line *away* from the 'sending' church *to* some faraway unreached 'mission field,' but rather curving back to it throughout."[13] This is what Saayman calls the "boomerang effect" of Christian mission, in which local churches can never be the same again if they are willing to open their congregational life to influences from the whole of which they are a part: "For too long Christians . . . have conceived of the missionary journey only as a linear progression from 'here' to 'there'—Jerusalem, Samaria, the ends of the earth."[14] If, at one level, "glocalization" has to do with the impact of the global on the local, then this linear paradigm of mission needs to be replaced with one that acknowledges the contribution that those in the "majority world" can offer to the local church setting, sometimes in dramatic and spectacular ways. In the United States, a pastor in Michigan made a number of visits to Africa, bringing a number of Ugandans back to his city to help them establish their deliverance ministry. An invitation by another pastor to lay church leaders in Ghana has led to them setting up a similar ministry in Ghanaian Presbyterian churches in the Bronx. American film-maker James Ault, who recently produced a two-DVD set of films

---

11. Volf, *Exclusion and Embrace*, 21. See chapter 11 for a fuller discussion of Volf's notion of "social agents" and the "will to embrace."

12. Yong, *Hospitality and the Other*, 134.

13. Saayman, "Missionary by its Very Nature."

14. Saayman, "Subversive Subservience."

on Christianity in Ghana and Zimbabwe called *African Christianity Rising*, claims that the force of the explosion of Christianity in Africa "will be felt throughout the world and in American society through our immigrant communities and through their relationships with churches of the African diaspora, which would include African-American, West Indian, and Puerto Rican. It will connect with Pentecostalism and with folk religion, including fundamentalism, that sees the spirit world as very active in material life."[15]

Symbiotic Relationship

Indeed, as Oscar García-Johnson points out, "immigrant communities are now carriers of the leading energy for missions and religious transformation."[16] Echoing Saayman's "boomerang effect," a number of immigrant faith-communities have become vessels of renewal, "bouncing back to the Global North" as catalysts of evangelism and church planting, agents of cultural, social, and economic adaptation between immigrants and the majority society, strategic partners in societal development, and leaders of grassroots movements in advocacy and justice. García-Johnson discerns in this trend the dialectics necessary for the sustenance of Christian faith, embodying what Vásquez and Marquardt call a parasitic relationship in which "popular religion and religious institutions are engaged in a complex, if asymmetrical, interplay that leads to innovation, ambiguity, and heterogeneity."[17] This symbiotic relationship between the institutional and the non-institutional offers an opportunity for the home church to function as a stable local space for transnational Christians who simultaneously desire to remain connected to their native culture. At the same time this hybrid ecclesiology offers a renewal of life and energy for the whole congregation, such that Christ is experienced in the midst of the plurality of cultures, and where worship, evangelism, preaching, and mission require "multiple levels of cultural sensitivity and theologizing."[18] These, for García-Johnson, are the marks of a truly glocal church, where local practices are exercised in a global way.

---

15. Interview in Sheahen, "How Africa's Churches are Changing Christianity."
16. García-Johnson, "Mission within Hybrid Cultures," 119.
17. Vásquez and Marquardt, *Globalizing the Sacred*, 10.
18. García-Johnson, "Mission within Hybrid Cultures," 120.

Porous borders have led to an increase in the number of multiethnic communities in many other parts of the world. In their research on "hidden solidarities" in British society, Spencer and Pahl note that immigrants from different backgrounds and cultures enter a myriad micro-social worlds, each with their own histories, values, and priorities. Critiquing those who interpret contemporary social life as fragmented and individualized, with family life, civic engagement, and communal values on the point of collapse, they argue from their studies that community is in fact alive and well in modern Britain, in which the notions of friendship, altruism, and reciprocity are still very much in evidence.[19] Claiming that Britain is a "community of communities"—and the same might be said of other countries today where multiculturalism is a growing feature of the social landscape—Ray Pahl observes that "a Lithuanian migrant working in Aberdeen will have a very different experience of the host society from a newly arrived Bangladeshi in Tower Hamlets, a Pakistani in Bradford or a Turk in Stoke Newington. The immigrant taxi driver in Newport who much prefers the 'atmosphere' there to working in Cardiff is recognizing the practical significance of local variations."[20]

Paralleling these local variations is the diversity implicit in the multiethnic, multicultural fabric that now stretches across many parts of the world, given expression in local settings where different ethnic groups congregate, more often than not in distinctive social groups. The rich tapestry of *multiculturalism* afforded here, characterized by a mosaic of cultures coexisting side by side, has its polar opposite in *assimilation* in which immigrant minorities, instead of remaining apart, blend seamlessly into the host culture, so that citizenship, language and even identity are shaped and determined by their country of adoption. *Interculturalism* is a compromise between multiculturalism and assimilation, lying midway between these two ends of the spectrum and "may include the use of integration policies and efforts to water down excessive distinctiveness or segregation, for example in urban concentrations of minority groups. It is sympathetic towards people from immigrant families perceiving themselves as having a hybrid identity, who feel Anglo-Indian, or French-Algerian or German-Turkish for example."[21]

---

19. Spencer and Pahl, *Rethinking Friendship*.
20. Pahl, "Hidden Solidarities," para. 3.
21. Emerson, *Interculturalism*, 3.

Whilst a number of factors—notably the emergence of radical Islam minorities in several European countries—have led in some quarters to the verdict that the multicultural project has failed, it is generally recognized that some form of intercultural integration is necessary if we are to live at ease with one another within complex local multiethnic communities. Of course, the process of adaptation is two-way. Lung-kwong Lo points out that when we encounter different cultures and ethnic communities, "there are tendencies for these communities, on the one hand, to absorb influences that naturally fit and enrich their lives. On the other hand, the communities tend to resist those things that are alien to them, and they often compartmentalize things that can be enjoyed and celebrated as different. It is by such differences that the identities and values of individuals and communities are embodied."[22]

Systems Thinking

Soong-Chan Rah is a professor of evangelism and church growth in Chicago who founded a multiethnic, urban church focused on living out the values of racial reconciliation and social justice in their neighborhood. He laments the captivity of the church to Western cultural trappings: "Too often, ethnic minorities are asked to put aside their discomfort to come and sit at the white table. The rules of the table have already been set and there's not a whole lot of room, but come and sit at *our* table. We won't change the way we interact with one another and we still need to maintain the white majority, but it still would be nice to have an Asian face or a black face sit at *our* table."[23] He argues the case for "cultural intelligence" in those situations that are characterized by multiethnic diversity: each local context demands an awareness of the different ways that unfamiliar cultures function so that church members do not respond in a negative or indifferent knee-jerk fashion to the new realities facing them. This implies a willingness to examine our own values, presuppositions, and prejudices in order to detect any cross-cultural insensitivities that might lie under the surface. In particular, suggests Rah, we need to shift from a linear thinking style to a more holistic systems thinking approach in multiethnic ministry, grounded in a willingness to learn from others whose lives are shaped by influences and cultural backgrounds very dif-

---

22. Lo, "Paul and Ethnicity," 184–85
23. Rah, *The Next Evangelicalism*, 121, author's italics.

ferent from our own. So the local cannot be insulated from the realities of the global environment.

But so too can the global be shaped by what happens at the local level. In 1961 Edward Lorenz, Professor of Meteorology at Massachusetts Institute of Technology, accidentally discovered the so-called "butterfly effect" in his computer simulations of weather patterns whilst seeking a shortcut in his programming.[24] The phenomenon, technically known as "sensitive dependence on initial conditions," has been popularized in the phrase, "the flap of a butterfly's wings in Brazil can set off a tornado in Texas" and it ultimately gave rise to the sciences of chaos and complexity, competitors to the predictable ordered linearity assumed in scientific activities. Whilst the location of the butterfly, the consequences, and the location of the consequences have varied according to who tells the story, the point is clear enough in the context of the present discussion: what we do at the local level can have a significant influence on the global picture. Or, in van Engen's words, "A glocal perspective of the universe recognizes that the smallest stone thrown into a pond causes ripples that shake the earth."[25]

In an interview in *Christianity Today*, Bob Roberts, the lead pastor of a church in Texas out of which over a hundred other churches have been planted, shared about his vision of glocal churches, based upon the premise that "the main players in overseas kingdom work are not trained cross-cultural missionaries or NGO professionals, but laypeople who take their current expertise (whether it be teaching, plumbing, electronics, or so forth) and use it to serve people in other nations."[26] However, this interpretation of "glocal," whilst challenging a model of mission predicated on those who have been specifically trained to engage in intercultural ministry in the mission-field, still has a strong "missionary" ring to it. In fact, Roberts views congregational members as an army of missionaries sitting in the pews who need to be mobilized. Thus those who have specific talents and time to offer are encouraged to move beyond the physical borders of their own comfort zones and serve in far-flung corners of the globe under the guidance of the Holy Spirit. This, for Roberts, is what discipleship—or "T-Life": transformed life—is all about, and this is what

---

24. For a compelling account of Lorenz's discovery, see Gleick, *Chaos*, 11–31.
25. Van Engen, "The Glocal Church," 159.
26. Interview in Galli, "Glocal Church Ministry," para. 3.

he writes about in two recent books on the topic.[27] But precisely because of its lack of distinctiveness—though evidently transformative, Roberts' "glocalization" paradigm is not as revolutionary as it might seem at first blush—it is perhaps not the most appropriate way to interpret glocalization in terms of the impact of the local on the global.

Globalization from Below

In a book on community development subtitled "Community-based Alternatives in an Age of Globalization," Frank Tesoriero suggests that glocalization is really the process of "globalization from below." Typically the effects of globalization, as a social, political, and economic reality, have been in a top-down direction, some good but many not so good. He acknowledges the inevitability of this process, but laments that "its emphasis on economics at the expense of social and environmental issues means that it does not take account of many things that directly affect the lives of people and communities."[28] Accordingly, globalization from below "seeks to implement a form of globalisation that is democratic and participatory, which is about issues of direct concern to people—including economic sustainability, social justice, and human rights—and which seeks to empower rather than disempower local communities."[29] There are some obvious ways in which this goal might be achieved, such as buying products that benefit skilled craftspeople from some of the world's poorest communities, engaging in improved recycling practices that help to save rainforests, buying fair trade coffee and clothing, and supporting micro financing enterprises that assist the poor to become self-sufficient. These are all bottom-up actions that have a global impact, and they represent areas that many local churches can actively promote as they seek to model responsible global citizenship: thinking globally and acting locally.

The notion of global citizenship means that Christians cease to be parochial in their outlook, and make every effort to understand the times in which they live (1 Chr 12:32). In the same way that an awareness of other cultures enables the local church to respond sympathetically and sensitively to different ethnic groups on their doorstep, so does

---

27. Roberts, *Transformation*; Roberts, *Glocalization*.
28. Tesoriero, *Community Development*, 183.
29. Ibid., 183.

an awareness of the international and global environment—economic, political, social, religious, and spiritual—help to shape and give meaning to how the local church might function as an agent of transformation beyond its own localized setting. It reflects a paradigm that "seeks to perceive the world through the lens of the simultaneous interaction, the interweaving influences, the dynamic, always changing, multidimensional interrelatedness of the global and the local."[30]

This bottom-up way of looking at globalization has implications too for how we do theology. Theology is not an enterprise that happens outside particular contexts. The Catholic theologian Neil Darragh argues that ministry engagement demands that we seek a balance between implicit and explicit theology.[31] "Implicit theology" is the dogma, the theological understanding we inherit, perhaps unconsciously, as we journey through life and ministry. Much of this may not be very carefully thought through—hence the importance of making explicit the beliefs to which we adhere, so opening them to correction, revision, or affirmation. Exposure to different cultural interpretation of texts will necessarily challenge the way we think about our own received interpretation, thus offering new insights that may lead to a different theological perspective. Exercises in contextual theology are not so much a matter of adaptation as about wrestling with "fundamental differences of perspective, divergent ways of conceiving what the gospel is about."[32] David Augsburger illustrates this with reference to a group made up of Africans and Western missionaries who were asked to identify the main point of the story of Joseph in the Old Testament: the Africans interpreted the narrative as a model of tribal identity, of a young man who never forgot his family; the Westerners saw Joseph as an individual whose example of faithfulness to God represents a model of personal strength.[33] Augsburger comments that whilst both meanings are legitimate, we need to acknowledge both in order to establish a responsibly inclusive theology, rather than a neutral theology (which is actually a "homeless theology"): "The beginning point for pastoral theology must be both local—with a particular case, person, instance—and universal—with all humankind, human culture,

---

30. Van Engen, "The Glocal Church," 159.
31. Darragh, "Theology from Elsewhere."
32. Mudge and Poling, *Formation and Reflection*, xx–xxi.
33. Augsburger, *Pastoral Counseling*, 81–82.

and human history. Awareness of both the universal and the particular offers a constant corrective and directive to creative theologizing."[34]

Understandably, the creative revisioning of theology suggested here may be perceived by some as a threat to orthodoxy, and whilst it has the potential to lead to spurious hermeneutics, it nonetheless represents a journey that we need to make if we are to be faithful to the spirit of glocalization. *Theologia viatorum*—doing theology "on the way"—must never be understood as an enterprise that seeks to impose one theology "from above" on all others. Rather, it seeks to draw from the insights of those whose interpretive lens may be very different from our own, especially if they come from different cultural contexts. To be contextual requires a methodological rather than a theological modification, requiring us to seek new truths even at the expense of previously held understandings. This methodological transformation is central to an understanding of ministry as *praxis* in its shift away from a propositional, dogmatic approach to one that has its roots in a willingness to learn from others. Instead of telling others, we listen to them. Christian ministry therefore demands a willingness to engage in paradigm shifts in order to creatively interact with people whose perceptions of reality may be very different from our own. The missionary theologian Vincent Donovan quotes some advice given to him by a young person in an American university: "In working with young people in America, do not try to call them back to where they were, and do not try to call them to where you are, as beautiful as that place might seem to you. You must have the courage to go with them to a place that neither you nor they have ever been before."[35]

God-in-Context

The "glocalization" concept reminds us that God is a God-in-context, who lives and moves amongst his people, whose story is not a story in isolation, but one that interacts with every human story across the globe. There are many advantages in starting with the local context as we "do theology": we are required to listen in a way that helps us to truly understand what is going on in a particular setting. Rather than taking the gospel and trying to work it into the context, it may be far more fruitful to start with the context and work backwards from that to the gospel, and

---

34. Ibid., 73.
35. Donovan, *Christianity Rediscovered*, vii.

then ask: what has the gospel to say in this situation or that set of circumstances? Such an approach is not to argue for a model of ministry that permits the context to set the agenda for the Christian church: as van Engen points out, "the atomization of a plurality of local theologies violates the oneness of the church, the unity of the Holy Spirit, the singularity of the gospel, and the unity of all Christians who read the same Bible."[36] The challenge facing all who engage in intercultural ministry is to enter into the interweaving social, political, and economic currents that flow between the global and the local without falling into either cultural naïvety or dogmatic fundamentalism, and without losing the prophetic cutting-edge that can so easily be blunted by a concentration on the particular at the expense of the unifying centre of Christ.

An Indian evangelist once said: "Do not bring us the gospel as a potted plant. Bring us the seed of the gospel, and plant it in our soil." Charles Kraft recounts his experience as a field missionary in northern Nigeria: he was frequently jolted by the perspectives of his Nigerian brethren, whose language and culture continually challenged his own way of seeing and doing things. Gradually he became aware that his growing attempt to "integrate my anthropological understandings with my theological understandings was opening my mind to the probability that God wanted to lead the Nigerians in their attempts to be faithful to Christ in a way different from the way he wanted to lead me and my people."[37] Theology should be "an ever-renewed re-interpretation to the new generations and peoples of the given Gospel, a re-presentation of the will and the way of the one Christ in a dialogue with new thought-forms and culture patterns."[38] Bruce Olson tells of a fascinating encounter with two warriors of the Motilone Indian tribe in Colombia, amongst whom he was working as a missionary.[39] The Motilones were a feared tribe, hostile to outsiders, but Olson befriended them and lived amongst them. By respecting their culture, and accepting their legends and understanding of life, he discovered that God was willing to work through the prophecy of a Motilone shaman in order to reveal Christ to these Indians. This remarkable event is characteristic of the unpredictable and surprising Spirit, who is ever at work in the cultures of the world to make Christ known. However,

36. Van Engen, "The Glocal Church," 174.
37. Kraft, *Christianity in Culture*, 8.
38. Sundkler, *Christian Ministry in Africa*, 211.
39. Olson, *Bruchko*.

the possibility of a diminution of the Christian message is never far away. In certain liberation-theology contexts, for example, the exodus tradition focusing on Moses has become more important than the story of Jesus. Robert Schreiter traces the rise of many independent churches in Africa and observes that "their grasp on traditional Christianity seems to have been lost."[40] In some regions of Africa, for example, older independent churches in the rural areas practise polygamy, citing its presence in the Old Testament. Reformers think the church should be tolerant of men who took several wives before they converted to Christianity and now feel committed to them. Others, however, vow that no amount of "enculturation"—faith taking root in a new culture—should permit the church to bend on the issue. An even more extreme example of enculturation permits the incorporation of tribal religions into African Christianity.

Where should the line be drawn? This is the constant challenge facing all who are committed to incarnational ministry in a pluralist and ethnically diverse world. As have we have already seen, cross-cultural ministry is not restricted to overseas activity: ethnicity and multiculturalism are domestic realities in many nations today, demanding sensitivity to world views that are frequently ignored in the practice of Christian ministry. In the great cities of the world, many different philosophies of life jostle with each other in a rich mixture of human experience and endeavor. It is precisely because authentic Christian ministry is incarnational, directed towards individuals and people-groups whose perceptions of reality and belief systems are very different from our own, that we must allow the new insights stimulated by the dynamic dialectic of glocalization—both global and local—to inform the way we do ministry today.

---

40. Schreiter, *Constructing Local Theologies*, 102.

14

"Now I know in part, then I shall know fully"
–The Apostle Paul

A New Song to Sing

In *Celebrating Life*, I wrote that the task of the church is not just about being relevant, learning to speak the language of the culture, but more critically about being prophetic in its redemptive presence in the world.[1] The danger of identifying passionately with the political struggle for liberation or of immersing ourselves in the diverse cultural contexts that surround us is, as we saw in chapter 10, that of assimilation. We become so like those around us that we cannot speak prophetically into their lives. When we see that beginning to happen, we need to take fresh stock of our lives and re-orient ourselves within the creative tension of the "now" and "not yet" of the kingdom of God: we acknowledge that though there is much that is good and wholesome in the world, there is also much that is corrupt and corrupting. The duality between light and darkness will not go away until that day when the old order of things has passed away, when "every tear is wiped from our eyes," and when there will be "no more death or mourning or crying or pain" (Rev 21:4). But until that day, we celebrate the truth that God has not deserted his world.

In the midst of the suffering, injustice, and evil that pervade this present world, it is perhaps understandable that some may opt for what

---

1. Buxton, *Celebrating Life*, 195.

Miroslav Volf calls a "thinned-out" or "idle" faith, rather than a prophetic faith. Faith becomes idle, he suggests, when in our fragility and shortcomings we succumb to the lure of temptation, the subtle power of systems to control our lives—such as the financial market or a military unit—or a misinterpretation of faith as simply a crutch, a "soothing opiate." Faith's work, he writes, "may get restricted to a narrow sphere—to the life of the soul, to private morality, to family matters, or to church life. As a result, faith becomes idle in important domains in which it, as a prophetic faith, should be active."[2] And faith's action—its energy and vibrancy—is most powerfully and truly expressed when it is applied to our daily lives, giving us meaning and purpose within the larger story of God's involvement in and with his creation. Because of all that God has done for us in Christ, each of us has a new song to sing, the song of the redeemed, but we do not sing as those who have no part of the life of the world. "Praying in the Spirit and interest in life drive one another on,"[3] writes Jürgen Moltmann, and it is this ongoing tension between prayer and meditation, on the one hand, and solidarity with the imperfections and brokenness of this world, on the other, that marks our call to live life in the overlap between heaven and earth.

The Eschatological "Not Yet"

In his outstanding theological exploration of Christian eschatology, *Theology of Hope*, Moltmann asks the question: does hope cheat man of the happiness of the present? Challenging the view that memories of the past and hopes for the future cause us to pass over the happiness of the present so that we are *never wholly in the present*, he points to the promises of God—or perhaps we should say the God of promise?—who "calls into being the things that are not" (Rom 4:17). When we stake our hope on the *creator ex nihilo* it "becomes the happiness of the present when it loyally embraces all things in love, abandoning nothing to annihilation but bringing to light how open all things are to the possibilities in which they can live and shall live."[4]

Recalling our discussion in chapter 3 of Moltmann's distinction between *futurum* (which emphasizes that which arises out of the present)

---

2. Volf, *A Public Faith*, 14.
3. Moltmann, *Church in Power of Spirit*, 284.
4. Moltmann, *Theology of Hope*, 32.

and *adventus* (which has to do with that which comes into the present out of the future), we should be mindful that the two ideas, though distinct, are not to be pulled apart as if they have nothing to do with each other. The ultimate new thing of God's promise—*novum ultimum*—can never *issue* from the old precisely because it is predicated on the radical, astonishing, and transforming new thing that God has done in Christ. However, God's new creation is not discontinuous with the old: indeed, it "does not annihilate the old but gathers it up and creates it anew.... The *creatio nova* is therefore the new creation of this one, the creation which is perishing from sin and injustice."[5] The new is recognizable in that it has some similarity to that which has gone before, but it contains more, something richer and deeper and more meaningful. This continuity in the midst of discontinuity speaks to us of the God who is faithful to his creation, from *creatio originalis* to *creatio nova*.

C. S. Lewis expresses this continuity quite marvelously in the closing pages of *The Last Battle*, the final book in his *Chronicles of Narnia*. The Pevensie children have just arrived in the new Narnia, and the Lord Digory—who is introduced in *The Magician's Nephew*, the first book in the chronology of Narnia—consoles Lucy, who is struggling with the difference all around her: "You need not mourn over Narnia, Lucy. All of the old Narnia that mattered, all the dear creatures, have been drawn into the real Narnia through the Door. And of course it is different; as different as a real thing is from a shadow or as waking life is from a dream."[6] Lewis continues:

> It is as hard to explain how this sunlit land was different from the old Narnia as it would be to tell you how the fruits of that country taste. Perhaps you will get some idea of it if you think like this. You may have been in a room in which there was a window that looked out on a lovely bay of the sea or a green valley that wound away among mountains. And in the wall of that room opposite to the window there may have been a looking-glass. And as you turned away from the window you suddenly caught sight of that sea or that valley, all over again, in the looking glass. And the sea in the mirror, or the valley in the mirror, were in one sense just the same as the real ones: yet at the same time they were somehow different—deeper, more wonderful, more like places in a story: in a story you have never

---

5. Moltmann, *Coming of God*, 29.
6. Lewis, *Last Battle*, 195.

heard but very much want to know. The difference between the old Narnia and the new Narnia was like that. The new one was a deeper country: every rock and flower and blade of grass looked as if it meant more.[7]

But not only is the "now" continuous in a time-forward direction with the "not yet": the eschatological "not yet" illuminates the present because it has to do not just with ultimate reality, but with what the philosopher Ingolf Dalferth calls "the fundamental normative orientation of our *present life* in terms of its final end and ultimate points of reference."[8] It is therefore more appropriate to define eschatology as that which expresses the *goal* of all creation, human and physical, rather than specific, identifiable last things in a chronological sense: death, judgment, heaven, and hell. And so, with "the raising of Christ from the dead, the future of the new creation sheds its lustre into the present of the old world, and in 'the sufferings of this present time' kindles hope for new life."[9] As noted in chapter 10, our calling as Christians is to live redemptively *in* the world because we are looking forward to experiencing it in all its glorious fullness in the new creation of God's promise.

Ethic of Risk

How then can Christian churches effectively make their mark in the world, speaking prophetically into the public arena, whilst at the same time pointing towards a future hope founded in the ultimate purposes of God? Let me offer in this final chapter a compelling vision for Christian life, grounded in a spirituality of hope that finds expression in local communities of faith proclaiming the gospel of Christ crucified and working for peace and justice, seeking to make a genuine difference in the lives of others *because they delight in them as those with whom they share a common humanity*. Sharon Welch is a philosopher and theologian who acknowledges the difficulties of trying to achieve one's aspirations for "the good life" for those whose lives are lived on the margins: "It is easier to give up on long-term social change when one is comfortable in the present—when it is possible to have challenging work, excellent health care and housing, and access to fine arts. When the good life is

---

7. Ibid., 195-96.
8. Dalferth, "Eschatological Roots," 157, my italics.
9. Moltmann, *Coming of God*, 28.

present or within reach, it is tempting to despair of its ever being in reach for others and resort merely to enjoying it for oneself and one's family."[10] This tendency towards numbness in our response to the plight of others resonates with Volf's "idle faith," and leads Welch to propose an "ethic of risk" that finds its source in the hopes and memories embedded in community life, evocative of the Appreciative Inquiry process discussed in earlier chapters of this book. Her ideas are based on the recognition that we are rarely able to achieve what we would like, and so we need to focus on possibilities rather than outcomes, embracing risk rather than the certainty of success. This, she suggests, is more likely to happen when love for individuals is our primary motivation, rather than engaging in idealized programs of social change. And for that we need one another.

Welch's focus on community life is, I suggest, important in sustaining a Christian vision of hope for others, especially in the light of the mainstream church's drift to the margins of social life, particularly evident in the Western world. This is not to counsel giving up on institutional church structures, and opting for Moravian-style *ecclesiolae in ecclesia*—"little churches within the church"—as the only form of church life. I suggested in chapter 6 that there is a place for some form of overarching structure in order to ensure that the historic "good deposit" of the gospel is not diluted or corrupted in the understandable desire to communicate the Christian faith in a world of swirling change and desperate need. Furthermore, if they are open to *semper reformanda*, mainstream denominational structures have both the capacity and the authority to safeguard against any potential drift towards heresy or manipulative leadership within small self-contained *ecclesiolae*.

If the spread of Christianity—or any other religion, for that matter—has more to do with the local than the corporate, resulting from the witness of those on the ground rather than from the pronouncements of those who occupy positions of power and influence in society, then local communities of faith daring to live lovingly and riskily—generously giving and forgiving as the Spirit enables—will offer the hope that the world truly needs, a hope that is grounded in the gospel of Jesus Christ. Challenging the assumption that the church should exert its influence from the centres of power, Volf reminds us that the early Christian communities, persecuted and on the margins, were "at most a bit of a thorn in

---

10. Welch, *Feminist Ethic of Risk*, 15.

society's flesh"[11] as they celebrated hope in God and proclaimed joyfully the resurrected Lord. It is unrealistic, he claims, for the contemporary church to bewail its lack of influence and attempt to wield power from the centre rather than from the margins. Andrew Brown, a religion writer for the UK newspaper *The Guardian*, suggests in a recent blog that the Church of England is already disestablished in all the ways that really matter. His solution? "What the Church of England needs to do is to re-establish itself in the ordinary life of the country. Its instinct is obviously to do this with grand gestures, speeches, proclamations, and debates, but this is entirely wrong. Instead of pretending it is a single coherent entity with clearly defined opinions and policies—something which simply isn't true and never will be—it should just forget about the national level and get on with things locally."[12] What matters, he claims, is not doctrine but how faith plays out in everyday life in the local communities in which we are placed.

In sympathizing with Brown's thesis, I do not want to suggest that doctrine is unimportant—in fact, throughout this book we have been addressing a range of Christian doctrinal positions, such as the doctrines of the Trinity, incarnation, and atonement, and demonstrated their contribution to an understanding of the Christian faith. But doctrinal *beliefs* need to be set alongside the most fundamental and central faith statement in Christianity, which is centred on a *person*: "For I resolved to know nothing while I was with you except Jesus Christ and him crucified" (1 Cor 2:2). The apostle Paul was captivated not by a set of doctrines, but by Jesus Christ. This is the faith position that pastor and theologian Greg Boyd espouses in his book *Benefit of the Doubt*, fittingly sub-titled *The Idol of Certainty*. He argues that "in sharp contrast to certainty-seeking faith, the kind of faith that Scripture encourages us to embrace is a faith that invites us to boldly raise questions, to honestly embrace ambiguity, and to fearlessly entertain doubt,"[13] a journey that he shares candidly with the reader. This is what I have attempted to do in a modest way in each chapter of this book, offering snapshots as we journey on a road that offers the promise of a richer and more rewarding awareness of the contours of Christian belief and practice.

---

11. Volf, *A Public Faith*, 78.
12. Brown, "Church of England," para. 4.
13. Boyd, *Benefit of the Doubt*, 72.

Seeking Truth

As stated in chapter 1, the underlying premise sustained throughout this book is that many pastors—like Greg Boyd—are tired of simplistic certainties, often associated with formulae for church growth, and narrow, dualistic "either-or" thinking; what they are looking for, and what they need, is permission to live with uncertainty, with mystery, ambiguity, and paradox. However, I have also sustained the unwavering thesis that there is a centre to hold fast to, a conviction to affirm, even as we acknowledge a boundary that is necessarily uncertain . . . and that centre is Jesus Christ. In resisting claims to knee-jerk denominational allegiance and mechanically-recited doctrinal "certainties," and holding fast to the truth of Christ crucified, perhaps more important than *claiming* truth in our personal faith journey is *seeking* truth. As Volf points out, we do in fact need boundaries to establish our discrete Christian identity, but they should be permeable: so we do well to listen to the voices of other truth-seekers, even from within other religious traditions. The upshot of this is that "encounters with others don't serve only to assert our position and claim our territory; they are also occasions to learn and to teach, to be enriched and to enrich, to come to new agreements and maybe reinforce the old ones, and to dream up new possibilities and explore new paths."[14]

So, in the midst of uncertainty we hold fast to the certainty of Christ, in whose steps we are called to follow as witnesses to his goodness, grace, and forgiveness: hence the title of this book. Towards the end of his first epistle to the Christians at Corinth Paul acknowledges the limitations of our understanding: "Now I know in part; then I shall know fully, even as I am fully known" (1 Cor 13:12). As Christians, we are citizens of both this world and the next: we live life in the overlap between this age and the age to come, and they make sense only if we see them as belonging together. And, as we have already noted, God has committed himself to putting everything to rights again, not by demolishing physical creation, but by renewing it in his promised new creation. His redeeming grace is at work throughout history bringing this future about, and one way in which we might understand this happening today has to do with Tom Wright's four "voices" that echo in the human subconscious: "the longing for justice, the quest for spirituality, the hunger for relationships, and the delight in beauty."[15]

---

14. Volf, *A Public Faith*, 133.
15. Wright, *Simply Christian*, x.

"Now I know in part, then I shall know fully" 215

Actually, argues Wright, these four voices point us towards God because they have their source in him: they are expressions of the one voice which alone can lead us out of the multiple alienations and frustrations of human existence into an authentic and specifically Christian way of life. When we respond to these echoes, however faint they may be, we are opening ourselves to the activity and energy of the Spirit of grace who knows no boundaries in reaching and restoring broken humanity. This is what grace means—it is the unmeasured and unmeasurable goodness of God who takes the initiative in putting everything right again. That is our true Christian hope, and those who name Christ as Lord are privileged to participate in the gracious work of the Spirit who is ever at work doing just that—putting everything to right again. Taking an eschatological perspective, Wright suggests that these four "voices," which have to do with justice, spirituality, relationships, and beauty, may actually help us to glimpse the glorious possibilities of the new creation opened up to us in Christ. Perhaps, then, we might interpret these voices as "echoes of the Spirit," whose inclusive love for all people compels him to participate in every field of human endeavor precisely because they are "highways into the centre of a reality which cannot be glimpsed, let alone grasped, any other way."[16]

> Perhaps art can help us to look beyond the immediate beauty with all its puzzles, and to glimpse that new creation which makes sense not only of beauty but of the world as a whole, and ourselves within it. Perhaps.
> The artist can then join forces with those who work for justice and those who struggle for redemptive relationships, and together encourage and sustain those who are reaching out for a genuine, redemptive spirituality.[17]

This vision of God's future, a future in which all people are invited to participate in the final divine self-glorification, is the substance of Christian hope. It is a vision that demands imagination in the face of mystery, for none of us in our finitude can fully grasp all that God has prepared for his beloved creation. At the beginning of this book, I suggested that this implies paying attention to "what is" in a way that takes us beyond observation and into *participation*, an "abduction"—to use Daniel Hardy's term—that is grounded in a generous and humble appreciation

---

16. Ibid., 235.
17. Ibid., 236.

of what we *don't* know as much as what we do know. Accordingly, we have reflected in these pages on the mystery that surrounds the eschatological vision, the fundamentally ineffable *presence* that lies beyond human experience. But a mystery, in all its ambiguity and paradox, that we now know in part . . . but will one day know fully in all its beauty and glory. And so in the strength and wisdom of the Spirit, and with all the passion and love we can muster—continuing to work out our salvation with fear and trembling, for it is God who works in us to will and to act according to his good purpose (Phil 2:12-13)—we take that which we have been given by God and plant it in the soil in which we ourselves have been placed. And we also, as in the words of the "Romero Prayer" cited at the very beginning of this book, "water seeds already planted, knowing that they hold future promise."

Compelling Vision

This demands both imagination and faith, for we are those who have received seeds to plant and water, and we often lack the faith to believe that they will turn into fully-grown trees in which many birds will find a home (Matt 13:31-32). But, as Eleazer Fernandez points out, though our seeds may be small, "in the seed there is a promise, which is often, as the lines of a hymn express it, 'unrevealed until its season, something God alone can see.'"[18] As communities of faith and "citizens of the new tomorrow," we are privileged to nurture these seeds in hope until they burst forth with the full and generous life of God, a God who is patiently "waiting for his image, his echo, his response in us."[19] This is the eschatological vision of humanity, which is at the same time a cosmic vision for all creation, that David Bentley Hart presents to us when he writes of "the advent within history of the possibility of a new, Christlike self, the form of one's true self, *for which one was created and toward which one stretches out*, the proper 'essence' that one has never yet possessed."[20] For Hart, this essence of human being—perhaps we should say human "becoming"—embraces the particular and celebrates difference, so that true reconciliation is ultimately true *justice* in which "the other will always be

---

18. Fernandez, *Burning Center, Porous Borders*, 349.
19. Moltmann, *Source of Life*, 41.
20. Hart, *Beauty of the Infinite*, 398, my italics.

blessed with an infinite regard and charged with an infinite worth."[21] In this ultimate realization of the "not yet" kingdom of God, no one voice will dominate: all will contribute to a Spirit-inspired polyphony, a harmony of multiple voices all contributing to Hart's "beauty of the infinite," when God will be "all in all." Indeed, the summons to emulate the generous and hospitable inclusiveness of the Trinity, whose embrace leaves no one out, is precisely why we need communities of faith who are willing to live vulnerable, risky lives, embracing those who are different from us, welcoming strangers, and blessing even those who are our enemies. This is not something we can do alone—we need one another.

In an intriguing exploration of the musical term *polyphony*—which technically refers to multiple tones and sequences played simultaneously, overlapping each other in such a way that no one note is so dominant that it renders another mute—David Cunningham links the concept to trinitarian theology, suggesting that "Christianity proclaims a polyphonic understanding of God—one in which *difference* provides an alternative to a monolithic homogeneity, yet without becoming a source of confusion. Attention to any one of the Three does not imply a diminished role for the others; all three have their distinctive melodies, and all are 'played' and 'heard' simultaneously without damage to God's unity."[22] For Cunningham, "the communion that informs and underwrites our common bond of humanity" is an expression of "the perfect, polyphonic communion of the inner life of God."[23]

It is this compelling vision of seeing all things finally united within the inner life of God for which we labor in Christian ministry, living out our lives in the public space as we participate as grace-filled faith communities in God's immeasurably loving and healing work in the world. We glimpse it surely but dimly through the eyes of faith, *surely* because our hope is built on nothing less than the crucified and resurrected Christ in whom our common bond of humanity is perfected, but *dimly* because in our finitude we cannot yet see the fullness of all that God has purposed and in our weakness and sinfulness we are too easily consumed by trivial hopes rather than the hope of the gospel. As those who confess the Christian faith, we claim with faith's certainty the sure and certain hope of the resurrection to eternal life, confident that there will come

---

21. Ibid., 411.
22. Cunningham, *These Three Are One*, 129, author's italics.
23. Ibid., 164.

a day when "every tear is wiped from our eyes," when there will be "no more death or mourning or crying or pain" (Rev 21:4). But until that day, we do well to confess faith's uncertainties in the midst of life's ambiguities and contradictions, acknowledging that "there must always be a prominent element of modesty, or even tentativeness and hesitancy, in what we profess concerning the knowledge of God."[24]

---

24. Hall, *What Christianity Is Not*, 12.

Bibliography

Abrams, M. H. *The Mirror and the Lamp: Romantic Theory and the Critical Tradition.* New York: Oxford University Press, 1953.
Alexander, Denis. *Creation or Evolution: Do We Have to Choose?* Oxford: Monarch, 2008.
Anderson, Ray Sherman. *Minding God's Business.* Grand Rapids: Eerdmans, 1986.
———. *The Soul of Ministry: Forming Leaders for God's People.* Louisville, KY: Westminster John Knox, 1997.
———. *Theological Foundations for Ministry: Selected Readings for a Theology of the Church in Ministry.* Edinburgh: T. & T. Clark, 1979.
Armstrong, Karen. *The Case for God: What Religion Really Means.* London: Bodley Head, 2009.
Astley, Jeff. *Ordinary Theology: Looking, Listening, and Learning in Theology.* Aldershot, UK: Ashgate, 2002.
Astley, Jeff, and Leslie J. Francis. *Exploring Ordinary Theology: Everyday Christian Believing and the Church.* Farnham, UK: Ashgate, 2013.
Athanasius. *On the Incarnation: The Treatise De Incarnatione Verbi Dei.* Crestwood, NY: St. Vladimir's Seminary, 1993.
———. "Select Works and Letters: Introductory to Texts from the Gospels on the Incarnation." *Christian Classics Ethereal Library*, 1031–42. Online: http://www.ccel.org/ccel/schaff/npnf204.pdf.
Augsburger, David W. *Pastoral Counseling across Cultures.* Philadelphia: Westminster, 1986.
Augustine. *The Works of Saint Augustine: A Translation for the 21st Century.* Translated by Edmund Hill. Brooklyn, NY: New City, 1990.
Bacon, Francis. *The New Atlantis.* Minneapolis: Filiquarian, 2007.
Balthasar, Hans Urs von. *Dare We Hope "That All Men Be Saved"? With a Short Discourse on Hell.* San Francisco: Ignatius, 1988.
Bancewicz, Ruth. *Test of Faith: Spiritual Journeys with Scientists.* Eugene, OR: Wipf & Stock, 2010.
Banks, Robert J. *Paul's Idea of Community.* Surry Hills, NSW: Anzea, 1979.
Barron, Robert E. *The Priority of Christ: Toward a Postliberal Catholicism.* Grand Rapids: Brazos, 2007.
Barth, Karl. *Church Dogmatics Vol. 1, Part 1. The Doctrine of the Word of God.* Translated by Geoffrey Bromiley. Edinburgh: T. &. T. Clark, 1936.

———. *Church Dogmatics Vol. 2, Part 2 The Election of God*. Translated by Geoffrey Bromiley. Reprint. London: T. & T. Clark, 2009.

———. *Church Dogmatics Vol. 4, Part 1 The Doctrine of Reconciliation*. Translated by Geoffrey Bromiley. Edinburgh: T. & T. Clark, 1956.

———. *Church Dogmatics Vol. 4, Part 3.2 The Doctrine of Reconciliation*. Translated by Geoffrey Bromiley. Edinburgh: T. & T. Clark, 1962.

Bauckham, Richard. *The Bible and Ecology: Rediscovering the Community of Creation*. Waco, TX: Baylor University Press, 2010.

———. "The Rich Man and Lazarus: The Parable and the Parallels." *New Testament Studies* 37.2 (1991) 225–46.

Belcher, Jim. *Deep Church: A Third Way beyond Emerging and Traditional*. Downers Grove, IL: InterVarsity, 2009.

Bell, Rob. *Love Wins: A Book about Heaven, Hell, and the Fate of Every Person Who Ever Lived*. New York: HarperOne, 2011.

Benner, David G. *Care of Souls: Revisioning Christian Nurture and Counsel*. Grand Rapids: Baker, 1998.

Bloesch, Donald G. *Jesus Christ: Savior & Lord*. Downers Grove, IL: InterVarsity, 1997.

Bloom, Allan David. *The Closing of the American Mind*. New York: Simon and Schuster, 1987.

Boff, Leonardo. *Trinity and Society*. Maryknoll, NY: Orbis, 1988.

Boli, John, and Frank J. Lechner. *The Globalization Reader*. Oxford: Blackwell, 2004.

Boyd, Gregory A. *Benefit of the Doubt: Breaking the Idol of Certainty*. Grand Rapids: Baker, 2013.

Branson, Mark Lau. *Memories, Hopes, and Conversations: Appreciative Inquiry and Congregational Change*. Herndon, VA: Alban Institute, 2004.

Brown, Andrew. "The Church of England's Unglamorous, Local Future." *The Guardian* (26 December 2013). No pages. Online: http://www.theguardian.com/commentisfree/andrewbrown/2013/dec/26/church-of-england-unglamorous-local-future.

Brown, Robert McAfee. *Spirituality and Liberation: Overcoming the Great Fallacy*. Philadelphia: Westminster, 1988.

Browning, Elizabeth. *Aurora Leigh: A Poem in Nine Books*. New York: Crowell, 1883.

Bruce, Ian. "Plato's Theory of Forms." No pages. Online: http://www.ccs.neu.edu/course/com3118/Plato.html.

Bussey, Peter. "Mystery and Ignorance." *Society and Christian Belief* 23.1 (2011) 3–21.

Buxton, Graham. *Celebrating Life: Beyond the Sacred-Secular Divide*. Milton Keynes, UK: Paternoster, 2007.

———. *Dancing in the Dark: The Privilege of Participating in the Ministry of Christ*. Carlisle, UK: Paternoster, 2001.

———. "In Praise of Mystery." In *Conversations at the Edges of Things: Reflections for the Church in Honor of John Goldingay*, edited by Francis Bridger and James T. Butler, 58–66. Eugene, OR: Pickwick, 2012.

———. *The Trinity, Creation and Pastoral Ministry: Imaging the Perichoretic God*. Paternoster Theological Monographs. Milton Keynes, UK: Paternoster, 2005.

Buxton, Graham, et al. *God and Science: In Classroom and Pulpit*. Preston, Australia: Mosaic, 2012.

Byrne, Brendan, SJ. "Creation Groaning: An Earth Bible Reading of Romans 8.18–22." In *Readings from the Perspective of Earth*, edited by Norman C. Habel, 193–203. Sheffield, UK: Academic, 2000.

Chevalier, Tracy. *Girl with a Pearl Earring*. London: HarperCollins, 2000.
Christie, Ann, and Jeff Astley, "Ordinary Soteriology: A Qualitative Study." In *Empirical Theology in Texts and Tables: Qualitative, Quantitative and Comparative Perspectives*, edited by Leslie J. Francis et al., 177–96. Leiden: Brill, 2009.
Church of England. *The Alternative Service Book 1980*. London: Hodder & Stoughton, 1980.
Clapp, Rodney. *A Peculiar People: The Church as Culture in a Post-Christian Society*. Downers Grove, IL: InterVarsity, 1996.
Collins, James C., and Jerry I. Porras. *Built to Last: Successful Habits of Visionary Companies*. New York: HarperCollins, 1997.
Cunningham, David S. *These Three Are One: The Practice of Trinitarian Theology*. Oxford: Blackwell, 1999.
Dalferth, Ingolf U. "The Eschatological Roots of the Doctrine of the Trinity." In *Trinitarian Theology Today: Essays on Divine Being and Act*, edited by Christoph Schwöbel, 147–70. Edinburgh: T. & T. Clark, 1995.
Darragh, Neil. "Theology from Elsewhere." *South Pacific Journal of Mission Studies* 2 (November 1991) 2–8.
De Bono, Edward. *Parallel Thinking: From Socratic Thinking to de Bono Thinking*. New York: Viking, 1994.
Deeks, David. *Pastoral Theology: An Inquiry*. London: Epworth, 1987.
DeYoung, Kevin, and Ted Kluck. *Why We're Not Emergent: By Two Guys Who Should Be*. Chicago: Moody, 2008.
Donovan, Vincent. *Christianity Rediscovered: An Epistle from the Masai*. London: SCM, 1985.
Douthat, Ross Gregory. *Bad Religion: How We Became a Nation of Heretics*. New York: Free, 2012.
Drane, John William. *Cultural Change and Biblical Faith: The Future of the Church*. Carlisle, UK: Paternoster, 2000.
Dunn, James D. G. *Unity and Diversity in the New Testament: An Inquiry into the Character of Earliest Christianity*. London: SCM, 2005.
Eagleton, Terry. "Lunging, Flailing, Mispunching." *London Review of Books* 28.20, October 2006, 32–34.
Edwards, Denis. *Jesus the Wisdom of God: An Ecological Theology*. Maryknoll, NY: Orbis, 1995.
Eiseley, Loren. *The Immense Journey: An Imaginative Naturalist Explores the Mysteries of Man and Nature*. New York: Vintage, 1957.
Eliot, T. S. "Choruses from 'The Rock'" (Chorus I). In *Selected Poems*, 107–27. London: Faber and Faber, 1961.
Emerson, Michael. *Interculturalism: Europe and Its Muslims in Search of Sound Societal Models*. Brussels: Centre for European Policy Studies, 2011.
Fee, Gordon D., and Douglas K. Stuart. *How to Read the Bible for All Its Worth: A Guide to Understanding the Bible*. Grand Rapids: Zondervan, 1982.
Fernandez, Eleazer S. *Burning Center, Porous Borders: The Church in a Globalized World*. Eugene, OR: Wipf & Stock, 2011.
Fiddes, Paul S. "Learning from Others: Baptists and Receptive Ecumenism." *Louvain Studies* 33.1/2 (2008) 54–73.
———. *Participating in God: A Pastoral Doctrine of the Trinity*. London: Darton Longman & Todd, 2000.

Foster, Claire, and Rowan Williams. *Sharing God's Planet: A Christian Vision for a Sustainable Future.* London: Church House, 2005.
Frei, Hans W., et al. *Types of Christian Theology.* New Haven: Yale University Press, 1992.
Fretheim, Terence. *Creation Untamed: The Bible, God, and Natural Disasters.* Grand Rapids: Baker Academic, 2010.
Friend, Howard. "Leading from the Bottom Up: Bureaucracy and Adhocracy." In *Leadership in Congregations,* edited by Richard Bass, 41–53. Herndon, VA: Alban Institute, 2007.
Fromont, Paul. "Rublev's Icon: Contemplating the Trinity, Inwardly and Outwardly," 1–4. Online: http://prodigal.typepad.com/prodigal_kiwi/files/paul_fromont_rublevs_icon_contemplating_the_trinity_inwardly_and_outwardly.pdf.
Frye, Marilyn. "In and Out of Harm's Way: Arrogance and Love." In *The Politics of Reality: Essays in Feminist Theory,* 53–83. Trumansburg, NY: Crossing, 1983.
Fuller, Michael. *Atoms and Icons: A Discussion of the Relationships between Science and Theology.* London: Mowbray, 1995.
Furnham, A., and T. Ribchester. "Tolerance of Ambiguity: A Review of the Concept, Its Measurement and Applications." *Current Psychology: Research & Reviews.* 14.3 (1995) 179–99.
Galli, Mark. "Glocal Church Ministry." *Christianity Today,* August 2, 2007. No pages. Online: http://www.christianitytoday.com/ct/2007/july/30.42.html.
García-Johnson, Oscar. "Mission within Hybrid Cultures: Transnationality and the Glocal Church." In *The Gospel after Christendom: New Voices, New Cultures, New Expressions,* edited by Ryan K. Bolger, 113–26. Grand Rapids: Baker Academic, 2012.
Gardner, Anne. "Ecojustice: A Study of Genesis 6.11–13." In *The Earth Story in Genesis,* edited by Norman C. Habel and Shirley Wurst, 117–29. Sheffield, UK: Academic, 2000.
Gay, Craig M. "Plurality, Ambiguity, and Despair in Contemporary Theology." *Journal of the Evangelical Theological Society* 36.2 (1993) 209–27.
Giberson, Karl, and Francis S. Collins. *The Language of Science and Faith: Straight Answers to Genuine Questions.* Downers Grove, IL: InterVarsity, 2011.
———. "Where It All Comes Together: The Beginning of Wisdom." In *Research News and Opportunities,* July/August 2001, 4.
Giles, Kevin. *What On Earth Is the Church? An Exploration in New Testament Theology.* North Blackburn, Australia: Dove, 1995.
Gilkey, Langdon. "God." In *Christian Theology: An Introduction to Its Traditions and Tasks,* edited by Peter C. Hodgson and Robert H. King, 108. Philadelphia: Fortress, 1985.
Gleick, James. *Chaos: Making a New Science.* New York: Viking, 1987.
———. *Faster: The Acceleration of Just about Everything.* London: Abacus, 2000.
Godin, Seth. *Tribes: We Need You to Lead Us.* New York: Portfolio, 2008.
Goldingay, John. *Authority and Ministry.* Bramcote, UK: Grove, 1976.
Goldsman, Akiva. "A Time to Kill: Summation by Jake Brigance." No pages. Online: http://www.angelfire.com/il/jilliannichole/atimetokill.html.
Gollings, Richard. "Planting Covenant Communities of Faith in the City." In *God So Loves the City: Seeking a Theology for Urban Mission,* edited by Charles van Engen and Jude Tiersma, 125–42. Monrovia, CA: MARC, 1994.

Gomez, Drexel. *True Union in the Body? A Contribution to the Discussion within the Anglican Communion concerning the Public Blessing of Same-Sex Unions*. Colorado Springs: Anglican Communion Institute, 2002.
Green, Sidney L. *Beating the Bounds: A Symphonic Approach to Orthodoxy in the Anglican Communion*. Eugene, OR: Wipf & Stock, 2013.
Greenwood, Robin. *Transforming Priesthood: A New Theology of Mission and Ministry*. London: SPCK, 1994.
Grenz, Stanley. *Revisioning Evangelical Theology: A Fresh Agenda for the 21st Century*. Downers Grove, IL: InterVarsity, 1993.
Grenz, Stanley J., and John R. Franke. *Beyond Foundationalism: Shaping Theology in a Postmodern Context*. Louisville, KY: Westminster John Knox, 2001.
Gunton, Colin E. *The Doctrine of Creation: Essays in Dogmatics, History and Philosophy*. Edinburgh: T. & T. Clark, 1997.
Habel, Norman C. *Readings from the Perspective of Earth*. Sheffield, UK: Academic, 2000.
Hall, Douglas John. *Imaging God: Dominion as Stewardship*. Grand Rapids: Eerdmans, 1986.
———. *Thinking the Faith: Christian Theology in a North American Context*. Minneapolis: Augsburg, 1989.
———. *What Christianity Is Not: An Exercise in "Negative" Theology*. Eugene, OR: Cascade, 2013.
Hampson, Peter. "How to Walk a Tightrope." Society for Christian Psychology. No pages. Online: http://christianpsych.org/wp_scp/how-to-walk-a-tightrope/.
Hardy, Daniel. *Wording a Radiance: Parting Conversations on God and the Church*. London: SCM, 2010.
Hare, R. M. *Plato*. Oxford: Oxford University Press, 1982.
Harper, Michael. *A New Way of Living: How the Church of the Redeemer, Houston, Found a New Life-Style*. London: Hodder and Stoughton, 1973.
Harris, Brian. *The Tortoise Usually Wins: Biblical Reflections on Quiet Leadership for Reluctant Leaders*. Milton Keynes, UK: Paternoster, 2013.
Harrison, Michael, and Christopher Stuart-Clark. *The Oxford Book of Christmas Poems*. Oxford: Oxford University Press, 2010.
Hart, David Bentley. *The Beauty of the Infinite: The Aesthetics of Christian Truth*. Grand Rapids: Eerdmans, 2003.
Haught, John. *Mystery and Promise: A Theology of Revelation*. Collegeville, MN: Liturgical, 1993.
Hocking, William. *The Meaning of God in Human Experience: A Philosophic Study of Religion*. New Haven: Yale University Press, 1912.
Holmes, Peter R. *Trinity in Human Community: Exploring Congregational Life in the Image of the Social Trinity*. Milton Keynes, UK: Paternoster, 2006.
Horrell, David G. *The Bible and the Environment: Towards a Critical Ecological Biblical Theology*. Oakville, CT: Equinox, 2010.
Horrell, David G., et al. *Ecological Hermeneutics: Biblical, Historical and Theological Perspectives*. London: T. & T. Clark, 2010.
Horton, Michael Scott. *Power Religion: The Selling out of the Evangelical Church?* Chicago: Moody, 1992.
Houghton, John. Foreword to "Dried Up, Drowned Out," edited by Hazel Southam. Tearfund 2012 Report. Online: http://tilz.tearfund.org/~/media/files/tilz/research/dried%20up%20drowned%20out%202012%20-%20full%20report.pdf.

Houston, James M. *I Believe in the Creator*. London: Hodder and Stoughton, 1979.
Humphrey, Edith M. "The Gift of the Father." In *Trinitarian Theology for the Church: Scripture, Community, Worship*, edited by Daniel Treier and David Lauber, 79–102. Downers Grove, IL: InterVarsity, 2009.
Hunsinger, George. *Disruptive Grace: Studies in the Theology of Karl Barth*. Grand Rapids: Eerdmans, 2000.
Huxley, Aldous. *The Doors of Perception*. New York: Harper, 1954.
James, William. *Pragmatism: A New Name for Some Old Ways of Thinking*. Indianapolis: Hackett, 1981.
Johnson, Elizabeth A. *She Who Is: The Mystery of God in Feminist Theological Discourse*. New York: Crossroad, 1992.
Johnson, Steven. *Emergence: The Connected Lives of Ants, Brains, Cities, and Software*. New York: Scribner, 2001.
Johnston, Philip S. *Shades of Sheol: Death and Afterlife in the Old Testament*. Leicester, UK: InterVarsity, 2002.
Keller, Catherine. "The Last Laugh: A Counter-Apocalyptic Meditation on Moltmann's *The Coming of God*." *Theology Today* 54.3 (1997) 381–91.
Killen, Patricia O'Connell, and John De Beer. *The Art of Theological Reflection*. New York: Crossroad, 1996.
Kimball, Dan. *They Like Jesus but Not the Church: Insights from Emerging Generations*. Grand Rapids: Zondervan, 2007.
Kinast, Robert L. *Let Ministry Teach: A Guide to Theological Reflection*. Collegeville, MN: Liturgical, 1996.
Kraft, Charles H. *Christianity in Culture: A Study in Dynamic Biblical Theologizing in Cross-Cultural Perspective*. Maryknoll, NY: Orbis, 1979.
Kuhrt, Stephen. *Tom Wright for Everyone: Putting the Theology of N. T. Wright into Practice in the Local Church*. London: SPCK, 2011.
Küng, Hans. *Eternal Life? Life after Death as a Medical, Philosophical, and Theological Problem*. Garden City, NY: Doubleday, 1984.
Kushner, Lawrence. *Honey from the Rock: An Introduction to Jewish Mysticism*. New Anniversary Edition. Woodstock, VT: Jewish Lights, 2000.
L'Engle, Madeleine. *Walking on Water: Reflections on Faith and Art*. Colorado Springs: Waterbrook, 2001.
LaCugna, Catherine Mowry. *God for Us: The Trinity and Christian Life*. San Francisco: HarperSanFrancisco, 1991.
Lawrence, D. *Reflections on the Death of a Porcupine and Other Essays*. Cambridge: Cambridge University Press, 1988.
Leach, John. *Liturgy and Liberty*. Monrovia, CA: MARC, 1989.
Lewis, C. S. *A Grief Observed*. San Francisco: Harper & Row, 1961.
———. *An Experiment in Criticism*. Cambridge: Cambridge University Press, 1961.
———. *Mere Christianity*. London: Collins, 2012.
———. *The Last Battle*. London: HarperCollins, 2005.
Liederbach, Mark, and Seth Bible. *True North: Christ, the Gospel, and Creation Care*. Nashville: B. & H. Academic, 2012.
Lincoln, Andrew T. "The Letter to the Colossians." In *The New Interpreter's Bible, Volume XI: 2 Corinthians–Philemon*, edited by J. Paul Sampley et al., 551–669. Nashville: Abingdon, 2000.

Lo, Lung-kwong. "Paul and Ethnicity: The Paradigm of Glocalization." In *Jesus and Paul: Global Perspectives in Honor of James D. G. Dunn for his 70th Birthday*, edited by B. J. Oropeza et al., 184–98. London: T. & T. Clark, 2009.

MacDonald, Gregory. "Introduction: Between Heresy and Dogma." In *"All Shall be Well": Explorations in Universalism and Christian Theology, from Origen to Moltmann*, edited by Gregory MacDonald, 1–25. Eugene, OR: Cascade, 2010.

———. *The Evangelical Universalist*. Eugene, OR: Cascade, 2006.

Marcel, Gabriel. *Being and Having*. Translated by Katharine Farrer. Collins: London, 1965.

———. *Creative Fidelity*. New York: Noonday, 1964.

McDougall, Joy Ann. "The Return of Trinitarian Praxis? Moltmann on the Trinity and the Christian Life." *The Journal of Religion* 83.2 (2003) 177–203.

McDowell, John C. "A Passion for Holiness." No pages. Online: http://www.geocities.ws/johnnymcdowell/Rowan_Williams.html

McFague, Sallie. *Super, Natural Christians: How We Should Love Nature*. Minneapolis: Fortress, 1997.

McGavran, Donald. *Understanding Church Growth*. Grand Rapids: Eerdmans, 1980.

McGrath, Alister E., "A Better Way: The Priesthood of all Believers." In *Power Religion: The Selling Out of the Evangelical Church?* edited by Michael S. Horton, 301–13. Chicago: Moody, 1992.

———. *A Scientific Theology Vol. 1, Nature*. Edinburgh: T. & T. Clark, 2001.

———. *The Passionate Intellect: Christian Faith and the Discipleship of the Mind*. Downers Grove, IL: InterVarsity, 2010.

———. *The Re-Enchantment of Nature: Science, Religion and the Human Sense of Wonder*. London: Hodder & Stoughton, 2003.

McKnight, Scot. *The King Jesus Gospel: The Original Good News Revisited*. Grand Rapids: Zondervan, 2011.

McLaren, Brian D. *A Generous Orthodoxy*. Grand Rapids: Zondervan, 2004.

———. *A New Kind of Christianity: Ten Questions That Are Transforming the Faith*. New York: HarperOne, 2010.

Miles, Margaret. *Augustine on the Body*. Reprint. Eugene, OR: Wipf & Stock, 2010.

Moltmann, Jürgen. *Experiences in Theology: Ways and Forms of Christian Theology*. Minneapolis: Fortress, 2000.

———. "From the Closed World to the Infinite Universe." In *Science and Wisdom*, 158–71. Minneapolis: Fortress, 2003.

———. "God and Space." In *Science and Wisdom*, 111–26. Minneapolis: Fortress, 2003.

———. *The Church in the Power of the Spirit: A Contribution to Messianic Ecclesiology*. London: SCM, 1977.

———. *The Coming of God: Christian Eschatology*. Minneapolis: Fortress, 1996.

———. *The Crucified God: The Cross of Christ as the Foundation and Criticism of Christian Theology*. New York: Harper & Row, 1974.

———. *The Experiment Hope*. Philadelphia: Fortress, 1975.

———. *The Future of Creation: Collected Essays*. Philadelphia: Fortress, 2007.

———. *The Source of Life: The Holy Spirit and the Theology of Life*. Minneapolis: Fortress, 1997.

———. *The Spirit of Life: A Universal Affirmation*. Minneapolis: Fortress, 1992.

———. *The Trinity and the Kingdom of God: The Doctrine of God*. London: SCM, 1981.

———. *Theology of Hope: On the Ground and the Implications of a Christian Eschatology.* London: SCM, 1967.
Moore, Geoff. "Geoff Moore: A Fuller Unity." No pages. Online: http://www.faithandleadership.com/qa/geoff-moore-fuller-unity.
Mouw, Richard J. *Uncommon Decency: Christian Civility in an Uncivil World.* Downers Grove, IL: InterVarsity, 1992.
Mudge, Lewis Seymour, and James N. Poling. *Formation and Reflection: The Promise of Practical Theology.* Philadelphia: Fortress, 1987.
Muir, John, and Linnie Marsh Wolfe. *John of the Mountains: The Unpublished Journals of John Muir.* Boston: Houghton, Mifflin, 1938.
Murray, Paul D. "Receptive Ecumenism and Catholic Learning: Establishing the Agenda." *International Journal for the Study of the Christian Church* 7.4 (2007) 279–301.
Nelstrop, Louise. *Evaluating Fresh Expressions: Explorations in Emerging Church: Responses to the Changing Face of Ecclesiology in the Church of England.* Norwich, UK: Canterbury, 2008.
Netland, Harold A. "Introduction: Globalization and Theology Today." In *Globalizing Theology: Belief and Practice in an Era of World Christianity*, edited by Craig Ott and Harold A. Netland, 14–34. Nottingham, UK: Apollos, 2007.
Newton, Isaac. *The Correspondence of Isaac Newton.* Cambridge: Cambridge University Press, 1961.
Olson, Bruce. *Bruchko.* Lake Mary, FL: Charisma House, 2006.
Olthuis, J. "Dancing Together in the Wild Spaces of Love: Postmodernism, Psychotherapy, and the Spirit of God." *Journal of Psychology and Christianity* 18.2 (1999) 140–52.
Packer, J. I. *Knowing God.* London: Hodder & Stoughton, 2005.
Pahl, Ray. "Hidden Solidarities." *Prospect* (September 24, 2006). No pages. Online: https://www.prospectmagazine.co.uk/magazine/hiddensolidarities/
Pannenberg, Wolfhart. *Systematic Theology.* Vol. *1.* Edinburgh: T. & T. Clark, 1991.
Pascal, Blaise. *Pensées.* Mineola, NY: Dover, 2004.
Patton, John. *Pastoral Care in Context: An Introduction to Pastoral Care.* Louisville, KY: Westminster/John Knox, 1993.
Pelikan, Jaroslav. *The Christian Intellectual.* London: Collins, 1966.
Pembroke, Neil. *The Art of Listening: Dialogue, Shame, and Pastoral Care.* London: T. & T. Clark, 2002.
Peterson, Eugene H. *Christ Plays in Ten Thousand Places: A Conversation in Spiritual Theology.* Grand Rapids: Eerdmans, 2005.
———. *Five Smooth Stones for Pastoral Work.* Grand Rapids: Eerdmans, 1992.
———. "Pastors and Novels." In *Subversive Spirituality*, 185–92. Vancouver: Regent College, 1994.
———. *Working the Angles: The Shape of Pastoral Integrity.* Grand Rapids: Eerdmans, 1987.
Phillips, J. *Your God is Too Small.* New York: Macmillan, 1953.
Pickard, Stephen K. *Seeking the Church: An Introduction to Ecclesiology.* London: SCM, 2012.
———. *Theological Foundations for Collaborative Ministry.* Farnham, UK: Ashgate, 2010.
Pinnock, Clark H. "From Augustine to Arminius: A Pilgrimage in Theology." In *The Grace of God, the Will of Man: A Case for Arminianism*, 15–30. Grand Rapids: Zondervan, 1989.

———. *Most Moved Mover: A Theology of God's Openness.* Carlisle, UK: Paternoster, 2001.
Piper, Don, and Cecil Murphey. *90 Minutes in Heaven: A True Story of Death and Life.* Grand Rapids: Revell, 2004.
Pitt-Watson, Ian. *A Primer for Preachers.* Grand Rapids: Baker, 1986.
Plato. *The Republic.* Translated by H. D. P. Lee. London: Penguin, 1955.
Pohl, Christine D. *Making Room: Recovering Hospitality as a Christian Tradition.* Grand Rapids: Eerdmans, 1999.
Polkinghorne, J. *Science and Christian Belief: Theological Reflections of a Bottom-up Thinker.* London: SPCK, 1994.
———. *Serious Talk: Science and Religion in Dialogue.* Valley Forge PA: Trinity, 1995.
Rah, Soong-Chan. *The Next Evangelicalism: Releasing the Church from Western Cultural Captivity.* Downers Grove, IL: InterVarsity, 2009.
Rahner, Karl. *Foundations of Christian Faith: An Introduction to the Idea of Christianity.* New York: Seabury, 1978.
———. *Hearers of the Word.* New York: Herder and Herder, 1969.
Ramankutty, N., et al. "Comparing the Yields of Organic and Conventional Agriculture." *Nature* 485.7397 (2012) 229–32.
Ratzinger, Joseph, and Hans Urs von Balthasar. *Mary, the Church at the Source.* San Francisco: Ignatius, 2005.
Reid, Duncan. "Setting Aside the Ladder to Heaven: Revelation 22.1—22.5 from the Perspective of Earth." In *Readings from the Perspective of Earth*, edited by Norman C. Habel, 232–45. Sheffield, UK: Academic, 2000.
Rendle, Gilbert R., and Alice Mann. *Holy Conversations: Strategic Planning as a Spiritual Practice for Congregations.* Bethesda, MD: Alban Institute, 2003.
Roberts, Bob. *Glocalization: How Followers of Jesus Engage the New Flat World.* Grand Rapids: Zondervan, 2007.
———. *Transformation: How Glocal Churches Transform Lives and the World.* Grand Rapids: Zondervan, 2006.
Roberts, David. "Our Materialism Disguises a Deeper Problem." No pages. Online: http://grist.org/article/materialism-and-material/.
Robinson, John A. T. *In the End, God.* London: Fontana, 1968.
———. *Honest to God.* London: SCM, 1963.
Robinson, Marilynne. *Home.* London: Virago, 2008.
Rogers, Eugene F. "The Stranger as Blessing." In *Knowing the Triune God: The Work of the Spirit in the Practices of the Church*, edited by James J. Buckley and David S. Yeago, 265–83. Grand Rapids: Eerdmans, 2001.
Ryken, Leland. *The Liberated Imagination: Thinking Christianly about the Arts.* Wheaton, IL: Shaw, 1989.
Saayman, Willem. "Missionary by its Very Nature." *Missionalia* (2000). No pages. Online: http://www.reocities.com/missionalia/saayma00.htm.
———. "Subversive Subservience." *Missionalia* (1997). No pages. Online: http://www.reocities.com/missionalia/saayman.htm.
Sachs, J. R. "Apocatastasis in Patristic Theology." *Theological Studies* 54.4 (1993) 617–40.
Saint Augustine. *City of God.* New York: Penguin, 1972.
Sanders, John. "A Summary of Openness Theology." Open Theism Information Site. No pages. Online: http://opentheism.info/open-theism/.

———. "Historical Considerations." In *The Openness of God: A Biblical Challenge to the Traditional Understanding of God*, edited by Clark H. Pinnock et al., 59–100. Downers Grove, IL: InterVarsity, 1994.

———. *The God Who Risks: A Theology of Providence*. Downers Grove, IL: InterVarsity, 1998.

Santmire, Paul H. *The Travail of Nature: The Ambiguous Ecological Promise of Christian Theology*. Philadelphia: Fortress, 1985.

Schilling, Harold. *The New Consciousness in Science and Religion*, Philadelphia: United Church, 1973.

Schreiter, Robert J. *Constructing Local Theologies*. Maryknoll, NY: Orbis, 1985.

Scott, Nancy. "Dueling with Dualism." McKenzie Study Center, Gutenberg College. No pages. Online: http://msc.gutenberg.edu/2001/02/dueling-with-dualism/.

Seamands, Stephen. *Ministry in the Image of God: The Trinitarian Shape of Christian Service*. Downers Grove, IL: InterVarsity, 2005.

Sheahen, Laura. "How Africa's Churches are Changing Christianity." Beliefnet.com. No pages. Online: http://www.beliefnet.com/Faiths/Christianity/2005/08/How-Africas-Churches-Are-Changing-Christianity.aspx?p=1.

Sine, Tom. *The New Conspirators: Creating the Future One Mustard Seed at a Time*. Downers Grove, IL: InterVarsity, 2008.

Sleeth, J. Matthew. *24/6*. Carol Stream, IL: Tyndale House, 2012.

SmartStorming. "The Power of Divergent and Convergent Thinking." No pages. Online: http://smartstorming-blog.com/the-power-of-divergent-and-convergent-thinkingguide-your-groups-thinking-process-to-new-heights-of-productivity/.

Snyder, Howard A., and Joel Scandrett. *Salvation Means Creation Healed: The Ecology of Sin and Grace*. Eugene, OR: Cascade, 2011.

Somerville, Margaret. *The Ethical Imagination: Journeys of the Human Spirit*. Toronto: House of Anansi, 2006.

Spencer, Liz, and R. E. Pahl. *Rethinking Friendship: Hidden Solidarities Today*. Princeton, Princeton University Press, 2006.

Spender, Stephen. *The Making of a Poem*. New York: Norton, 1962.

Stark, Rodney. *What Americans Really Believe: New Findings from the Baylor Surveys of Religion*. Waco, TX: Baylor University Press, 2008.

Steiner, George. *Real Presences: Is There Anything in What We Say?* London: Faber and Faber, 1989.

Steyn, Mark. "Rummy Speaks the Truth, Not Gobbledygook." *The Telegraph*. No pages. Online: http://www.telegraph.co.uk/comment/personal-view/3599959/Rummy-speaks-the-truth-not-gobbledygook.html.

Strudwick, Vincent. "'Towards an Anglican Covenant': A Response from Inclusive Church." Inclusive Church.net. No pages. Online: http://www.anglicancommunion.org/commission/covenant/docs/Inclusive%20Church%20%20Towards%20an%20Anglican%20Covenant.pdf.

Sundkler, Bengt. *The Christian Ministry in Africa*. London: SCM, 1960.

Tacey, David. *Re-Enchantment: The New Australian Spirituality*. Pymble, Australia: HarperCollins, 2000.

Talbott, Thomas. *The Inescapable Love of God*. Parkland, FL: Universal, 1999.

———. Tom Talbott's Site. No pages. Online: http://www.willamette.edu/~ttalbott/.

Taylor, Daniel. *The Myth of Certainty: The Reflective Christian and the Risk of Commitment*. Downers Grove, IL: InterVarsity, 1999.

Taylor, John Vernon. *The Go-Between God: The Holy Spirit and the Christian Mission.* London: SCM, 1972.
Tertullian. *Tertullian on the Testimony of the Soul and On the "Prescription" of Heretics.* London: SPCK, 1914.
Tesoriero, Frank. *Community Development: Community-Based Alternatives in an Age of Globalisation.* Frenchs Forest, Australia: Pearson Australia, 2010.
Thielicke, Helmut. *Theological Ethics, Volume 2 – Politics.* Grand Rapids: Eerdmans, 1979.
Thoreau, Henry David. *Walden: An Annotated Edition.* Boston: Houghton Mifflin, 1995.
Tickle, Phyllis. *The Great Emergence: How Christianity Is Changing and Why.* Grand Rapids: Baker, 2008.
Tiersma, Jude. "What Does It Mean to be Incarnational When We are Not the Messiah?" In *God So Loves the City: Seeking a Theology for Urban Mission*, edited by Charles van Engen and Jude Tiersma, 7–25. Monrovia, CA: MARC, 1994.
Tillich, Paul. *The Shaking of the Foundations.* New York: Scribner's Sons, 1948.
Torrance, Alan J. "*Creatio ex Nihilo* and the Spatio-Temporal Dimensions, with Special Reference to Jürgen Moltmann and D. C. Williams." In *The Doctrine of Creation: Essays in Dogmatics, History and Philosophy*, edited by Colin E. Gunton, 83–104. Edinburgh: T. & T. Clark, 1997.
Torrance, James B. "The Place of Jesus Christ in Worship." In *Theological Foundations for Ministry: Selected Readings for a Theology of the Church in Ministry*, edited by Ray S. Anderson, 348–69. Edinburgh: T. & T. Clark, 1979.
———. *Worship, Community & the Triune God of Grace.* Downers Grove, IL: InterVarsity, 1996.
Torrance, Thomas F. *Theology in Reconstruction.* London: SCM, 1965.
Toulmin, Stephen. *Cosmopolis: The Hidden Agenda of Modernity.* Chicago: University of Chicago Press, 1992.
Tournier, Paul. *The Adventure of Living.* New York: Harper, 1965.
Tucker, Frank. *Intercultural Communication for Christian Ministry.* Adelaide: Tucker, 2007.
Turner, Steve. *Imagine: A Vision for Christians in the Arts.* Downers Grove, IL: InterVarsity, 2001.
Underhill, Evelyn. *The Spiritual Life.* Harrisburg PA: Morehouse, 1997.
Untener, Ken. "Archbishop Oscar Romero Prayer: A Step Along the Way." United States Conference of Catholic Bishops. No pages. Online: http://www.usccb.org/prayer-and-worship/prayers/archbishop_romero_prayer.cfm.
van Engen, Charles E. "The Glocal Church: Locality and Catholicity in a Globalizing World." In *Globalizing Theology: Belief and Practice in an Era of World Christianity*, edited by Craig Ott and Harold A. Netland, 157–79. Nottingham, UK: Apollos, 2007.
Vanhoozer, Kevin J. "What is Everyday Theology? How and Why Christians Should Read Culture." In *Everyday Theology: How to Read Cultural Texts and Interpret Trends*, edited by Kevin J. Vanhoozer et al., 15–60. Grand Rapids: Baker Academic, 2007.
Vanier, Jean. *Community and Growth.* Homebush, Australia: St. Paul, 1979.
Vásquez, Manuel A., and Marie Friedmann Marquardt. *Globalizing the Sacred: Religion across the Americas.* New Brunswick: Rutgers University, 2003.

Veith, Gene. *Reading between the Lines: A Christian Guide to Literature*. Wheaton, IL: Crossway, 1990.
Volf, Miroslav. *After Our Likeness: The Church as the Image of the Trinity*. Grand Rapids: Eerdmans, 1998.
———. *Exclusion and Embrace: A Theological Exploration of Identity, Otherness, and Reconciliation*. Nashville: Abingdon, 1996.
———. *A Public Faith: How Followers of Christ Should Serve the Common Good*. Grand Rapids: Brazos, 2011.
Wagner, C. *Your Church Can Be Healthy*. Nashville: Abingdon, 1979.
Wainwright, Elaine M. "A Transformative Struggle towards the Divine Dream: An Ecofeminist Reading of Matthew 11." In *Readings from the Perspective of Earth*, edited by Norman C. Habel, 162–73. Sheffield, UK: Academic, 2000.
Walsh, Brian J., and Richard J. Middleton. *The Transforming Vision: Shaping a Christian World View*. Downers Grove, IL: InterVarsity, 1984.
Ward, Keith. *Divine Action*. London: Collins, 1990.
Ware, Kallistos. *The Orthodox Church*. London: Penguin, 1993.
Watkins, Jane Magruder, and Bernard J. Mohr. *Appreciative Inquiry: Change at the Speed of Imagination*. San Francisco: Jossey-Bass/Pfeiffer, 2001.
Watts, Rikki. "What Does It Mean to be Saved?" In *Working Together* (2002). No pages. Online: http://www.ea.org.au/site/defaultsite/filesystem/documents/Theological/watts.pdf
Welch, Sharon D. *A Feminist Ethic of Risk*. Minneapolis: Fortress, 1990.
Wheatley, Margaret J. *Leadership and the New Science: Discovering Order in a Chaotic World*. San Francisco: Berrett-Koehler, 1999.
White, Lynn. "The Historical Roots of Our Ecologic Crisis." *Science* 155.3767 (1967) 1203–7.
Wilde, Caleb. "Why 99% of Pastors are Universalists . . . at Funerals." See http://www.churchleaders.com/pastors/pastor-how-to/153575-caleb-wilde-why-99-of-pastors-are-universalists-at-funerals.html
Williams, Rowan. "To What End are we Made?" In *Who Is This Man? Christ in the Renewal of the Church*, edited by Jonathan Baker and William Davage, 1–22. New York: Continuum, 2006.
Wittgenstein, Ludwig. *Culture and Value: A Selection from the Posthumous Remains*. Oxford: Blackwell, 1998.
Wittmer, Michael. *Heaven Is a Place on Earth: Why Everything You Do Matters to God*. Grand Rapids: Zondervan, 2004.
Wright, N. T. *Surprised by Hope*. London: SPCK, 2007.
———. *Bringing the Church to the World*. Minneapolis: Bethany House, 1993.
———. *Simply Christian: Why Christianity Makes Sense*. San Francisco: HarperSanFrancisco, 2006.
———. *The Way of the Lord*. London: Triangle, 1999.
———. *Luke for Everyone*. London: SPCK, 2001.
Yong, Amos. *Beyond the Impasse: Toward a Pneumatological Theology of Religions*. Grand Rapids: Baker, 2003.
———. *Hospitality and the Other: Pentecost, Christian Practices, and the Neighbor*. Maryknoll, NY: Orbis, 2008.
Zizioulas, John. *Being as Communion: Studies in Personhood and the Church*. Crestwood, NY: St. Vladimir's Seminary, 1985.

Names Index

Abrams, M. H., 165, 165n18
Acton, Lord, 168
Alexander, Denis, 179n7
Anderson, Ray S., 41, 41n25, 94, 94n1, 94n2
Anselm, Saint, 65
Aristotle, 167
Arius, 20
Armstrong, Karen, 6, 6n9, 7n13, 14, 14n31
Astley, Jeff, 139, 139n43, 139n44, 139n45
Athanasius, Saint, 20, 20n5, 55, 55n12
Auden, W. H., 161
Augsburger, David, 204, 204n33
Augustine, Saint, 65, 124, 126, 126n6, 151, 151n21, 176
Ault, James, 198

Bacon, Francis, 187, 187n39
Balthasar, Hans Urs von, 9n23, 74, 74n39
Bancewicz, Ruth, 178n6
Banks, Robert, 132, 132n26
Barron, Robert E., 56n14
Barth, Karl, 38-39, 38n12, 54, 54n8, 59, 59n21, 66, 72-73, 73n36, 97, 166, 172, 172n31
Bauckham, Richard, 68, 68n21, 182, 182n19, 186-87, 186n35, 187n38
Baxter, Richard, 87
Belcher, Jim, 83, 83n18, 87, 88, 89
Bell, Rob, 74, 74n40, 75
Benner, David, G., 108, 108n39

Betjeman, John, 12
Bible, Seth, 186, 187n37
Bloesch, Donald G., 34n5
Bloom, Allan, 86, 86n25
Boff, Leonardo, 97, 107, 108n37, 134, 134n32
Boli, John, 192n1
Boyd, Gregory A., 213, 213n13, 214
Branson, Mark L., 116-18, 116n7, 117n11, 118n12, 136, 136n36
Brown, Andrew, 213, 213n12
Brown Robert McA., 149, 149n17, 167-68, 168n20
Browning, Elizabeth B., 13, 13n27, 173, 173n1
Bruce, Ian, 147, 147n13
Brueggemann, Walter, 149
Brunner, Emil, 66
Bussey, Peter, 6, 6n10
Butterfield, Herbert, 9-10
Buxton, Graham, 3n5, 5n8, 23n12, 33n2, 37n9, 53n7, 102n19, 115n5, 131n24, 144n8, 158n3, 179n8, 180n12, 208n1
Byrne, Brendan, 185, 185n30

Chesterton, G. K., 30, 192, 193
Chevalier, Tracy, 163, 164n13
Christie, Ann, 139n43
Clapp, Rodney, 144, 144n7
Clement of Alexandria, 66
Coleridge, Samuel T., 14
Collins, Francis S., 179n8
Collins, James C., 28, 29n28

names index

Cook, Jerry, 25
Cunningham, David S., 97, 97n6, 98, 98n9, 105, 105n32, 217, 217n22

Dalferth, Ingolf U., 211, 211n8,
Darragh, Neil, 204, 204n31
Dawkins, Richard, 177
Dearden, John, 1
De Beer, John, 21–23, 21n7, 22n9, 23n13, 25, 25n17
De Bono, Edward, 27–28, 27n23
Deeks, David, 165, 165n19
Descartes, René, xvi
DeYoung, Kevin, 67–68, 68n18, 82, 82n17, 87, 87n28
Dickinson, Emily, 183
Diodore of Tarsus, 66
Donovan, Vincent, 8, 8n19, 205, 205n35
Douthat, Ross G., 84, 84n19
Drane, John W., 157n2
Dunn, James D. G., 99, 99n12
Dyer, Mark, 78

Eagleton, Terry, 177n5
Edwards, Denis, 182, 182n17
Einstein, Albert, xvi
Eiseley, Loren, 189–90, 190n45
Eliot, George, 162
Eliot, T. S., 1–3, 2n4
Emerson, Michael, 200n21
Emerson, Ralph W., x, 111, 115

Farnham, A., xviin7
Fee, Gordon D., 195–96, 196n9
Fernandez, Eleazer S., 216, 216n18
Fiddes, Paul S., 46, 47n33, 89n32, 96, 97n4, 102, 128, 128n14, 136, 136n39
Foster, Claire, 60n22
Francis of Assisi, 176, 179
Francis, Leslie J, 139n45, 140n46
Franke, John R., xi, 158n4
Frei, Hans W., 81, 81n13
Fretheim, Terence, 188n40
Friend, Howard, 125, 125n3
Fromont, Paul, 106, 106n34
Frye, Marilyn, 183n21

Fuller, Michael, 129, 129n19

Galileo, 178
Galli, Mark, 202n26
García-Johnson, Oscar, 199, 199n16, 199n18
Gardner, Anne, 185, 185n28
Gay, Craig M., xviin8
Giberson, Karl, 16, 16n36, 36, 179n8
Giles, Kevin, 88n31
Gilkey, Langdon, 34, 34n4
Gleik, James, 194, 194n5, 202n24
Godin, Seth, 30, 30n30
Goldingay, John, 126, 126n5
Goldman, Akiva, 21, 21n6
Gollings, Richard, 103, 103n24
Gomez, Drexel, 85n23
Green, Sidney L., 30n31
Greenwood, Robin, 127n7
Gregory of Nyssa, 66
Grenz, Stanley J., 23n11, 158, 158n4
Griffiths, Michael, 91
Grisham, John, 20
Gunton, Colin E., 128

Habel, Norman C., 180n11, 184–85, 184n27
Hall, Douglas J., 9, 9n21, 16, 16n37, 19, 19n2, 77n2, 181, 181n14, 186n32, 190, 190n46, 218n24
Hampson, Peter, 28, 28n27
Hardy, Daniel, 13-14, 14n30, 39, 41, 76–77, 77n1, 215
Hare, R. M., 145, 145n10, 146n11
Harper, Michael, 131, 131n25
Harris, Brian, 113, 113n2, 116n9, 125, 125n2
Harrison, Michael, 12n25
Hart, David B., 32, 45–46, 46n30, 216–17, 216n20
Haught, John, 8, 8n17, 15, 15n33, 41, 41n22
Heaney, Seamus, 167
Heraclitus, 146
Hocking, William, 6, 6n11
Holmes, Peter R., 97, 97n7
Hopkins, Gerard M., 141
Horrell, David G., 180n11

names index 233

Houghton, John, 188, 188n41
Houston, James M., 184n26
Humphrey, Edith M., 127-28, 127n10, 128n11
Hunsinger, George, 72, 72n34
Huxley, Aldous, 7, 7n15

Ireneaus, Saint, 176

James, William, 112, 112n1, 114, 114n3, 122
John Paul II, 179
Johnson, Elizabeth A., 57-58, 57n18
Johnson, Steven, 129n19, 130
Johnston, Philip S., 72, 72n33
Jung, Carl, 194

Kasper, Walter, 89
Keller, Catherine, 70, 70n27
Kierkegaard, Søren, 12
Killen, Patricia O'C., 21-23, 21n7, 22n9, 23n13, 25, 25n17
Kimball, Dan, 85, 85n24
Kinast, Robert L., 25, 25n18
Kluck, Ted, 67-68, 68n18, 82, 82n17, 87n28
Kraft, Charles H., 144n5, 206, 206n37
Kuhrt, Stephen, 91n36
Küng, Hans, 39, 40n18, 68n20
Kushner, Lawrence, 138, 138n42

LaCugna, Catherine M., 36, 36n7, 54n12, 97, 128
Lawrence, D. H., 7, 7n14
Leach, John, 81, 81n11
Lechner, Frank J., 192n1
Lemmel, Helen H., 142
L'Engle, Madeleine, 165, 165n17
Levitt, Theodore, 4, 30
Lewis, C. S., 12, 12n26, 31, 43, 87, 87n29, 89, 110, 110n44, 153, 160, 160n6, 210-11, 210n6
Liederbach, Mark, 186, 187n7
Lincoln, Andrew T., 67, 67n16
Lo, Lung-kwong, 201, 201n22
Lorenz, Edward, 202, 202n24
Luther, Martin, 10, 78, 84, 124, 126

MacDonald, Gregory, 53, 64, 64n8, 65n11, 66n14, 67n16, 68n19, 69n23, 71n32, 74, 74n41
MacDougall Joy A., 105, 105n31
Mann, Alice, 134, 134n31, 136n38
Marcel, Gabriel, 13, 13n28, 103, 103n22
Marquardt, Marie F., 199, 199n17
McDowell, John C., 2n3
McFague, Sallie, 182-83, 183n20, 183n22, 184, 184n25, 189, 189n43
McGavran, Donald, 10, 10n24
McGrath, Alister E., 6, 29, 29n29, 125, 125n1, 126, 126n4, 150n19, 189, 189n44, 191n48
McKnight, Scot, 27, 27n22, 48, 49-50, 49n2, 53, 59
McLaren Brian D., 56, 56n13, 57, 57n17, 80, 80n9, 81n12, 86-87, 86n27
Middleton, Richard J., 144, 144n6, 152n24
Miles, Margaret, 151, 151n22
Milton, John, 160
Mohr, Bernard J., 116n6
Moltmann, Jürgen, 18-19, 19n1, 38141, 39n16, 40n19, 40n20, 40n21, 41n24, 46, 46n32, 62, 62n1, 70-71, 70n24, 71n28, 71n31, 72, 76, 91, 91n35, 97-98, 98n8, 104, 104n29, 108, 108n38, 132-33, 132n27, 154, 154n31, 181, 181n13, 183, 183n24, 186, 186n33, 209-10, 209n3, 209n4, 210n5, 211n9, 216n19
Moore, Geoff, 137-38, 137n41
Mouw, Richard J., 85, 86, 86n26, 171, 171n30
Mudge, Lewis J., 204n32
Muir John, 190, 190n47
Murphey, Cecil, 66n12
Murray, Paul D., 136, 137n40

Nelstrop, Louise, 82n15
Netland, Harold A., 193, 193n2
Newbigin, Lesslie, xn1
Newton, Isaac, 6-7, 6n12

names index

Obama, Barack, 93
Olson, Bruce, 206, 206n39
Olthuis, James, xvii, xviin10, 109, 109n41, 110n43
Origen, 66, 150

Packer, J. I., 54, 54n11
Pahl, Raymond E., 200, 200n19, 200n20
Palmer, Parker, 96
Pannenberg, Wolfhart, 39, 39n17
Parmenides, 146
Parry, Robin, 53, 61, 64-65, 68, 71, 73
Pascal, Blaise, 8, 8n18
Patton, John, 96, 96n3
Peirce, Charles, 112
Pelikan, Jaroslav, xvi, xvin4
Pembroke, Neil, 103, 103n21
Peterson, Eugene H., 14, 14n32, 108, 109n40, 162, 162n10, 193n3, 193-95, 194n6
Phillips, J. B., 32, 32n1
Philo of Alexandria, 150
Picasso, Pablo, 166
Pickard, Stephen K., 102n17, 126, 127, 127n8, 127n9, 128-29, 128n12, 129n15, 129n16, 130, 130n22, 135n35
Pinnock, Clark H., 35, 35n6, 37, 44, 44n26, 44n27
Piper, Don, 66, 66n12
Pitt-Watson, Ian, 100, 100n14
Plato, 20, 35, 144-48, 145n9, 145n10, 147n12, 147n13, 150
Pohl, Christine D., 103, 103n23
Poling, James N., 204n32
Polkinghorne, John, 26, 26n19, 26n20
Porras, Jerry I., 28, 29n28
Protagoras, 125
Pseudo-Dionysius, 35
Pythagoras, 146

Rah, Soong-Chan, 201, 201n23
Rahner, Karl, 38-39, 39n13, 39n14, 40-41
Ramankutty, N., 141n1
Ratzinger, Joseph, 9, 9n23
Reid, Duncan, 185, 185n29

Rendle, Gilbert R., 134, 134n31, 136n38
Ribchester, T., xviin7
Roberts, David, 180n10
Roberts, Bob, 202-3, 203n27
Robinson, Marilynne, 8, 9n20
Robinson, John A. T., 62, 62n3, 66, 67n15
Rogers, Eugene F., 97n5
Romero, Oscar, 1
Rublev, Andrei, 106
Rumsfeld, Donald, x, xv, xvi
Ryken, Leland, 161, 162n9

Saayman, Willem, 198, 198n13, 198n14, 199
Sachs, J. R., 66n13
Sanders, John, 45n28, 45n29, 148, 148n14, 150
Santmire, Paul H., 143, 143n3, 175-76, 176n3, 179, 180, 180n12, 181
Scandrett, Joel, 180n11
Schilling, Harold, xviin3, 8, 8n16
Schreiter, Robert J., 207, 207n40
Schwarz, Christian, 101
Scott, Nancy, 149, 149n15
Scotus, Duns, 163
Seamands, Stephen, 99-101, 99n11, 101n15
Sheahan, Laura, 199n15
Sine, Tom, 81-81, 81n14, 82n16
Sleeth, J. Matthew, 60, 60n23
Smith, Elizabeth, 135n34
Snyder, Howard H., 180n11
Socrates, 18, 25, 145
Somerville, Margaret, 5, 5n7
Spencer, Liz, 200, 200n19
Spender, Stephen, 163, 163n12
Stark, Rodney, 84n21
Steiner, George, 156, 164, 164n16
Steyn, Mark, xvn1
Strudwick, Vincent, 85n22
Stuart, Douglas K., 195-96, 196n9
Sundkler, Bengt, 206n38

Tacey, David, 185-86, 186n31

names index

Talbott, Thomas, 63–65, 63n4, 63n5, 64n9, 66
Taylor, Daniel, 24, 24n16
Taylor, John V., 197, 107n36
Teilhard de Chardin, Pierre, 7
Tennyson, Alfred, 34
Tertullian, 111, 141, 150, 150n18
Tesoriero, Frank, 203, 203n28
Thales, 145
Theodore of Mopsuestia, 66
Thielicke, Helmut, 169, 169n21
Thimell, Daniel, 95
Thoreau, Henry D., 190–91, 191n49
Tickle, Phyllis, 78–79, 78n4, 78n5, 133, 133n30
Tiersma, Jude, 2, 2n2
Tillich, Paul, 16, 16n35
Torrance, Alan J., 38, 38n10
Torrance, James B., 80n10, 105n33
Torrance, Thomas F., 90, 90n33
Toulmin, Stephen, xvi, xvin5
Tournier, Paul, 22n8
Tucker, Frank, 19, 19n3
Turner, Steve, 164, 164n14

Underhill, Evelyn, 181–82, 182n16
Untener, Ken, 1, 2n1

Van Engen, Charles E., 197n10, 202, 202n25, 204n30, 206, 206n36
Vanhoozer, Kevin J., 156, 156n1
Vanier, Jean, 103, 104n25
Vásquez, Manuel A., 199, 199n17
Veith, Gene, 161, 161n8

Volf, Miroslav, 36, 37n8, 93, 102n20, 104, 104n27, 128, 128n13, 169–71, 170n24, 171n28, 198, 198n11, 209, 209n2, 212–13, 213n11, 214, 214n14

Wagner, Peter, 10, 10n24
Wainwright, Elaine M., 143, 143n4
Walsh, Brian J., 144, 144n6, 152n24
Ward, Keith, 188–89, 189n42
Ware, Kallistos, 74, 74n38
Watkins, Jane M., 116n6
Watts, Ricki, 174, 174n2
Welch, Sharon, 211–12, 212n10
Wesley, Charles, 12
Wheatley, Margaret J., 118n11, 130, 130n21
White, Lynn, 176, 176n4, 179–80, 179n9
Wilde, Caleb, 75, 75n42
Wiles, Maurice, 85
Willard, Dallas, 49
Williams, Rowan, xviin11, 60n22
Wittgenstein, Ludwig, 28, 28n26
Wittmer, Michael, 154, 154n30
Wright, N. T., 27n22, 33n3, 48, 49n1, 52, 52n6, 56, 56n15, 67, 67n17, 68, 70–71, 70n26, 71n30, 91, 91n37, 142, 142n2, 152-3, 152n26, 214–15, 214n15

Yong, Amos, 159, 159n5, 198, 198n12

Zizioulas, John, 78, 78n3, 133, 133n29